これがネイティブ発想!

100の超基本名詞で広がる
英語コロケーション 2500

クリストファ・バーナード 著
Christopher Barnard

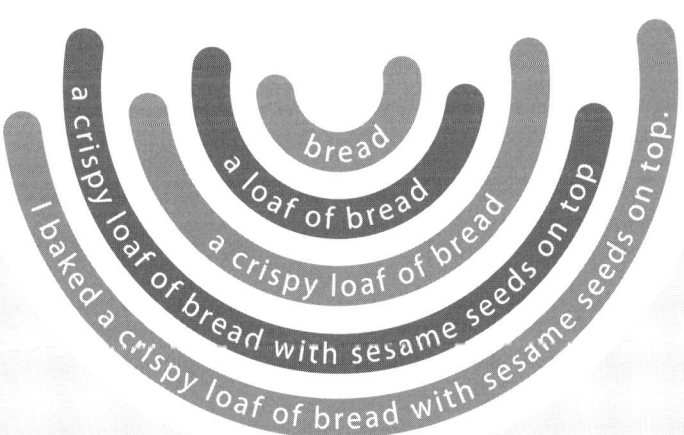

bread
a loaf of bread
a crispy loaf of bread
a crispy loaf of bread with sesame seeds on top
I baked a crispy loaf of bread with sesame seeds on top.

はじめに

英語は名詞中心にマスターすべき！

　本書は、「名詞の文法」すなわち「名詞のパターン」について書かれたものです。

　外国語を勉強するなら、動詞をマスターしなくては……私たちはふつうこう考えます。これはきわめて自然なことでしょう。母語であれ、どんな言語であれ、私たちが関わり合うのは、「<u>起こる</u>出来事、<u>ふるまう</u>方法、<u>目にする</u>現象、<u>感じる</u>感情、<u>心に抱く</u>考え、<u>述べる</u>言葉、<u>存在する</u>物体、<u>住んでいる</u>世界」などなのですから。

　英語学習においても、みなさんが主に関心があるのは、動詞の文法的なパターン（動詞の語法）をマスターすることでしょう。そうするとみなさんは、'give something to someone' や 'want someone to do something' や 'like＋-ing' などのような多様なパターンを記憶しなければならないことになります。

　冒頭で私は、私たちが住んでいる世界に関わる動詞に下線を引きました。しかし、上の文は下線の引き方を変えれば異なった見方をすることができます：

起こる<u>出来事</u>、ふるまう<u>方法</u>、目にする<u>現象</u>、感じる<u>感情</u>、心に抱く<u>考え</u>、述べる<u>言葉</u>、存在する<u>物体</u>、住んでいる<u>世界</u>

　本書は、このように下線を引いた事柄、すなわち動詞やその語法よりも、**名詞を中心として英語全体のボキャブラリーを広げること**を狙う本です（本書ではこのような考え方を**「名詞の文法」**と呼び

ます)。本書に登場するのは、さまざまな出来事や物体、物事、感情、思考、言葉などを表す名詞です。

**テレビ、服、男と女、幸福、天気、愛、コンピュータ、
休日、季節、仕事、事故、自動車、生活、ファッション、
趣味、食物、ダイエット、環境、顔、困難 ...**
(television, clothes, man and woman, happiness, weather, love, computer, holiday, season, work, accident, car, life, fashion, hobby, food, diet, environment, face, difficulty ...)

さらにもう80、合計100の名詞が登場します。

今までは言語について、「動詞が名詞(そしてその他の言葉)を文の中に連れてくる」と考えるのが一般的でした。本書で私は180度異なるアプローチを取ることにします。すなわち、

「名詞が動詞(そしてその他の言葉)を文の中に連れてくる」

のです。英文は従来のように動詞中心ではなく、名詞を中心として作り上げることができるのです。本書では、約2500もの実例をあげてその仕組みをお見せします。

本書を思う存分活用して、みなさんが自分の興味のあることを自由に話し、書き、読み、理解できるようになることを願います。

2010年4月

クリストファ・バーナード
Christopher Barnard

目 次

はじめに — *2*
本書の構成と使い方 — *6*
名詞の文法とコロケーション — *12*
「引用形」の活用法 — *16*
100の名詞の選択 — *18*

生活空間の核となる100の名詞 — *23*
The 100 Core Nouns In Your Lifespace

001 ACCIDENT ……………… *24*
002 AGRICULTURE /INDUSTRY ……………… *26*
003 AIM ……………… *28*
004 AMBULANCE/FIRE BRIGADE /POLICE …… *30*
005 APOLOGY ……………… *32*
006 ART ……………… *34*
007 BATH ……………… *36*
008 BEHAVIOUR ……………… *38*
009 BOOK ……………… *40*
010 BOSS ……………… *42*
011 CAR [AUTO (MOBILE)] … *44*
012 CELLPHONE [MOBILE PHONE] ……… *46*
013 CHANCE ……………… *50*
014 CHANGE ……………… *52*
015 CHARACTER ……………… *54*
016 CHILD ……………… *56*
017 CLOTHES ……………… *58*
018 COMPANY ……………… *60*
019 COMPUTER ……………… *62*
020 COUNTRY/COUNTRYSIDE ……………… *64*
021 COUNTRY/NATION ……… *66*
022 DAY/NIGHT ……………… *68*
023 DEATH ……………… *70*
024 DEPARTMENT STORE/ SUPERMARKET ……… *72*
025 DIET ……………… *74*
026 DIFFICULTY ……………… *76*
027 DINNER/LUNCH ……… *78*
028 DISASTER ……………… *80*
029 DREAM ……………… *82*
030 DRINK (酒類) ……………… *84*
031 DRINK (清涼飲料) ……… *86*
032 ECONOMY ……………… *88*
033 EDUCATION ……………… *90*
034 ELECTRICITY/GAS/WATER ……………… *92*
035 EMOTION ……………… *94*
036 E-MAIL/INTERNET ……… *96*
037 ENJOYMENT ……………… *98*
038 ENVIRONMENT ……… *100*
039 EVENING/MORNING …… *102*
040 FACE ……………… *104*
041 FAILURE ……………… *106*
042 FAMILY ……………… *108*

043	FASHION ... *110*	072	MEETING ... *168*
044	FISH/MEAT ... *112*	073	MISTAKE ... *170*
045	FITNESS ... *114*	074	MONEY ... *172*
046	FOOD ... *116*	075	MOVIE ... *174*
047	FRIENDSHIP ... *118*	076	MUSIC ... *176*
048	FRUIT /VEGETABLE ... *120*	077	NEWSPAPER [PAPER] ... *178*
049	GOVERNMENT ... *122*	078	PARCEL [PACKAGE] ... *180*
050	GROWTH ... *124*	079	PET ... *182*
051	HAIR ... *126*	080	POLITICS ... *184*
052	HAPPINESS ... *128*	081	QUALITY/QUANTITY ... *186*
053	HEALTH ... *130*	082	RELIGION ... *188*
054	HOBBY ... *132*	083	ROAD ... *190*
055	HOLIDAY ... *134*	084	SEASON ... *192*
056	HOME ... *136*	085	SEA/SEASIDE ... *194*
057	HOSPITAL ... *138*	086	SHOPPING ... *196*
058	HOTEL ... *140*	087	SLEEP ... *198*
059	HOUSEWORK ... *142*	088	SOCIETY ... *200*
060	HUSBAND/WIFE ... *144*	089	SPORT ... *202*
061	IDEA ... *146*	090	STRESS ... *204*
062	ILLNESS ... *148*	091	SUCCESS ... *206*
063	INTEREST ... *150*	092	TECHNOLOGY ... *208*
064	KINDNESS ... *152*	093	TELEVISION ... *210*
065	LANGUAGE ... *154*	094	THANKS ... *212*
066	LIE/TRUTH ... *156*	095	TIME ... *214*
067	LIFE ... *158*	096	TRAIN ... *216*
068	LOVE ... *160*	097	TRAVEL ... *218*
069	LUCK ... *162*	098	WEATHER ... *220*
070	MAN/WOMAN ... *164*	099	WEEKEND ... *222*
071	MARRIAGE ... *166*	100	WORK ... *224*

索 引 — *226*

本書の構成と使い方

1 本書の構成

100の核となる名詞 (Core Nouns) がアルファベット順に配列されています。(100の名詞の選択についてはp.18を参照)

各項目は見開き2頁で、項目ごとの構成は以下のとおりです。

(1) 見出し語 (Core Noun) と解説

見出し語：原則として1語ですが、'man/woman'のようにまとめて提示したほうが有用と思われる場合はペアで掲げてあります。

C と U：名詞は「数えられる名詞」と「数えられない名詞」の二種類に分類されますが、これを本書では、C (Countable: 数えられる名詞) と U (Uncountable: 数えられない名詞) の記号で示しました。両方の用法を持ち、頻度に差がある場合は、頻度の低いほうを薄く示してあります。例えば、'C U' はその名詞が「数えられる名詞」として用いられる場合が多いことを示しています。

文法・語法情報：文法や語法面での注意事項や日本と英語圏での文化的な差異に関わる情報を適宜加えました (✱印で表示)。

相互参照項目：あわせて学習すると効果的な他のCore Nounsを最後に '>>' で示してあります。

(2) コロケーション (見出し語をもとにした語句・表現)

続けて、それぞれのCore Nounをもとに広がる典型的かつ多様な語句・表現 (コロケーション) を和文→英文の順にあげました。必要に応じて、次のような〈ラベル〉で分類してあります。

▶ ～ (Core Noun) から広がるボキャブラリー

それぞれのCore Nounが作り出す表現のバリエーションを示し

ました。

例えば、(001) ACCIDENTの項目では、〈accidentから広がるバリエーション〉というラベルの下に 'a fatal accident'（致命的な事故）や 'an accident that caused serious injury'（ひどいけがを負わせた事故）など 'accident' が他のどんな形容詞や名詞（句）と結びついてバリエーションを作り出すかがわかります。

これにより、Core Nounをもとにした**形容詞や名詞（句）に関わるボキャブラリーの増強**がはかれます。

また、動詞（句）とそれぞれのCore Nounの結びつきを、フレーズや文の形で示しました。（※ 名詞表現と動詞表現を別々のラベルでまとめている場合もあります）

例えば、ACCIDENTの項目では、'avoid' や 'reduce' や 'witness' が 'accident' と結びつきやすいことがわかります。

逆にここから、それぞれの動詞の典型的な用法を知ることにもなり、**動詞に関わるボキャブラリーの増強**がはかれます。

▶ 関連表現

ここは、何らかの形でそれぞれのCore Nounと関連のある語句を用いた表現を集めてあります。

例えば、(010) BOSSの項目では 'bossy' という派生語を用いた表現があります。(015) CHARACTERの項目では、'character' に関わる別の名詞表現やコロケーションを集めてあります。

▶ 決まり文句

ここにはCore Nounに関連した典型的なことわざ、名言やイディオム的な表現、格言などを集めてあります。

▶ **それぞれの項目独自のラベル**

これらの他にも項目に応じて適宜、独自のラベルを設けてあります。どれも自明のものですが、少しだけ例をあげておきましょう。

(013) CHANCEの項目では、'chance'のもつ複数の概念をはっきりさせるために、「機会」「見込み」「偶然の一致」それぞれに関わる表現に分けて用例をあげました。

(074) MONEYの項目では、「入ってくる金」と「出ていく金」という2つのラベルを設けました。これにより、私たちが'money'についてどのよう考え、'money'という言葉をどのように用いているのかがわかります。

▶ **その他の注意点**

・**名詞以外の用法**：名詞には形容詞（例：a pet dog）や副詞（例：I went home.）として用いられる場合もあり、本書でもそれらの用法を含めて扱い、特に注意が必要な場合はコメントを添えました。

・**CとUの典型例**：用例の後ろに小さくつけた C や U は、その用例が〈解説〉で示した C あるいは U としての典型的な例であることを示しています。それぞれ各項目1～2例を選んであります。

・**イディオムの指摘**：用例中で重要なイディオムを形作っている部分には下線を施し、それが分かれている場合は点線でつないで注意を喚起しました。

・**語法を示す記号**：本書では☞の記号に続けて、Core Nounと結びつく形容詞や動詞がさらに他の語句と結びつく例を示しました。これにより、Core Nounをもとにしてさらに表現が広がっていくことがわかるでしょう。また、注意すべき語句については簡単な説明を施しましたが、その中では次のような略号を用いました。

sb = somebody：「人」を表す語句が続くことを示す

sth = something：「物」あるいは「事」を表す語句が続くことを示す

spl = some place：「場所」を表す語句が続くことを示す

stm = some time：「時間」を表す語句が続くことを示す

(3) ストーリー

ここは上にあげた文法情報やコロケーションが多く含まれた、まとまりのある文章を示しました。これにより、それぞれのCore Nounを含む**さまざまな語句・表現を一つの体系として頭に深く認識させることができます**。

2 本書の使い方

本書はこれと決まった使い方はありません。ここの説明をとばして、すぐに23頁からの本文を読み始めてもかまいませんし、どこからどのように取り組んでも効果の上がるように設計されています。

しかし、以下の提案にしたがって取り組めば、さらに無駄なく効果的に学習を進めることができると思います。

*

読者のみなさんが本書で示したフレーズや文を覚えることができれば、英語を読んだり、聞いたりするうちにそれらに出くわす機会が頻繁にあることに気づくでしょう。その理由は、それらのフレーズや文が英語で最もよく用いられるコロケーションの例だからです。

また、このコロケーションは話す・書くときにも「そのまま使える」英語のかたまり (chunk) なのです。（コロケーションの重要性とその取り扱いについては、p.12からを参照）

英語でもどんな言語でも、ばらばらに覚えないで、このような「かたまり」ごとに覚えてゆけばアウトプットも非常に楽になります。なぜなら、「ジグソーパズル」を組み合わせるような複雑な作業から脳が解放されるからです。

　上級レベルの読者の方は、さらに学習効果を上げるために、本書のフレーズや文を使って、「ストーリー」に変更を加えていくことをお勧めします。すでに「ストーリー」に使われている表現を置き換えたり、そこに足していったりするのです。

　理想を言えば、みなさんが本書のフレーズや文を使って、自分独自の新しいストーリーを作り出すことができれば完ぺきでしょう。

　本書は、最初から順を追って取り組んでいってもかまいませんが、自分の興味のある項目から拾い読みしていくのもいいでしょう。

　お勧めの学習法は、どこからでもかまいませんから、どれか1つの項目（Core Noun）をまず徹底的に学習することです。そして「相互参照」（>>）を利用して次々に関連する項目（Core Noun）に取り組んでいきましょう。

　こうすればみなさんは知らず知らずのうちに、すべての項目を楽しみながら学習することができるのです。これが最も効果的で無駄のないやり方でしょう。

　例えば、みなさんの目に最初にとまったのが(058) HOTELの項目だとします。みなさんは次のように進んでいくはずです。

HOTEL >> HOLIDAY >> WEEKEND >> ENJOYMENT >> HAPPINESS >> EMOTION >> BEHAVIOUR >> CHARACTER >> KINDNESS

　また、(016) CHILDの項目からならこう進むはずです。

CHILD >> FAMILY >> HOME >> HUSBAND/WIFE >> ENJOYMENT >> HAPPINESS

　このようにしてみなさんは、名詞から名詞へ、まるで「ガイド付きのツアーで生活空間をめぐっていく」ような体験をすることができるわけです。

　お気づきと思いますが「HOTEL発のツアー」も「CHILD発のツアー」もENJOYMENTを通ることになります。生活空間の中のさまざまな名詞は、特にその中心部分（すなわち生活空間の核付近）では、程度の差はあれ互いに密接に結びついているのです。

　さらに言えば、英語の単語、イディオム、文法などはばらばらに存在しているのではなく、互いに密接に結びついた1つのシステムのようなものを構成しているのです。

　英語を最も速くマスターするには、「検定試験などで高得点をあげるためだけに、1000単語を覚えたり、よく出るイディオムを暗記したり、文法を学んだり」しても意味がありません。

　最善の方法は、英語というシステムを構成する要素の結びつきを理解し、その結びつきを用いて英語を使える範囲を徐々に広げていくことなのです。

　みなさんの興味に応じて、本書は何千通りものツアーを用意しています。どうぞご自由にお楽しみください！

名詞の文法とコロケーション

1 「名詞の文法」とは何か？

本書では、「言語は名詞を中心として広がっていく」という考え方を**「名詞の文法」**と呼ぶことにします。

実際は、この「名詞の文法」を次の4つのレベルに分けて考えるといいでしょう。

◆ 第1レベル

これは**名詞が文中で名詞としての機能を果たすために必要とされる最低限の文法**です。

例えば、もし私たちが、'I like bread.'（私はパンが好きです）や'Bread is baked in an oven.'（パンはオーブンで焼かれます）のように、パンを「パンというもの（＝物質）」として、あるいは「パン一般」について、述べているのなら、単に 'bread' と言うことができます。

しかし、'bread' は他の言葉を一緒に連れてくる場合のほうがはるかに多いのです。英語では 'I want bread.' と言うことは実際にはありません。このような場合、英語では、

I want	some		（私は	パン	
	a piece of			パン一切れ	
	a loaf of			パン一斤	
	two loaves of			パン二斤	
	a slice of	bread.		パン一枚	がほしい）

などと言わなければなりません。このように、'bread' について意味のあることを述べたり、文法的に正しい英文を作ろうとする場合、'bread' は他の言葉を一緒に文中に連れてくることになるのです。

◆ 第2レベル

次のレベルは、'bread' の前に付いて、'bread' について私たちに多くのことを教えてくれる言葉です。

次のように、これらは基本的に形容詞や形容詞句です。

a crispy loaf of bread　（パリパリしたパン一斤）
a thin slice of bread　　（薄いパン一枚）
some stale bread　　　（古くなったパン）

◆ 第3レベル

次は 'bread' の後に付く言葉に関わるレベルです。

a crispy loaf of bread with sesame seeds on top
（ゴマのせのパリパリしたパン一斤）

この場合、'bread' の右に説明を加えることにより、私たちは 'bread' について面白い言い方をしたことになります。

◆ 第4レベル

次のレベルは、上の 'a crispy loaf of bread with sesame seeds on top' と共に用いられる**最も典型的な動詞**を教えてくれます。この句からまず思い浮かぶのは 'bake' という動詞です。そうすると、

I baked a crispy loaf of bread with sesame seeds on top.
（私はゴマのせのパリパリしたパンを一斤焼いた）

という文ができることになります。本書で私がみなさんに伝えた

かったのは、まさにこのアプローチなのです。

　私が本書に収録したフレーズや文はこのアプローチにそって作り上げたものです。このアプローチにしたがえば、みなさんは身の回りの世界を英語で思い通りに楽しく表現することができるようになるでしょう。

　名詞がフレーズや文の核となるのです。動詞ではありません。

② コロケーションの重要性

　「名詞をもとにして英語を増強する」ことは、「コロケーション」(collocation) という考え方と密接に結びついています。

　では、「コロケーション」とは何でしょうか？　また、なぜそれほど重要なのでしょうか？

　英語で 'coffee' という言葉を聞いたり、見たり、あるいは言ったりする場合、かなりの確率の高さで 'drink' という言葉がその近くに現れます。

　つまり、'coffee' という言葉を聞いたとしたら、最初にネイティブスピーカーの頭に浮かぶのは、まず間違いなく 'drink' という言葉だろうということです。

　その他にはどんな言葉が浮かぶでしょうか？　いろいろあるとは思いますが、きっと次のようなものが含まれているはずです——'coffee cup' 'Kilimanjaro' 'strong' 'weak' 'coffee filter' 'sugar' 'milk' 'tea' 'cake' など。

　このような言葉と 'coffee' とが作る連語を「コロケーション」と呼んでいるのです。もちろん、その結びつきの度合いはそれぞれ異なります。

　コロケーションをマスターすることにより、それぞれの言葉（本

書では100の名詞を取り上げています)**をどのように使えばよいか手がかりをつかむことができるのです。**

本書で紹介したフレーズや文 (Core Nounを中心として作成したもの) はこのコンセプトに基づいています。

このようなアプローチは頭ごなしに単語を覚えさせようとする類のもの (例えば、「話す/読む/書く/聞くのに役立つ '1000語' を覚えましょう」など) と根本的に異なる、もしくは正反対のものです。

このやり方は、「単語を覚えれば覚えるほど英語が使えるようになる」という仮定に基づいています。

しかし、本書を手に取ったみなさんは、このようなやり方では自分の思ったことを自由に英語で言えるようにはならないことをうすうす感じているのではないでしょうか。

私のアプローチは、**少数の語と結びついている多数のコロケーションを使えるようにすることが英語マスターへの近道**だということです。そしてこれがもっとも無駄がなく効果的な学習法であると私は確信しています。

もちろん、このようにコロケーションを覚えていけば必然的に、上述の '1000語' を覚えてしまっているでしょう。その1000語はそれ自身がみなさんの覚えたコロケーションの一部だからです。

それらコロケーションの核となる単語の使い方を覚えることにより、間接的に膨大な数の単語を学んでいることになるのです。

コロケーションをもとにして英語に取り組めば、単語それぞれがもつ文法上の特徴を知ることになり、それにより単語と単語をどのようにつなげればよいのかが自然と頭に入ってゆきます。

単語ひとつひとつの意味を暗記する従来のやり方よりもはるかに効率的かつ実用的であることは、もうおわかりでしょう。

名詞の文法とコロケーション

「引用形」の活用法

　本書の用例（＝コロケーション）のほとんどのものが「引用形」(**citation form**) で提示されています。「引用形」とは、ある単語や表現についての主要な、そして最も重要な文法情報を短く簡潔に教えてくれる形です。しかし、それらの形から完全な文をつくるには、それらにさらに情報を与えてあげる必要があるのです（中には、すでに完全な文の形で示されているものもあります）。以下にその方法をいくつか例をあげて説明しましょう。

1. 引用形に主語と動詞を加える場合：

　　some bread

　この場合、'some' が 'bread' は不可算名詞であるという文法情報を教えてくれます。これを文の形にするには、主語と動詞が必要ですね。また、必要に応じて動詞の時制も変えなければなりません。

　　I ate some bread.（私はパンを食べた）

2. 不可算名詞の場合：

　'some bread' の 'some' は 'bread' が不可算名詞であることを教えてくれますから、「名詞の文法とコロケーション」で示したように、上の文を次のように変えてみてもよいでしょう。

　　I ate **a lot of** bread.（私はパンをたくさん食べた）
　　There is **only a little** bread in the house.
　　（家にはほんの少ししかパンがない）
　　I would like **a piece of** bread.（パンを一切れほしいのですが）

3. 冠詞：

引用形で示された名詞の前に付けられる冠詞は、'a /an' と 'the' の場合があります。これにより、その名詞がふつうどのように用いられるかがわかります。例えば、

have **a** clear idea　(p.146)

これにより、この表現は文中では次のように用いられることが多いことがわかります。

I **have a clear idea** of what you mean.
（あなたが何を言いたいかはっきりわかります）

しかし、次のように冠詞が 'the' である場合もあります。

do not have have **the** faintest idea　(p.147)

これにより、この表現は文中では次のように用いられることが多いことがわかります。

I did **not have the faintest idea**.
（まったく見当もつかなかった）

つまり、言葉の多くは、'bread' や 'idea' といった断片的な形ではなく引用形で提示されるのであり、引用形は本当の言語を用いるためのカギとなるものだということです。

100の名詞の選択

1 生活空間 (the lifespace) とは

　ご覧になればおわかりと思いますが、本書で私が取り上げた100の名詞はごく基本的なものです。

　それこそ無数の名詞の中からこれら100の名詞を選択した理由は、これらの名詞が実にさまざまな言葉（動詞、形容詞、前置詞、その他の名詞など）を「文の中に連れてくる」からです。

　この100の名詞がみなさんをかなりの上級レベルにまで導いてくれるはずです。

　膨大な数の名詞の中から核となる名詞を選び出すことは決してたやすい作業ではありません。これを行うにあたり、まず私は人間の「生活空間」(the lifespace) の潜在的なモデルを設定しました。

　「生活空間」を「**21世紀の現代社会における平均的な成人の社会的、個人的そして精神的な活動領域**」と定義します。

　話をわかりやすくするために、それを右図のようにごく単純化して図解してみましょう。

　●は生活空間の核（中心部分）を表しています。それぞれのアイテムは生活空間の核 (●) に近ければ近いほど、平均的な成人にとって生活の中での重要性が高くなるというわけです。

　例えば、'marriage'（結婚）は生活空間の核に近い位置にありますが、その反対語である 'divorce'（離婚）はそうではありません。'divorce' は私たちの生活において一般的にそれほど重要とは言えないからです。一方、'cellphone' (= cellular phone：携帯電話) は今や間違いなく生活空間の核に急接近しています。

　この核の付近に存在して、核を形成しているのが本書で扱う100の Core Nouns なのです。

　注意したいのは、核の付近に存在している名詞は 'food' や 'drink

現代人の潜在的生活空間

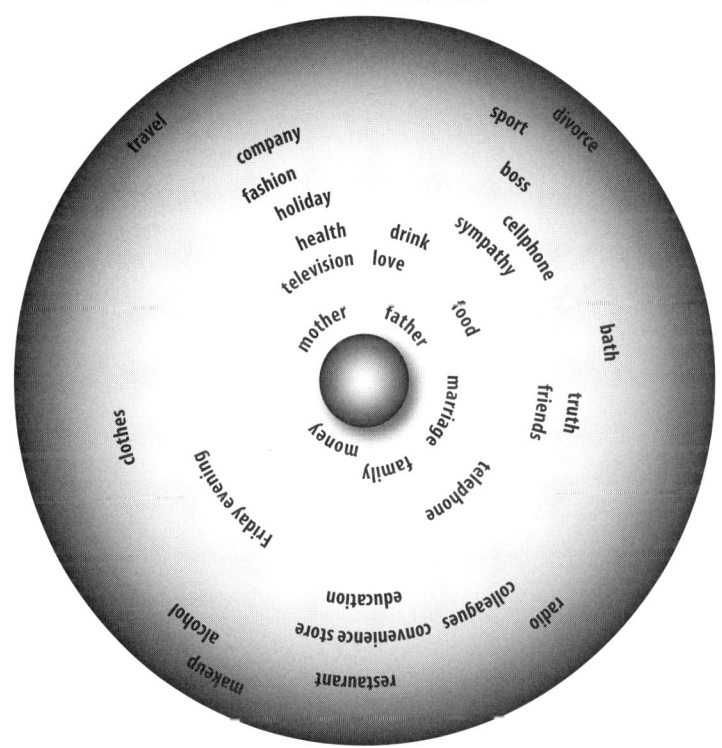

のようにはっきりした形をもつ名詞ばかりでなく、'truth' や 'love' のように抽象的な概念を表す名詞の場合もあることです。

これは、生活空間という考え方そして生活空間を構成する名詞群が、いわゆる「英語の最頻出〜語」のような考え方といかに異なるかを物語っています。

'hand' は英語において 'health' よりもよく用いられる言葉です。しかし、後者のほうが生活空間の核に近いのです。なぜなら、自分の健康に関心を絶やさない人は多いでしょうが、毎日自分の手のこ

とを意識的に考える人はほとんどいないでしょうから。

まとめると、

- 生活空間の核にある**100の名詞**を中心にして、どのように英語を増強することができるか
- それによって、自分が関心のある事柄（これが生活の中で重要な部分をしめるでしょう）について、どのように英語で話すことができるか

この2つをみなさんに示すことが本書の目的なのです。

実際、外国語が上達したと考えられるのは、その言語を使って生活空間の核となる領域について話す（理解する、読む、書く）ことができる、そしてさらに語学力が伸びていくにつれ、その領域の隙間を埋めたり、あるいは領域そのものを広げていけるようになることなのです。

みなさんが本書にまじめに取り組んでいけば、すべての項目を学習し終えたとき、みなさんの生活空間の英語は①のようなものになっているはずです。

そして、仮に本書に続編があったとして、さらに続けて500の名詞をマスターしたなら、②のように生活空間の密度はより高くなり、その範囲自体も広がりを見せているでしょう。

本書をひと通り学習すれば、みなさんは生活空間の中心をなす100の名詞をもとにボキャブラリーを大幅に増強することになります。**しかもそのボキャブラリーはどれもが、そのまますぐに使えるものばかり**なのです。

注：'lifespace' は通常 'life space' と2語でつづられますが、本書では、本書の中心となる新しい概念として1語でつづっています。

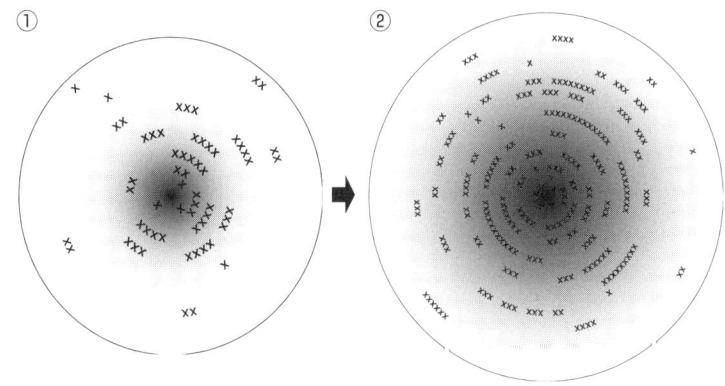

2 実際の生活空間地図

23頁に、本書で扱う100のCore Nounsが形づくる「実際の生活空間地図」を示しました。

この地図を見ればおわかりのように、私たちの生活空間は、最も基本的あるいは一般的なレベルでは、「モノと出来事の空間」「屋外の空間」「屋内の空間」の3つの空間に分けることができます。

これらの空間はそれぞれ、さらに2つずつに細分化され、下のようになります。

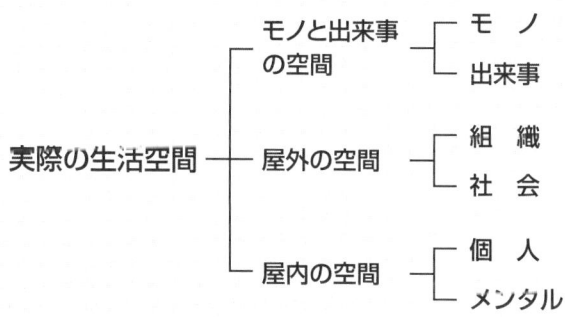

100の名詞の選択　21

100のCore Nounsはすべてこれら6つの生活空間区域のどれかに収まるのです。どの空間に分類するかはそれほど難しいことではありません。例えば、'car'は明らかに「モノ」ですし、'accident'は明らかに「出来事」です。

　もちろん、どこに分類すればよいか判断に迷う場合もあります。そのような場合は、その名詞の英語でのイメージや用いられ方を注意深く検討し、判断を下しました。

　このようにして、'television'は「モノ」の空間に、'cellphone'は「個人」の空間に収まりました。確かにどちらも「モノ」に分類することも可能ですが、'cellphone'はただの便利な物体以上の存在です。現在では多くの人たちが携帯電話を私生活の中心に位置づけています。しかし、テレビと聞くと、ただの物体（すなわち「モノ」）を連想するのがより一般的でしょう。

　誰もが自分だけの「生活空間地図」を持っています。しかし、次頁の地図はほとんどの人たちに共通する生活空間をかなりはっきりと描き出しています。

　この地図を頼りにみなさんは本書をCore NounからCore Nounへとナビゲートしていくことができます。そして、**自分が関心のある話題や日常生活での重要事項などついて、英語を自由に用いて話せるようになる**のです。

The 100 Core Nouns
In Your Lifespace
生活空間の核となる100の名詞

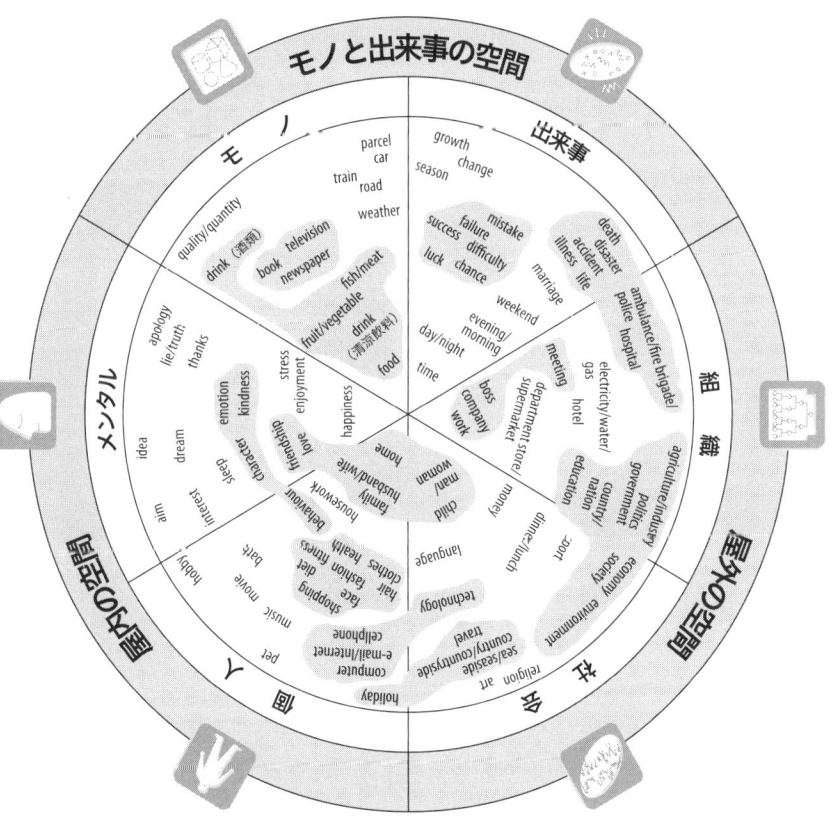

「生活空間」と「その核となる100の名詞」

　　は主要な関連グループを表している。これらは各 Core Noun で示した相互参照項目のうち重要なパターンのいくつかである。

001 ACCIDENT

> **事**故と偶然とは、さまざまな形で我々の生活空間についてまわる。まず、ここでは 'accident' と結びついて「事故」や「偶然」に関わる状況を表すさまざまな表現を紹介した。
>
> ✲ 'accident' は「事故」以外に「(ときによい意味の)意外な出来事」の意味で「偶然に関わる表現」にも用いられることに注意。'by accident'（偶然に）という副詞句でよく用いられる（この場合は無冠詞）。
>
> **>> AMBULANCE / FIRE BRIGADE / POLICE; CAR; DISASTER**

▶ accident から広がるボキャブラリー：名詞表現

- ❏ 重大な事故 ◯ a serious accident　☞ a serious matter「深刻な問題」
- ❏ ひどい事故 ◯ a terrible accident
- ❏ 致命的な事故 ◯ a fatal accident　☞ fatal「命にかかわる、きわめて重大な」
   a fatal mistake「致命的な [取り返しのつかない] 誤り」
- ❏ 船遊び中の事故 ◯ a boating accident
- ❏ (工場などで) 作業中の事故 ◯ an industrial accident
- ❏ 採鉱事故 ◯ a mining accident　☞ mining「採鉱(業)、採炭(業)」
- ❏ ひどいけがを負わせた事故
   ◯ an accident that caused serious injury
- ❏ 不注意によって起きた事故
   ◯ an accident that was caused by carelessness

▶ accident から広がるボキャブラリー：動詞表現

- ❏ 事故を避ける ◯ avoid accidents
- ❏ 事故を減らす ◯ reduce accidents
- ❏ 仕事中に事故に遭う ◯ have an accident at work
- ❏ 重大な事故を目撃する ◯ witness a serious accident
- ❏ 事故を警察に届ける ◯ report an accident to the police
   ☞ He reports to Mr Halford.「彼はハルフォード氏の部下である」
- ❏ メグはひき逃げ [当て逃げ] 事故の犠牲になった。
   ◯ Meg was the victim of a hit-and-run accident.
- ❏ 交通事故を起こした後で、車を止めるのを怠る (ひき逃げなど)

- ○ fail to stop after causing a traffic accident ☞ fail to do「〜し損なう」
- ❏ 事故の後に名前と住所を教えあう
  - ○ exchange names and addresses after an accident
- ❏ 事故の原因を調査する ○ investigate the cause of an accident
- ❏ 事故を起こしたことをボブに謝る
  - ○ apologize to Bob for causing an accident ☞ apologize to sb for sth「〈人〉に〈事〉を謝る[わびる]」

▶「偶然」に関わる表現

- ❏ 隠された宝物を偶然発見する
  - ○ discover hidden treasure by accident ☞ by accident「偶然(に)」
- ❏ うれしい偶然で解決を見つける
  - ○ find the solution by a happy accident ☞ 冠詞の有無に注意
- ❏ 爆弾は思いがけないときに爆発した。
  - ○ The bomb went off by accident. ☞ go off「爆発する」
- ❏ 我々がここで遭遇したのは決して偶然ではない。
  - ○ It is no accident that we have met here. ☞ It is no accident that ...「...は決して偶然ではない」

▶ ストーリー

I **have only had one traffic accident** in my life. I **failed to stop** where I should have. **Another car hit my car**. **It was my fault** entirely. **After the accident** I **phoned the police** and **reported it**. After that I **reported it to the insurance company**. The other driver was an old gentleman. He **had been driving** for fifty years, but **had never had an accident**. You can imagine how bad I felt!

(私は今までに交通事故を起こしたことが一度だけある。私は車を止めるべきところで止め損ねた。他の自動車が私の自動車にぶつかった。完全に私の責任だった。事故の後、私は警察に電話して事故を届け出た。その後、私は保険会社に届けた。相手の車を運転していた人は運転歴50年で、これまで一度も事故を起こしたことがない老紳士であった。私がどれだけ決まり悪かったか想像できるでしょう!)

002 AGRICULTURE Ⓤ / INDUSTRY ⒸⓊ

農業や工業は我々の生活空間を底辺から支えるものである。ここでは各種メディアによく登場する表現を中心に 'agriculture' と 'industry' のバリエーションを多く取り上げた。ⒸとⓊにも注意。

★ agriculture ☞ Ⓤ
★ industry
　特定の産業やそのタイプについて述べる場合 ☞ Ⓒ
　産業一般あるいは産業の分野について述べる場合 ☞ Ⓤ

>> ECONOMY; ENVIRONMENT; GOVERNMENT

▶ agriculture から広がるボキャブラリー

❑ 零細農業[自給自足農業] ◯ subsistence agriculture ☞ subsistence「(最低水準でのぎりぎりの)生活、生存」

❑ 農業、園芸、林業 ◯ agriculture, horticulture, and forestry

❑ 農業助成金 ◯ subsidies for agriculture ☞ subsidies「補助金、助成金」

❑ 肥沃な土壌の上に繁栄した農業
　◯ agriculture which flourished on fertile soils ☞ flourish「栄える」

❑ 灌漑により可能になった農業
　◯ agriculture made possible by irrigation ☞ irrigation「灌漑」

❑ 干ばつによる低い農業収穫高
　◯ low agricultural yields because of drought ☞ yield「収穫高」
　(a) drought [dráut]「干ばつ」

❑ 経済を農業に依存する国
　◯ a country whose economy relies on agriculture ☞ rely on「～に頼る」

❑ 農業に適さない[適した]地域
　◯ an area which is unsuitable [suitable] for agriculture

❑ 農業に科学的なアプローチを取り入れる
　◯ adopt a scientific approach to agriculture

▶ industry から広がるボキャブラリー

- ❏ 国営化産業 ◯ a nationalized industry [C] ☞ nationalize *sth*「〈物〉を国有化する」
- ❏ 伝統産業 ◯ a traditional industry
- ❏ 衰退 [斜陽] 産業 ◯ a decaying [declining] industry
- ❏ 重工業 ◯ heavy industry
- ❏ 製造業 ◯ manufacturing industry
- ❏ 鉄鋼産業 ◯ the iron and steel industry
- ❏ 軽織物産業 ◯ the light textile industry
- ❏ 化学薬品産業 ◯ the chemical and pharmaceutical industries
- ❏ 観光 (産) 業 ◯ the tourist industry
- ❏ 自動車産業の衰退 ◯ an economic decline in the car industry
- ❏ 産業でのロボット使用 ◯ the use of robots in industry [U]
- ❏ 産業と都市化の広がり ◯ the spread of industry and urbanization
- ❏ 産業に必要とされる人的資源 [労働力、人手]
  ◯ the manpower required for industry
- ❏ ある産業での生産性向上
  ◯ improvements in productivity in an industry

▶決まり文句

- ❏ 軍産複合体 ◯ the military-industrial complex
- ❏ 戦時中、女性たちが産業の担い手であった。
  ◯ Women kept the wheels of industry turning in the war.
  ☞ keep the wheels of *sth* turning「何かを円滑に進める」

▶ ストーリー

The spread of industry has been the story of the last two centuries. **There now exist industries**, like **the computer industry**, or **the telecommunications industry**, which did not exist a hundred years ago.
(産業が広がりを見せたのは、ここ2世紀の話である。現在は、コンピュータ産業や遠距離通信産業のように、100年前には存在しなかった産業が存在する。)

AGRICULTURE / INDUSTRY

003 AIM

> 目的と目標がなければ何をやっても成果は上がらない。ここでは、さまざまな目的・目標とその達成に関わる頻出表現を多数紹介した。
> ✱目的も目標も英語では 'aim' であるが、日本語では「目標」は「目的を達成するために設けためあて」(『広辞苑』より)であり、文脈に応じて訳出が変わる場合もあることに注意して以下の用例を見てほしい。
> **>> DREAM; IDEA; INTERNET**

▶ aim から広がるボキャブラリー：名詞表現

- ❏ 主な目的 ◯ the main aim
- ❏ 基本的な目的 ◯ the basic aim
- ❏ 潜在的な目的 ◯ an underlying aim ☞ underlying「隠された、基礎的な」
- ❏ 全体的な目的 ◯ the overall aim ☞ overall「(名の前で) 全体 (として) の」
- ❏ 一般的な目的 ◯ the general aim
- ❏ 最初の目的 ◯ the initial aim ☞ initial「(名の前で) 最初の」
- ❏ さしあたっての目標 ◯ the immediate aim ☞ immediate「(名の前で) 目下の、即座の」
- ❏ 短期的目標 ◯ a short-term aim
- ❏ 長期的目標 ◯ a long-range aim
- ❏ 究極の目的 ◯ the ultimate aim
- ❏ 明確な目的 ◯ a clear aim
- ❏ 理想主義的な目的 ◯ an idealistic aim
- ❏ 賞賛に値する目的 ◯ an admirable aim ☞ admirable qualities「すばらしい特色」
- ❏ 達成可能な目標 ◯ an achievable aim
- ❏ 人生における自分の目標 ◯ my aim in life
- ❏ 政策の公式な目的 ◯ the stated aim of government policy
- ❏ ガンの治療法を発見することが目的の研究
  ◯ research whose aim is to discover a cure for cancer
  ☞ research「研究、探求、調査」は U　a cure for sth「〈病気、問題〉の治療法 [薬]、解決策」

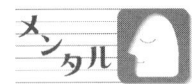

▶ aim から広がるボキャブラリー：動詞表現

- (明確な) 目標がない ◯ have no (clear) aim
- (長期的な) 目標を立てる ◯ set up an (a long-range) aim
- 金持ちで有名になるという目的を果たす
  ◯ fulfil my aim of becoming rich and famous
- 勝つことを目標にレースに参加する
  ◯ enter a race with the aim of winning ☞ with the aim of doing「…することを目標 [目的] として」
- テストでミスをしないという私の目的を達する
  ◯ achieve my aim of not making a mistake in the test
- その本の目的 [狙い] は読者を楽しませることである。
  ◯ The aim of the book is to amuse the reader.
- 私の目標は快適な生活を送ることである。
  ◯ My aim is to lead a comfortable life.
- 我が国はいまだその戦争目的をはっきりとさせていない。
  ◯ Our country has not made its war aims clear yet.

▶ ストーリー

You should **decide on what your main aims are in life**, and **how you will achieve them**. Do this by deciding what your **short-term**, **medium-term**, and **long-term aims** are. If you want to become a lawyer your **short-term aim** might be to get into a good law department in a good university. Your **medium term aim** might be to get As in all your courses. Your **long-term aim** will presumably be to pass the law exam.

(あなたは人生における自分の主たる目標が何であるか、そしてどのようにそれを達成するかを決めるべきである。自分の短期、中期、そして長期の目標を決めることによって、これを行うこと。もしあなたが弁護士になることを望むなら、短期の目標は良い大学の良い法学部に入ることかもしれない。中期の目標はすべての科目で優をとることかもしれない。長期の目標はおそらく司法試験に合格することになるであろう。)

AIM

004 AMBULANCE / FIRE BRIGADE Ⓒ / POLICE 複

救急車と消防隊そして警察署は、どれか一つが欠けても我々の安全な生活が脅かされる。ここでは、これらが活躍する「緊急の状況」に関わる表現を多数紹介した。特に 'police' を用いた頻出表現は多いので別にラベルを設けてまとめてある。

✲ a fire brigade (英) = a fire department (米)

✲ the police で「(複数の) 警察官」あるいは「警察署 (複数扱い)」

>> **ACCIDENT; CAR; DISASTER; HOSPITAL; ROAD**

▶「緊急の状況」に関わる表現

❏ 警察に電話をかける ➲ phone the police

❏ 電話で救急車を呼ぶ ➲ phone for an ambulance

❏ 地元の消防署に連絡する contact the local fire brigade

❏ 窃盗を警察に届ける ➲ report a burglary to the police

❏ 救急車で病院に緊急移送される

➲ be rushed to hospital by ambulance

❏ 有資格救急医療士の乗った救急車

➲ an ambulance with qualified paramedics [pæ̀rəmédiks]

☞ qualified「資格のある」

❏ 彼らはボブを担架に載せて救急車に運び入れた。

➲ They put Bob on a stretcher and put him in the ambulance.

❏ 火事の発生から消防団の到着までの重要な時間

➲ the critical period between the outbreak of a fire and the arrival of the fire brigade ☞ critical「重大な、危機的な」

❏ 消防団を待ち、飛び降りるのは最後の手段としてのみ

➲ wait for the fire brigade, and jump only as a last resort

☞ as a last resort「最後の手段として」

❏ ランプを点滅させたパトカー ➲ a police car with lights flashing

☞ an unmarked police car「覆面パトカー」

❏ 警察の発表では三人が行方不明だ。

➲ The police say that three people cannot be accounted for.

☞ not be accounted for「行方不明である」

組織

- 警察と救急車が現場に向かっている。
  - ○ The police and ambulance <u>are on their way</u>. ☞ be on *one*'s way「途中である」

▶ police から広がる表現

- 警察署 ○ a police station
- 警官 ○ a policeman / a police officer
- 刑事 ○ a police detective
- 機動隊 ○ the riot police
- 腐敗し役に立たない警察 ○ a corrupt and inefficient police force
  - ☞ a police force は警察組織全体を指す
- ボブは警察に尋問された。○ Bob was questioned by the police.
  - ☞ question「〜を尋問する、異議を唱える」
- 彼は警察署に拘留された。○ He <u>was held in police custody</u>.
  - ☞ in custody「収監されて、拘留中で」
- 彼は警察護衛のもと建物を後にした。
  - ○ He left the building <u>under police escort</u>. ☞ under escort「護衛されて」
- 警察は窃盗の容疑で彼を逮捕した。
  - ○ The police <u>arrested him for</u> burglary.
- 現在のところ、警察は容疑者を特定していない。
  - ○ <u>At present</u>, the police have no suspects. ☞ at present「現在、目下」

▶ ストーリー

Last night **the police arrested the man** they had been searching for since **the bank robbery** at XYZ Bank in ABC City. In this robbery, **more than ten million yen was stolen**. **The police had been searching for the suspected bank robber** for more than a month. **An anonymous telephone call led to his arrest**.

(昨夜、警察はABC市XYZ銀行での強盗事件発生以来捜索していた男を逮捕した。この強盗事件で1千万円以上が盗まれた。警察は1か月以上におよび容疑者の銀行強盗犯を捜索していた。匿名の電話が彼の逮捕につながった。)

005 APOLOGY C

> 謝罪に関わる意識が日本と英米（さらに英語圏の中でも）で差があるのは周知の事実である。英語では特に 'apology' に敏感であり、この語を用いた「謝罪しない」表現に慣れておくことも重要であろう。
> ✲ 'apology' は大まかではあるが、単数形か複数形かで以下のような違いがあり、単数形のほうが謝罪の気持ちが強く出ていると言える。
> - 単数形 ☞ 特定の事柄に対する謝罪
> - 複数形 ☞ 期待に添えないことへの言い訳や弁解
>
> **>> LANGUAGE; MISTAKE; THANKS**

▶ apology から広がるボキャブラリー：名詞表現

- 深くわびること ◯ profuse apologies ☞ profuse「熱心な、心からの」
- 平身低頭してわびること ◯ humble apologies
- 心からのおわび ◯ sincere apologies
- 公的な謝罪 ◯ a public apology
- 十分な謝罪 ◯ a full apology
- 適切な謝罪 ◯ a proper apology
- 簡単な謝罪 ◯ a brief apology

▶ apology から広がるボキャブラリー：動詞表現

- わびる；謝罪を申し出る ◯ offer apologies
- わびる ◯ make [give] an apology ☞「名詞表現」と組み合わせてみよう
- 謝罪を要求する ◯ demand an apology
- ボブは謝罪を繰り返した。 ◯ Bob repeated his apologies.
- 私はあなたに完全に謝らなければならない。
  ◯ I owe you a full apology. ☞ I owe him 10,000 yen「私は彼に1万円借りがある」
- 遅れたことをご容赦頂ければと存じます。
  ◯ Please accept my apologies for being late.
- 時間を守らなかったことをご容赦頂ければと存じます。
  ◯ Please accept my apologies for not being on time.
- 彼の声が謝罪めいてきた。 ◯ A hint of apology crept into his voice.

☞ a hint of sth「〈事〉の気配; 徴候」 creep into sth「(過失・失言などが)〈物事〉に徐々に現れてくる」

▶「謝罪をしないこと」に関わる表現

- ❏ わびを入れない ◯ offer no apologies
- ❏ わびるのを拒否する ◯ refuse to offer an apology
- ❏ しぶしぶおわびする ◯ make a grudging apology ☞ grudging「いやいやの、不承不承の」< grudge sth「〈物〉を与えるのを惜しむ、〈事〉をいやがる」
- ❏ 口先だけの謝罪しか受け取らない
  ◯ receive nothing but an insincere apology ☞ nothing but ...「ただ...だけ」(= only) insincere「誠意のない、心のこもっていない」
- ❏ 当然謝罪されるべきだ。◯ An apology is due. ☞ be due「当然与えられるべきだ」
- ❏ 何の謝罪も用意されていなかった。
  ◯ No apology was forthcoming. ☞ forthcoming「入手できる」
- ❏ 私は自分がしたことに対して弁解はしない。
  ◯ I make no apologies for what I have done.
- ❏ きちんとした謝罪を求める ◯ want a proper apology
- ❏ 書面での謝罪を要求する ◯ demand a written apology
- ❏ 謝罪の言葉を聞いていない ◯ hear no word of apology
- ❏ 謝罪と釈明を退ける ◯ dismiss an apology and explanation
  ☞ be unfairly dismissed「不当解雇される」

▶ ストーリー

Sometimes **giving a heartfelt** apology **can be very difficult**. However, even if we **do not want to apologize**, or **feel embarrassed about apologizing**, **it is usually better to make the** apology. We usually feel better after **apologizing sincerely**.

(時に心からの謝罪をすることが非常に難しいことがある。しかしながら、たとえ謝りたくない、あるいは謝ることが恥ずかしく感じるとしても、たいていは謝ったほうがよい。誠実におわびをすれば、たいていは気分が晴れるものである。)

APOLOGY

006 ART U

芸術は、現代社会における生活空間の充実に欠かせない要素である。ここでは芸術の種類に加えて、他の一般的な場面にも応用可能な「評価」に関わるさまざまな表現を 'art' をもとにして紹介した。
* 'art' は U 扱いであり、特定の具体的な芸術作品について述べる場合は 'a piece of art' または 'a work of art' などとしなければならない。C として複数形で用いられると次のように意味が異なるので注意。

例 the arts and the sciences (学問の) 文科系と理科系
the arts 総合芸術 (音楽、劇、映画、文学などを総合的に考える)

>> ENJOYMENT; HOBBY; INTERNET

▶ art から広がるボキャブラリー：名詞表現

- 美術 ◯ fine art
- 正真正銘の芸術 ◯ genuine art
- 現代芸術 ◯ contemporary art
- 抽象芸術 ◯ abstract art
- ポップアート ◯ pop art
- 現代芸術 ◯ modern art
- 韓国の現代芸術 ◯ modern Korean art
- アメリカの民芸 ◯ American folk art
- ルネッサンス芸術 ◯ Renaissance [rinéisns, rènəsá:ns] art
- 印象派の芸術 ◯ impressionist art
- 立体派芸術 ◯ cubist art
- 超現実主義 [シュールレアリスムの] 芸術 ◯ surrealistic art
- アール・ヌーボー ◯ art nouveau [á:r(t)nu:vóu]
- アール・デコ ◯ art deco [á:r(t)dékou]

▶「評価」に関わる表現

- 芸術の世界 ◯ the art world
- 芸術界 ◯ the art establishment
  ☞ the political establishment「政界」
- 美術評論家 ◯ an art critic

- 個人の芸術コレクション ◎ a private art collection
- 20世紀芸術のコレクション ◎ a collection of twentieth-century art
- 画廊を訪れる ◎ visit an art gallery
- 美術品の鑑定家になる ◎ become an art connoisseur [kɒnəsɔ́ːr]
- 芸術史を勉強する ◎ study the history of art
- 芸術品の競売[オークション]を開催する ◎ hold an auction of art
- ボブは芸術が本当にわかる人だ。◎ Bob can really appreciate art.
  ☞ appreciate sth「〈芸術など〉を鑑賞する、〈人物事〉の真価を認める」。「感謝する」の意味では〈人〉を目的語にとらない (No.036)
- 2千万円と評価された美術品を買う
  ◎ buy a piece of art valued at twenty million yen
  ☞ value sth at a million dollars「〈物〉を100万ドルと評価する」
- 盗まれた芸術作品を購入する ◎ purchase a stolen work of art
- 一つの芸術作品も国外へ輸出させない
  ◎ do not let a work of art be exported from the country
- 国に自分の芸術コレクションを寄付する
  ◎ donate my collection of art to the nation　☞ donate sth to sb「〈物〉を〈人〉に寄付する」
- 美術館に芸術品のコレクションを寄付する
  ◎ endow a museum with a collection of art works
  ☞ endow sb with sth「〈物〉を〈人〉に寄付する」 cf. He is endowed with genius.「彼は才能に恵まれている」

▶ ストーリー

I cannot really call myself **a real lover of art**. But I do **enjoy visiting art galleries and museums**. I cannot tell you if **a particular work of art** is an example of **such-and-such a school of art**, but I will be able to **tell you why I like it, or do not**.

(私はとても真の芸術愛好者ではない。しかし私は画廊と博物館を訪れるのが本当に楽しい。私はある特定の芸術作品が何々派に属すなどと判断することはできない。しかし、その作品を好きな、あるいは好きでない理由を述べることはできる。)

007 BATH　C

風呂は英米でも、入浴方法は異なれ日本同様リラックスするための場所であることに変わりなく、'bath'をもとにした表現は多い。
✲「風呂 に入る」「シャワーを浴びる」場合、英国では 'have a bath/shower' と言うが、米国で、'bathtub'(米) の違いがある。
✲「〜する」という場合 'have' と 'take' の両方を用いる表現が他にも多数あることに注意（必ずしも英米の差とは限らない)。

例 have [take] a walk / a nap / a sip / a bite /a look
散歩をする/昼寝をする/一口すする/少し食べる/ちょっと見る

>> HAIR; HOME

▶ bath から広がるボキャブラリー：名詞表現

❏ 専用の浴室 ⭘ a private bath
❏ 噴流式の風呂 ⭘ a whirlpool bath
❏ 泡風呂 ⭘ a bubble bath
❏ ちょうどいい湯加減の風呂 ⭘ a bath that is just right
❏ 熱すぎる風呂 ⭘ a bath that is too hot
❏ 生ぬるい風呂 ⭘ a bath with tepid water ☞ tepid「なまぬるい」 一般に hot＜warm＜tepid＜cool＜coldの順

▶ bath から広がるボキャブラリー：動詞表現

❏ 風呂の水を抜く；浴槽を空にする ⭘ empty a bath ☞ empty *sth*「〈入れ物〉を空にする」
❏ 湯船に水を入れる ⭘ run a bath ☞ run *sb* a hot bath「〈人〉に風呂を用意する」
❏ 湯船に水［湯］を張る ⭘ fill a bath
❏ 風呂をわかす ⭘ heat up a bath
❏ 風呂の湯加減をみる ⭘ test the bath
❏ 入浴する ⭘ have a bath
❏ 湯船に入る ⭘ get into the bath
❏ 入浴中である ⭘ be in the bath
❏ いい湯加減の風呂を楽しむ ⭘ enjoy a nice hot bath ☞ このniceは「十

分に、とても」の意味 *cf.* a nice long holiday「ちょうどいい長さの休日」
- 風呂から上がる ○ get out of the bath
- 子供風呂でゴム製のアヒル人形を浮かべる
  ○ float a rubber duck in the kids' bath

▶ 関連表現

- 子供の入浴時間 ○ the children's bathtime
- バスタオル ○ a bath towel
- 入浴・シャワー用のジェル ○ some bath and shower gel
- 入浴石けん ○ some bath soap
- デオドラント・スティック ○ a deodorant stick
- モイスチャークリーム ○ a body moisturizer

▶ 決まり文句

- 私は風呂に入りたい！ ○ I need a bath!
- 私たちは要らないものといっしょに大事なものを捨ててしまった。
  ○ We threw the baby out with the bath water.
  ☞ throw the baby out with the bath water「不要な物と一緒に大事な物を捨ててしまう」

▶ ストーリー

The bathroom was really luxurious. The walls **were covered in tiles** imported from Spain. **The bathtub** itself was carved from a single block of Italian marble. **The taps** were solid gold. I **got into the bath**, and **lay there for a full hour**. **When I got out, I felt really refreshed**. **There is nothing like a nice hot bath for relaxing you**.

(その浴室は本当に豪華であった。壁はスペインから輸入されたタイルで覆われていた。浴槽は一枚岩のイタリアの大理石から切り出されたものであった。蛇口は純金であった。私は風呂につかってまる1時間横たわった。風呂から上がったとき私は本当に気分爽快だった。リラックスするには、いい湯加減の風呂に優るものはない。)

008 BEHAVIOUR ⎵U⎵

「行動・ふるまい」を表す 'behaviour' [behavior《米》を含む表現は、次の3グループに分けて考えてみよう。この語が生活空間にしめる重要性が再認識されるはずだ。
① 「社会的な行動」: moral/criminal behaviour など
② 「生物学的な行動」: human/mating behaviour など
③ 「個人的な行動」: disruptive/selfish behaviour など(悪い意味になることが多い)

✸ 通常 U として用いられるが、社会学や行動学などで C として用い、「行動の形態」を意味する場合がある。
  例 observe certain behaviours in an animal
     動物のある種の行動を観察する

>> **CHARACTER; EMOTION; KINDNESS**

▶ behaviour から広がるボキャブラリー:名詞表現

- 道徳的な行為 ◎ moral behaviour ……………………………… ①
- 犯罪行動 ◎ criminal behaviour
- 白鳥の交尾(習性) ◎ the mating behaviour of swans ………… ②
- 社会的に是認された行動 ◎ socially acceptable behaviour
- 人間の行動 ◎ human behaviour
- 予想できない行動 ◎ unpredictable behaviour
- ばかげたふるまい ◎ irrational behaviour ☞ irrational「不合理な、無分別な」
- 自分の子供たちの望ましくないふるまい
  ◎ undesirable behaviour in my children ……………………… ③
- 子供の非協力的な態度 ◎ uncooperative behaviour in a child
- 秩序を乱す[破壊的な]行動 ◎ disruptive behaviour

▶ behaviour から広がるボキャブラリー:動詞表現

- 結婚生活において問題を引き起こす利己的な行動
  ◎ selfish behaviour which can lead to problems in a marriage
  ☞ lead to sth「〈事〉の結果になる、〈事〉を引き起こす」
- 攻撃的な行動を引き起こすテレビでの暴力

- ○ TV violence which causes aggressive behaviour
- ❏ ボブの態度を変えさせる ○ change Bob's behaviour
- ❏ 特定の行動パターンを説明する
    - ○ explain a particular pattern of behaviour
- ❏ 子供の行儀が悪い理由を探す
    - ○ <u>look for</u> the reasons for bad behaviour in a child
- ❏ 動物の生態を研究をする
    - ○ <u>carry out</u> research into animal behaviour ☞ carry /sth/ out「〈研究・実験など〉を実施する、行う」
- ❏ 政治家の行いを非難する
    - ○ <u>denounce</u> the behaviour of a politician ☞ denounce sb/sth「〈人/物事〉を非難する」
- ❏ 子供の行儀の良さを誉める
    - ○ <u>praise</u> a child <u>for</u> his [her] good behaviour
- ❏ 良い行いには報酬を与え、悪い行いを思いとどまらせる
    - ○ reward good behaviour and discourage bad (behaviour)

▶ 決まり文句

- ❏ パーティではできるだけ行儀をよくしなさい。
    - ○ <u>Be on your best behaviour</u> at the party.

▶ ストーリー

Yesterday, I took my four-year old daughter to the birthday party of one of her friends. She **is a little bit spoilt** and **used to getting her own way**, so I told her that she **had to be on her best behaviour**. Unfortunately, **her behaviour did not come up to my expectations**. To tell you the truth, she **behaved really badly**.

(昨日、私は4歳になる娘を彼女の友だちの誕生パーティに連れて行った。娘は少々甘やかされており、わがままを何とも思っていない。それで私は娘にできるだけお行儀よくしていなさいと言った。しかし残念ながら、娘は私の期待どおりにふるまってはくれなかった。それどころか彼女は本当に行儀が悪かったのだ。)

009 BOOK　C

> 本を扱う場面は生活空間で非常に多い。ここでは、本とそのつくりに関わるさまざまな表現や読書に関わる表現、そして 'book' を用いた決まり文句を中心に紹介する。
>
> ✼「本」としての 'book' 以外に、日本語の「録」「帳」「書」「鑑」は英語では 'book' で表される場合が多い。(以下の冠詞の違いにも注意)
>
> 例　an address book 住所録　　the (tele)phone book 電話帳
> 　　an instruction book 指導書　a yearbook 年鑑
>
> **>> NEWSPAPER; TELEVISION**

▶ book から広がるボキャブラリー：名詞表現

- ❏ 短編小説集 ● a book of short stories
- ❏ 美しいレイアウトの本 ● a book with a beautiful layout
- ❏ 情報が豊富な本 ● a book containing a lot of information
- ❏ 『英語を学ぼう』という書名の本 ● a book entitled '*Learn English!*'
- ❏ 読み出したらとまらない本 ● a book that I cannot put down
- ❏ 本の第二刷 ● the second printing of a book
- ❏ 本の新版 ● a new edition of a book
- ❏ 最近発売された本 ● a book recently put on sale ☞ put *sth* on sale 「〈物〉を売りに出す」
- ❏ ＸＹＺ社から刊行された本 ● a book published by XYZ Company

▶ book から広がるボキャブラリー：動詞表現

- ❏ 本をぱらぱらとめくって読む ● flick through a book
- ❏ 本屋で本を拾い読みする ● skim through a book in a bookshop
- ❏ 写真集をざっと眺める ● glance through a book of photos
- ❏ 初めから終わりまで本を読む ● read a book from cover to cover
- ❏ アマゾンからダウンロードして本を買う
  ● buy books by downloading them from Amazon
- ❏ 電子書籍をキンドル/iPadで読む
  ● read e-books on a Kindle / an iPad
- ❏ 参考書にあたる ● consult a reference book

- 本を読んで夜を明かす ◯ stay up all night reading a book
- 図書館から本を借りる ◯ check a book out of the library
- 本を検閲する ◯ censor a book
- いかがわしい本を発禁にする ◯ ban a pornographic book

▶ book のパーツ

- 表紙 ◯ the cover of a book
- カバー ◯ the (dust) jacket of a book
- 序文 ◯ the preface of a book
- はしがき ◯ the introduction of a book
- 第二章 ◯ the second chapter of a book
- 索引 ◯ the index of a book

▶決まり文句

- 裁判官は私に重い刑を下した。◯ The judge threw the book at me.
  ☞ throw the book at sb「〈人〉を可能な限りの厳罰に処す」
- ボブは機転が利かなくて、マニュアル通りにしかできない。
  ◯ Bob has so little imagination that he can only go by the book.
  ☞ go by the book「融通がきかない、規則通りにやる」
- 彼女はいわば本の虫だ。◯ She is, so to speak, a bookworm.
- 本は読んでみなければわからない [人は外見で判断してはいけない]。
  ◯ Don't judge a book by its cover.

▶ ストーリー

Someone said that they never **lent out their books** because all **theirs came from other people's libraries**. So, if a friend **admires your books** and starts to **take them down from the shelves**, looking at them, I suggest that you lead him or her away from **the bookshelf**.
(自分の本は絶対貸さない人たちがいたという。その理由は、その人たちの本はすべて他の人の蔵書から借りてきたものだったからだ。だから、もしあなたの友人があなたの所有する本を誉めて、それらを見ながら本棚から取り出し始めたら、その人を本棚から引き離すことを私はおすすめする。)

010 BOSS C

> 上下関係の重要さは、ファーストネームで呼び合うことが日本よりもふつうに行われる英語圏でも同様である。特に会社に勤めている限り避けて通れない 'boss' に関わる表現をまとめておこう。
>
> ✻ 'boss' は、'superior'（上役）のインフォーマルな表現にあたる。この語を使うことにより、肩書きで呼ぶのを避けることができ、堅苦しさが少なくなるという点で便利な言葉である。日本語の「ボス」にあるような、やや横柄なイメージはない点に注意。
>
> **>> COMPANY; WORK**

▶ boss から広がるボキャブラリー：名詞表現

- 会社のトップ ○ the boss of the company
- 我々の課の前の上司 ○ the former boss of our department
- ワンマンの上司 ○ an autocratic boss ☞ autocratic「独裁的な、横暴な」
- 威張り散らす上司 ○ a bullying boss ☞ bully sb「〈人〉をいじめる」
- 優柔不断な上司 ○ an indecisive boss

▶ boss から広がるボキャブラリー：動詞表現

- 上司を悩ませる ○ annoy the boss
- 上司が私に割り当てた仕事をする
  ○ do the work assigned to me by my boss ☞ assign sth to sb「〈物事〉を〈人〉に割り当てる」
- 上司をセクハラで告発する
  ○ accuse the boss of sexual harassment ☞ accuse sb of sth「〈人〉を〈何かのかど〉で訴える、非難する」
- 上司は辞めるべきである。○ The boss should resign.
- 上司は仕事を失った。○ The boss lost his job.
- 上司は私を解雇した［クビにした］。○ The boss fired me.
- 上司は私を他の課に異動させた。
  ○ The boss transferred me to another section.
- 上司は私に2週間の無給休暇をくれた。
  ○ The boss gave me two weeks' unpaid leave. ☞ a paid vacation

「(長めの) 有給休暇」 maternity leave「出産休暇」

❏ 上司は責任を負うべき者である。

　◯ The boss is the one who should take responsibility.

❏ 彼女は (その下で) 働きやすい上司である。

　◯ She is a good boss to work for. ☞ work for a bank「銀行勤めをする」

❏ 命令を下すのは俺だということをみんな忘れていないだろうな。

　◯ I want to remind everyone who the boss is.

　☞〈決まり文句〉You are the boss.

❏ 私は彼が上司だとは知らなかった。

　◯ I did not realize that he was the boss. ☞ realizeは「事実やものごとの重要性についてはっきり理解する、悟る」という意味

▶決まり文句

❏ なにかと威張り散らす兄 ◯ a very bossy elder brother

❏ 私をこき使ってばかりいる妹

　◯ a younger sister who is always bossing me around

　☞ boss sb around「〈人〉をこき使う、あごで使う」

❏ あなたが決めてください [あなたの言うとおりにします]。

　◯ You are the boss.

❏ 彼らに誰が実権をもっているか [一番偉いか] 思い知らせてやる。

　◯ I'll show them who is boss.

▶ ストーリー

Mr. Tanaka, **the manager of our section**, is **a pretty good boss to work for**. **Our previous boss was very indecisive**, and **would not treat everyone equally**. He **would assign work in a rather unfair way**. Mr. Tanaka **assesses our work fairly**. **Our former manager** did not.

(うちの課の課長、田中氏はとても働きやすい上司である。我々の前の上司は非常に優柔不断で皆を公平に扱わず、仕事の割り当て方も公正とは言えなかった。田中氏は我々の仕事を公正に評価する。前の課長はそうではなかった。)

011 CAR [AUTO(MOBILE)]　　　　　Ⓒ

米国は「車社会」と言われるほど、自動車が生活空間で最もよく用いられる移動手段である。車の状態や部品、乗車・運転に関して行う動作を英語でどう表現するのか、ここで確認しておこう。
＊ オートバイも含め、すべての「原動機付き輸送機」をカバーする語は '(motor) vehicle' である。これと関連して、'bike' は 'bicycle'(自転車)を意味し、'motorbike'(オートバイ)の意味になるのはきわめて文脈や状況がはっきりしている場合だけであることに注意。

>> ACCIDENT; ROAD; TRAIN; TRAVEL

▶ car から広がるボキャブラリー：名詞表現

❏ 非常に静かな自動車 ◯ a very quiet car
❏ 現代的な合成素材で作られた自動車
　　◯ a car made with modern composite materials
❏ 修理状態のよくない自動車 ◯ a car in a bad state of repair
❏ 空気抵抗が少ないように設計された自動車
　　◯ an aerodynamically designed car ☞ aerodynamically「空気力学的に」
❏ ハイブリッドカーへの政府からの補助金
　　◯ a government subsidy for hybrid cars ☞ subsidy「補助金、援助金」
❏ 走行距離の短い中古車 ◯ a secondhand car with low mileage
❏ cars in the fast lane, nose to tail
　　◯ 高速レーンで数珠つなぎになって(渋滞して)いる自動車 ☞ nose to tail = bumper-to-bumper《米》
❏ 最近の自家用車の減少
　　◯ the recent decrease in the number of private cars

▶ car から広がるボキャブラリー：動詞表現

❏ 車に乗り込む / 車から出る ◯ get into a car / get out of a car
❏ 車をガレージにバックで入れる ◯ back my car into the garage
　☞ back sth/sb「〈物〉を後退させる /〈人〉を支援する」
❏ 高そうな車で乗りつける ◯ pull up in an expensive looking car
　☞ pull up「(車が)一時停止する」

モノ

- 駐車場に駐車する ○ park my car in a car park
- 車のドアをバタンとしめる ○ slam the car door loudly
- 車をコントロールできなくなる ○ lose control of a car
- 2台の車は急にそれて、次に衝突した。
    ○ The two cars swerved, and then collided.
- 車のコントロールを取り戻す ○ recover control of a car
- 車の排気ガスを削減する ○ cut emissions from cars
- 車を整備に出す ○ have my car serviced
- 車のエンジンを調整する ○ tune up the engine of my car
- 新車を買うためにローンを組む ○ take out a loan to buy a new car
- 古い車を(下取りに出して)ハイブリッドカーに買い換える
    ○ trade in my old car for a hybrid one

▶ car のパーツ

- 点火装置；イグニッション ○ the ignition
- ヘッドライト ○ the headlights ☞ 複数形に注意
- ワイパー ○ the wipers ☞ 複数形に注意
- ブレーキ ○ the brake
- アクセル ○ the accelerator
- クラッチ ○ the clutch
- スピードメーター ○ the speedometer [spidómətər]

▶ ストーリー

British and American words for **cars** (should I say **automobiles**?) are rather different. A British (and Japanese) **bonnet** is an American **hood**; an American (and Japanese) **trunk** is a British **boot**. But no one will understand 'the handle', since this is '**the steering wheel**' in English.

('car'に関する言葉('automobile'と言うべきか)は英国と米国でかなり異なる。英国(そして日本)の'bonnet'(ボンネット)は米国では'hood'であり、米国(そして日本)の'trunk'(トランク)は英国では'boot'である。しかし、「ハンドル」を英語で'handle'と言っても誰もわからないだろう。なぜならこれは英語では'steering wheel'と言うからだ。)

CAR [AUTO(MOBILE)]

012 CELLPHONE [MOBILE PHONE] ･･･ C

> 携帯電話は間違いなく現代社会を象徴するアイテムの一つであり、すでに生活空間の核に最も近い部分に近づきつつある。その進化はいまだ止まらない。こういった状況を踏まえ、この項では特別に4頁を割いて携帯電話とその使用に関わる幅広い表現を紹介した。
>
> ✻ 'cellphone' は米語（俗称 'cell'、正式には 'cellular phone'）で、英国では 'mobile (phone)' と言う。
>
> ✻ 'cellphone' を「(携帯電話という) 技術」ではなく、特に「(実際に使う) もの」としてとらえる場合は、'handset' がほぼ同義の言葉として使われる。
>
> ✻ 従来の電話は '<u>the</u> (tele)phone' と言うが、携帯電話の場合は、'<u>my</u> [his, her など] cellphone' と言うことが多いことにも注意。
>
> **>> COMPUTER; E-MAIL / INTERNET; TECHNOLOGY**

▶ cellphone の種類と機能

❏ 手のひらにぴったり収まる携帯電話
  ○ a handset that <u>fits in to</u> the palm of your hand
❏ 動画再生画面付き携帯 ○ a handset <u>equipped with</u> a video screen
  ☞ be equiped with *sth*「〈物〉が装備されている、〈事〉が身についている」
❏ 見やすいディスプレイのついた携帯電話
  ○ a handset with a display that is easy to read
❏ カメラ付き携帯電話 ○ a cellphone with a built-in camera
❏ ワンセグチューナー付き携帯電話
  ○ a cellphone equipped with a One-Seg digital TV tuner
❏ ハンドヘルド・コンピュータにもなる携帯電話
  ○ mobile phones that are handheld computers
❏ ケータイの迷惑電話 [メール] 対策機能
  ○ the nuisance-block function on my cell
❏ 世界標準である携帯電話の技術
  ○ a cellphone technology that is the global standard
❏ ケータイがないために友達ができない学生
  ○ a student who cannot <u>make friends</u> because he has no mobile

▶ 「cellphone の使い方」に関わる表現

- メグとケータイで話す ◎ talk to Meg on my cell
- 耳に携帯電話をあてたまま歩き回る
  ◎ walk round with a cellphone glued to my ear ☞ be glued to *sth*
  「〈物〉にくっついて離れない」
- (携帯)電話にしゃべりながら運転する
  ◎ drive a car while chatting into a phone
- 携帯電話をとってダイヤルボタンを押す
  ◎ pick up my handset and press the dial button
- 携帯電話の確認ボタンを押す
  ◎ press the confirm button on my mobile
- ケータイをマナーモードにする ◎ set my cell to silent mode
- 携帯電話でEメールをやりとりする
  ◎ exchange e-mails over our cellphones
- 携帯電話で文章を送る ◎ send a text message by cellphone
- 携帯電話を使って情報をダウンロードする
  ◎ download information using a cellphone
- 携帯電話でインターネットに接続する
  ◎ connect to the Internet with a mobile
- 今使っている番号で海外でも携帯電話を使う
  ◎ use a mobile overseas with my usual number
- 自分への電話を他の携帯電話に転送してもらう
  ◎ have my calls forwarded to another mobile
- 空港でレンタル携帯電話を受け取れます。
  ◎ You can pick up your rental handset at the airport.
- おじいちゃんがペースメーカーをつけているのでケータイを切った。
  ◎ I turned off my cell because Grandpa has a pacemaker.

▶ 「料金の支払い」に関わる表現

- 基本料金として3,000円請求された。
  ◎ I was charged 3,000 yen as a base fee. ☞ charge *sb* $100「〈人〉に

100ドル請求する」（例文はこの受身形）

❏ 90分間の通話料（金）を含んだ基本料金
　◯ a base fee which includes 90 minutes of calls

❏ 指定の番号への通話に対して20％割引になる
　◯ get a discount of 20% off all calls for designated numbers
　☞ offは「〜から」の意味　designated「（名の前で）指定［指名］の」

❏ 未使用分の時間（基本料金）を翌月に繰り越す
　◯ roll over unused minutes [the unused basic charge] to next month　☞ roll /sth/ over to stm「（金）の返済をある時まで延期する」

❏ 通信料金は送受信されたデータ量のみに基づいて課金される。
　◯ Communications charges are based only on the amount of data volume sent and received.

❏ 普通の固定電話や他社の携帯へかけると高い。
　◯ Calling landline telephone numbers, or mobiles on other networks, is expensive.

❏ 一般的に言って、基本料金が高いほど通話料は安くなる。
　◯ Generally, the higher the base fee, the lower the call charges.

▶ 関連表現

❏ 電話番号をダイヤル / 入力する ◯ dial / input a phone number
❏ 長電話して電話を切る ◯ hang up after a long phone call
❏ 圏外にいる。◯ I am outside the service area. ☞ No Service「圏外」
❏ 都市部の外では受信状態が悪くなる。
　◯ Reception deteriorates outside urban areas.
❏ 国内に最も広いサービスエリアをもつ（携帯電話の）会社
　◯ the company which has the best coverage nationwide
❏ 広い販売網をもつ優れたキャリア
　◯ a good provider with a wide network of outlets
　☞ このproviderは携帯電話の会社（＝キャリア）のこと。outletは「小売店」
❏ 携帯電話の会社を変えても番号はそのまま
　◯ switch the company, and keep my number

- 着メロをダウンロードする ◯ download ring tones
- 着信拒否機能をオンにする activate the caller-block function
- かけ直したら出会い系サイトに接続された。
  ◯ I called back and was connected to a dating site.
- 短縮ダイヤルを使う ◯ use one-touch dialling
- 表示されない番号からの着信を拒否する機能
  ◯ a blocking feature that blocks calls from numbers that are not displayed
- 親指でEメールのメッセージを打つ
  ◯ tap out an e-mail message with my thumb ☞ tap /sth/ out |〈文字情報など〉を打ち出す」
- 機種変する ◯ change my cellphone
- 第5世代のアイフォーン ◯ a fifth generation iPhone handset
- 携帯電話をアイフォーンのようなスマートフォンに変える
  ◯ replace my cellphone for a smart phone like iPhone

▶ ストーリー

Cellular phones have changed our lives. Cellphones give us access to unimaginable amounts of information, which we **can download with our cellphones**. Cellphones are rapidly becoming, or might have already become, cameras, video cameras, and **small computers that can fit in to the palm of your hand**. However, certain kinds of accidents have increased because of **the spread of cellphones**. I often see people **driving while talking on their cellphones**. Children ride bicycles and cross the road **with phones glued to their ears**.

(携帯電話は私たちの生活を変えた。携帯電話によって私たちは想像もできないくらい多くの情報にアクセスし、それらをダウンロードできるようになった。携帯電話は急速にカメラやビデオカメラそして手のひらにぴったり収まるくらいの小さなコンピュータになりつつある。あるいは、もうなっているかもしれない。しかし、携帯電話の普及が原因である種の事故が増加している。私は携帯電話で話しながら運転している場面をしばしば見かける。子供たちは携帯電話を耳にあてながら自転車に乗ったり道路を渡ったりするのだ。)

013 CHANCE · · · · · · · · · · · · C U

「**チ**ャンス」はもはや日本語の一部になった感があるが、英語の'chance' は意味的に「機会・好機」「見込み」「偶然の一致」の3つのグループに大きく分かれる。「チャンス」の乱用は禁物である！

C U { 特定の機会について述べる場合 ☞ C
特に偶然の一致について述べる場合 ☞ U または 'a ～ chance' の形

>> FAILURE; LUCK; SUCCESS

▶「機会・好機」に関わる表現

- ❏ 私の最後のチャンス ◯ my last chance
- ❏ 千載一遇の好機 ◯ the chance of a lifetime
- ❏ その学生にもう一度チャンスを与える
  ◯ give the student a second chance
- ❏ これは遅れている仕事を片づけるチャンスだ。
  ◯ This is a chance to finish my overdue work. C
- ❏ 与えられたチャンスに飛びつく
  ◯ jump at a chance that has been offered me ☞ jump at the invitation「その招待に飛びつく」
- ❏ 絶好のチャンスを逃してしまう ◯ let a wonderful chance slip by
  ☞ slip by「(機会などが) 過ぎてしまう」
- ❏ バカなことをして、チャンスを台無しにする
  ◯ ruin my chances by doing something stupid
- ❏ 昇進のチャンスをぶちこわす ◯ wreck my chances of promotion
  ☞ wreck sth「〈事〉を台無しにする」
- ❏ 惜しいチャンスがたくさんあったラグビーの試合
  ◯ a rugby match that was full of missed chances ☞ miss a chance to do「～するチャンスを逃す」
- ❏ 我がチームは機会を逃さず勝利した。
  ◯ Our team took our chances well and won.

▶「見込み」に関わる表現

- ❏ an even chance ◯ 五分五分の見込み

- ❏ 宝くじを当てるという万に一つの可能性
  - ◯ a one in a million chance of winning in the lottery
- ❏ 事故が起きる可能性 ◯ the chances of an accident happening
- ❏ 勝利の可能性はごくわずかだ ◯ have only a small chance of victory
- ❏ 勝つ見込みは決してない ◯ never stand a chance of winning
- ❏ 我々が生き残る見込みはわずかである。
  - ◯ Our chances of survival are slim. ☞ a slim hope「わずかな希望」
- ❏ それは我々が成功するただ一度のチャンスだ。
  - ◯ It is our one and only chance of success.
- ❏ メグが来る見込みはほとんどない。
  - ◯ There is little chance of Meg coming.

▶「偶然の一致」に関わる表現

- ❏ まったくの偶然 ◯ sheer chance Ⓤ
- ❏ 運がよいこと ◯ a lucky chance
- ❏ 私たちはほんの偶然で友達になった。
  - ◯ We became friends by pure chance.
- ❏ 偶然の出会いが我々を友情に導いた。
  - ◯ A chance encounter led to our friendship.

▶ ストーリー

Life is a story of **chances that we missed** and **chances that we took**. When I think about it, I am here right now because of **nothing more than chance**. There are probably **many chances that I have let slip by**, without even noticing them. How many **chances of success have I ruined by saying the wrong thing at the wrong time**, or **not being in the right place at the right time**?

（人生はチャンスを逃したりつかんだりの物語である。考えてみると、私が今まさにここにいるのは偶然以外の何ものでもない。恐らく私が気づきさえしないで見逃したチャンスは多いだろう。間の悪いときに不適切なことを言ったり、時や場所が適切でなかったばかりに台無しにした成功のチャンスがどれだけあったことか。）

014 CHANGE C U

> 時代の流れは変化と共に進行し、現代ではその動きが加速度を増している。ここでは、'change' を用いた変化・変更に関わる表現を、変化の「出来事やその発生」としての面と、「様子やパターン」としての面の2つのグループに分けて整理・紹介した。「〜の変化」といった場合の前置詞にも注意しよう。
>
> C｛特定の変化やそのタイプについて述べる場合 ☞ C
> U｛変化一般について述べる場合 ☞ U
>
> **>> ECONOMY; TECHNOLOGY**

▶「出来事・発生」に関わる表現

- ❏ 突然の変更 ◎ an abrupt change C
- ❏ 不意の変更 ◎ a sudden and unexpected change
- ❏ 抜本的な改革 ◎ a radical change
- ❏ 劇的かつ全面的な変化 [改革] ◎ a dramatic and sweeping change
    - ☞ sweeping「広範囲にわたる」
- ❏ 通常の [定期的な] 変更 ◎ a regular change
- ❏ 常識的な範囲の変化 ◎ a sensible change
- ❏ 強調点の変更 ◎ a change in emphasis ☞ 前置詞に注意
- ❏ 自分の運が変わること ◎ a change in my fortunes ☞ 前置詞に注意
- ❏ 心変わり ◎ a change of mind
- ❏ 変化はしばしば起こるものだ。◎ Changes often take place.

▶「変化の様子やパターン」に関わる表現

- ❏ 変化のパターン ◎ a pattern of change
- ❏ 変化のプロセス ◎ the process of change
- ❏ ファッションの変化 ◎ a change in fashion ☞ 前置詞に注意
- ❏ 気候の変化 ◎ a change in the climate ☞ 前置詞に注意
- ❏ 広範囲にわたる環境の変化 ◎ widespread environmental changes
- ❏ たゆまぬ改良と変更 ◎ continuing improvement and change U
- ❏ 患者の容態の好転
    - ◎ a change for the better in the patient's condition ☞ for the

better「より良く、快方に」〈決まり文句〉の U 扱いの同様表現に注意
- 政局の大きな変化 ◎ a great change in the political situation
- 力の均衡の変化 ◎ a change in the balance of power
- めまぐるしく景気が変わる時代
    ◎ a time of rapid economic change
- 市場の急激な変動に対応できない企業
    ◎ a company that cannot cope with rapid change in the marketplace ☞ cope with *sth*「〈事〉に対応する」
- 社会の大きな変化をもたらした戦争
    ◎ a war which brought about great changes in society ☞ bring /*sth*/ about「〈物事〉をもたらす」
- 元の計画には多くの変更の余地がある。
    ◎ There is plenty of scope for change to the original plan.
    ☞ scope for *sth*「〈事〉をする余地、機会」

▶決まり文句

- 変化のすべてが必ずしも好い変化ばかりとは限らない。
    ◎ All change is not necessarily change for the better. U
- 物事は変化すればするほど、かえって変わらないもの。《動詞》
    ◎ The more things change, the more they remain the same.

▶ストーリー

In our company there is always **some kind of change going on**. We **have changes in office procedures, changes in the system of claiming expenses,** and so on. None of **these changes is beneficial**. The boss **likes change for the sake of change**. English has borrowed a proverb from French: **The more things change, the more they remain the same.**

(我が社では常に何らかの変更が行われている。業務上の手続きの変更や、諸経費請求の仕方の変更などである。これらの変更で有益なものは何もない。上司は変更のための変更が好きなのである。英語にはフランス語から借用したこんな格言がある:物事は変化すればするほど、かえって変わらないもの。)

015　CHARACTER　　　　　　　　Ⓒ Ⓤ

> **性**格や特性についての描写に 'character' を用いる表現は多い。一般的に 'character' は内面の特徴を表す。外見的な特徴である 'characteristics' の組み合わせが 'character' になるとも言える。ここでは個性を表す関連表現も多数紹介したので参考にしてほしい。
> ✽ 通常はⒸで用いられるが、以下のような違いがある。
> - 人が持っている具体的な性格について述べる場合 ☞ Ⓒ
> - 人格や品性や特性などについて誉めて述べる場合 ☞ Ⓤ
>
> **>> BEHAVIOUR; FRIENDSHIP; KINDNESS**

▶ character から広がるボキャブラリー：名詞表現

- 強烈な個性 ○ a strong character Ⓒ
- 軟弱な性格 ○ a weak character
- まっすぐな性格 ○ an upright character ☞ an upright posture「背筋をのばした姿勢」
- 立派な性格の男性 ○ a man with a fine character
- 社交好きな性格の女性 ○ a woman with a gregarious character
  ☞ gregarious「社交的な、人付き合いの良い」
- 愛らしい性格をしている ○ have a lovable character
- 風変わりな性格をしている ○ have an eccentric character
- 不愉快な性格をしている ○ have an obnoxious character
  ☞ obnoxious [əbnɔ́kʃəs | -nák-]「ひどく不快で気に障る」
- メグの家は多くの特色がある。
  ○ Meg's house has a lot of character. Ⓤ

▶ character から広がるボキャブラリー：動詞表現

- ボブの性格が大きらいだ ○ hate Bob's character
- 修養を積む ○ develop my character ☞ develop *sth*「〈性質・特徴など〉を持つようになる」
- 自分の性格を形成した経験
  ○ an experience which formed my character
- 誠実さと品格を問われる仕事

○ a job which requires sincerity and character
❏ メグの性格を反映する行動

○ behaviour that reflects Meg's character
❏ 自分らしくない [柄にもない] 行動をする ○ act out of character
☞ out of character「その人らしくない」
❏ メグの性格が表情に現れている。

○ Meg's character shows in her face.

▶ 関連表現

❏ ダイナミックな人 ○ a dynamic person
❏ 非常に如才ない人 ○ a very tactful person
❏ 機転が利かない人 ○ a tactless person
❏ 寛容な人 ○ a tolerant person
❏ 短気な人 ○ a short-tempered person
❏ カリスマ的な個性を持った人

○ a person with a charismatic personality
❏ 強烈な性格を持った人 ○ a person with a forceful personality
☞ personalityは、特に他人の目に映る個性や性格

▶ 決まり文句

❏ 彼は本当に (変わった) 面白いやつだ。

○ He's a real character.
❏ ここは (面白い) 特徴にあふれた町である。

○ This is a town which is full of character.

▶ ストーリー

Bill **has a very gentle character and charming personality**. He is **not a person who gets angry easily**, although he **can be very forceful** in expressing his opinions.
(ビルは非常に優しい性格と魅力的な個性を持っている。彼は、自分の意見を述べるさいは非常に強い口調になることもあるが、すぐに腹を立てたりするような人間ではない。)

CHARACTER

016　CHILD　C

> 子供への接し方は文化圏により異なる。英語には 'Children should be seen and not heard.'（子供は見てやるだけでよく、おしゃべりを聞いてやるべきではない→子供は大人の前にいてもよいが黙っているべきだ）ということわざがある。これは紀元前423年にギリシアの喜劇詩人アリストファネスによって書かれたものであるが、驚くべきことに彼自身がこれは古いことわざであると述べている。ここからもわかるように、西洋の文化は伝統的に日本よりも子供の不作法に厳しいのである。
>
> **>> FAMILY; HUSBAND / WIFE**

▶ child から広がるボキャブラリー：名詞表現

- ❏ 5人兄弟の末っ子 ◯ the youngest of five children
- ❏ 3人の息子がいる家族の長男
  ◯ the eldest child in a family of three sons
- ❏ 一人っ子 ◯ an only child
- ❏ 天才児 ◯ a gifted child ☞ gifted「(天賦の)才能のある」
- ❏ 神経過敏な子供 ◯ a sensitive child ☞ be sensitive about *sth*「〈事〉を気にしている」
- ❏ 早熟な子供 ◯ a precocious child ☞ precocious [prikóoʃəs]「早熟な、並はずれた」
- ❏ 障害児 ◯ children with special needs
  ☞ a special need「(障害者などに生じる)特殊ニーズ」

▶ child から広がるボキャブラリー：動詞表現

- ❏ 子供をつくることができない ◯ cannot have children
- ❏ (初夜に)子供を身ごもる
  ◯ conceive a child (on your wedding night)
- ❏ もうすぐ初めての子供が生まれる。◯ I am expecting my first child.
  ☞ 単に She is expecting.「彼女は妊娠している」
- ❏ 養子をとる ◯ adopt a child ☞ an adopted child「養子」
- ❏ 子供の世話をする ◯ care for a child
- ❏ 子供を育てる ◯ raise a child

- 子供にトイレのしつけをする ◎ toilet-train a child
- 子供を甘やかして駄目にする ◎ spoil a child
- 心の底から自分の子供を愛す ◎ love my child with all my heart
- 子供の成長を見る喜びを知る
    ◎ know the joy of seeing a child grow up

▶関連表現

- 私の妻は妊娠8か月である。 ◎ My wife is eight months pregnant.
- 生まれたばかりの子供 ◎ a newborn child
- よちよち歩きの子 ◎ a toddler
- 赤ん坊 ◎ a baby ☞ 2歳くらいまで
- 幼児 ◎ an infant ☞ 普通、7歳以下を指す
- 未就学児 ◎ a preschooler
- 十代前の子供 ◎ a preteen
- ティーンエイジャー ◎ a teenager ☞ 13～19歳
- 青年期の若者 ◎ an adolescent ☞ 普通、12～18歳を指す

▶決まり文句

- そんなことは誰にでもできる。そんなの朝飯前だ。
    ◎ Anyone can do that. It's child's play.
    ☞ child's play「簡単なこと、たかが知れたこと」(Ⅱ扱いに注意)

▶ストーリー

Jim and Mary **got married** and **were looking forward to having children**. But however hard they tried, Mary **did not get pregnant**. They decided to **adopt a child**. Soon after that Mary **got pregnant** and **had a baby**. Jim and Mary now **have two lovely children**.

(ジムとメアリーは結婚して、子供ができるのを楽しみにしていた。しかしいくらがんばってもメアリーは妊娠しなかった。彼らは養子をとることに決めた。そのすぐ後メアリーは妊娠して赤ん坊を生んだ。ジムとメアリーには今二人のかわいい子供たちがいる。)

CHILD

017 CLOTHES (複数形)

> 「衣服」を表すこの語 'clothes' は歴史的に見れば、その材料である 'cloth' (布) の複数形である。発音は 'close the door' と言うときの 'close' [klóuz] と同じでよい。
>
> ここでは、「衣服を着る/脱ぐ」行為に関わるさまざまな英語表現 (☞〈使い分けのポイント〉) や 'a pair [two pairs] of ～' の豊富なパターン (☞〈ストーリー〉に多数登場) を特によくマスターすること。
>
> **>> FACE; FASHION; HAIR**

▶ clothes から広がるボキャブラリー：動詞表現

- ❏ 服装の趣味が良い/悪い ◯ have good / bad taste in clothes
  - ☞ この taste は「センス、鑑賞 [判断] 力」の意味。次の a taste「好み、嗜好」と比較のこと。前置詞にも注意
- ❏ 高価な服を好む ◯ have a taste for expensive clothes
- ❏ カジュアルな服を着るのを好む ◯ like wearing casual clothes
- ❏ ボブは明るくファッショナブルな服を着ている。
  - ◯ Bob is dressed in bright, fashionable clothes.
- ❏ デザイナーズブランドの服を買うのを楽しむ
  - ◯ enjoy shopping for designer clothes ☞ shop for sth「〈物〉を買い求める」 designer は「有名デザイナー製作の、デザイナーブランドの」の意味の形容詞として用いられることがあることに注意
- ❏ しわだらけにならないように服を掛ける
  - ◯ hang up my clothes to stop them getting badly creased
  - ☞ creased「しわになった、折り目のついた」
- ❏ 破れて、しみのついた服 ◯ clothes which are torn and stained
- ❏ 一泊旅行のための着替え (の服) をカバン [スーツケース] に詰める
  - ◯ pack a change of clothes for an overnight trip
  - ☞ a change of underwear「下着の替え」

▶使い分けのポイント

- ❏ パジャマを脱いだ。《動作》 ◯ I took off my pyjamas.
- ❏ 服を着た。《動作》 ◯ I put on my clothes.

- 私はいつもはスカートをはいている。《状態》 ◎ I usually wear a skirt.
- 今日はジーンズをはいていた。《一時的状態》
  ◎ I was wearing jeans today.
- 今は服を着ている。《一時的状態》 ◎ I now <u>have on</u> my clothes.
- 医者は私にズボンをはいたままでいるように言った。
  ◎ The doctor told me to <u>keep my trousers on</u>.

▶関連表現

- 赤いストライプのダークブルーのシャツ
  ◎ a dark blue shirt with red stripes
- 黄色の水玉模様のライトグリーンのシャツ
  ◎ a light green shirt with yellow polka dots
- 横縞の入ったピンクがかったブラウス
  ◎ a pinkish blouse with horizontal stripes
- 縦縞の入った明るい赤のセーター
  ◎ a bright red sweater with vertical stripes
- 縞模様の赤茶けた色のシャツ
  ◎ a reddish-brown shirt with a striped pattern
- 美しい花柄のネクタイ ◎ a tie with a beautiful flowery pattern
- チェックのソックス1足 ◎ <u>a pair of</u> socks with a checked pattern

▶ストーリー

Clothes that **are made up of two parts** are either plural (**my shoes**, **my jeans**, etc.), or are referred to as '**a pair of shoes**', '**a pair of jeans**', etc. But even within this group, there are some that are dividable, and can exist as one (**a shoe**, **a stocking**), and others that cannot (not 'a jean', or 'a tight').

(2つの部分で構成されている衣類は複数形(my shoes, my jeansなど)で用いられるか、または 'a pair of shoes' (1足のくつ)、'pair of jeans' (1着のジーンズ) と言われる。しかしこういったグループの中でさえ、分割可能で一個として存在できるもの (a shoe (くつの片方), a stocking (ストッキング)) とその他のそうでないもの ('a jean' や 'a tight' とは言えない) がある。)

CLOTHES

018 COMPANY C

日本の社会は会社中心に回っていると言っても過言ではない。新聞やニュースで毎日のように登場する 'company' に関わる表現をマスターしよう。

✢〈動詞〉や〈ストーリー〉で取り上げた「経営」に関わる動詞はその他さまざまな組織や団体などとも用いられる。

  例 establish a political party 政党を結成する
    manage a restaurant 食堂を経営する

✢ 日本語で「社会法人」や「財団法人」などと使い分けがなされる表現は英語では 'corporation' で表されることに注意。

  例 日本住宅公団 → the Japan Housing Corporation

>> BOSS; WORK

▶ company から広がるボキャブラリー：名詞表現

- 持ち株会社 ◯ a holding company
- 親会社 ◯ a parent company ☞ a subsidiary (company)「子会社」
- 電力会社 ◯ a power company
- 保険会社 ◯ an insurance company
- エンジニアリングの会社 ◯ an engineering company
- 鉄道会社 ◯ a railway company
- 金融会社 ◯ a finance company
- 革新的な会社 ◯ an innovative [ínəvèitiv] company
- 倒産した会社 ◯ a bankrupt company ☞ go bankrupt「倒産する」
- 経営体制の整っていない会社
  ◯ a company with no proper management structure

▶ company から広がるボキャブラリー：動詞表現

- 企業戦略を立てる ◯ plan company strategy
- 非常に効率的に会社を運営する
  ◯ run a company very efficiently
- 会社が破産するまで経営する
  ◯ manage a company till it goes bankrupt

組織

- ❏ 友人何人かと会社を設立する
  - ○ <u>set up</u> a company with some friends
- ❏ establish an overseas company ○ 海外に会社を設立する
- ❏ 会社をたたむ以外に選択肢がない
  - ○ <u>have no choice but to</u> <u>wind up</u> a company ☞ have no choice but to do「～するより他ない」 wind /sth/ up「〈事〉を終わらせる」
- ❏ 倒産寸前の会社を救おうとする
  - ○ <u>try to</u> rescue a company <u>on the brink of</u> collapse ☞ on the brink of sth「〈事〉の瀬戸際で」
- ❏ 会社を引き継ぐ；会社を乗っ取る ○ <u>take over</u> a company
- ❏ 会社の25パーセントの株式を得る
  - ○ take a 25 percent stake in a company
- ❏ 会社に投資する ○ <u>invest in</u> a company ☞ invest time and energy in studying English「英語の学習に時間と精力を注ぎ込む」
- ❏ 会社の年次総会を開催する
  - ○ hold the annual general meeting of the company

▶ 関連表現

- ❏ 会社の自動車 ○ a company car
- ❏ 会社人間 ○ a company man
- ❏ 会社のロゴ ○ the company logo
- ❏ 会社法を学ぶ ○ study company law ☞ commercial law「商法」

▶ ストーリー

Ten years ago I **established a new company with a few friends**. None of us **had had any experience in managing a company**. But I think we have **run it very efficiently**. We **have expanded** to the stage where **the company employs three hundred people**.

（10年前に私は数名の友人と新しい会社を設立した。我々の誰も会社経営の経験がなかった。しかし我々は非常に効率的に運営してきたと思う。我々は会社が従業員300人を抱えるところまで発展したのだ。）

COMPANY

019　COMPUTER　　　　　　　　　　　Ⓒ

> 今や生活空間の一風景となった感のあるコンピュータだが、誰しもこれに関しては苦い経験があるのではないだろうか。ここでも「手こずる/使いこなす」という視点から、コンピュータに関わる生活表現を整理してある。英語で書かれたマニュアルやインターネットなどにもよく登場する表現である。「コンピュータで/に」という場合の前置詞の使い分けにも注意したい。
>
> **>> CELLPHONE; E-MAIL / INTERNET; TECHNOLOGY**

▶「手こずる状況」に関わる表現

❏ いつも自分のパスワードを忘れてしまう
   ◯ always forget my computer password
❏ コンピュータがクラッシュして大あわてする
   ◯ panic when the computer crashes
❏ コンピュータを再起動せねばならない
   ◯ have to reboot my computer
❏ コンピュータのコの字[初歩]も理解できない
   ◯ cannot understand the first thing about computers
   ☞ not understand [know] the first thing about *sth*「〈事〉について何もわからない[知らない]」
❏ コンピュータについてくる説明書の類(たぐい)が理解できない
   ◯ cannot understand the documentation which comes with the computer ☞ come with *sth*「(商品など)についている」
❏ アイコンをダブルクリックしても何も起こらない
   ◯ double click an icon and nothing happens
❏「強制終了」の仕方がわからない ◯ do not know how to 'force quit'
❏ タスクバーを右クリックしたらコンピュータがフリーズした。
   ◯ My computer froze when I right clicked on the task bar.
❏ コンピュータ・ネットワークはダウンしている。
   ◯ The computer network is down.

▶「使いこなす状況」に関わる表現

- コンピュータを使い始める ◯ log in [on] to a computer
- コンピュータの使用を終了する ◯ log off [out of] a computer
- コンピュータで情報にアクセスする
  ◯ access information by computer ☞ access to としないこと
- コンピュータによって(外部の)情報を取り出す[検索する]
  ◯ retrieve information via a computer ☞ retrieve sth「〈情報〉を検索する、何かを取り戻す」via sth「〈事〉によって、〈事〉を通して」
- ネットワーク上の共有ファイルにアクセスする
  ◯ access shared files on a network ☞ share sth「〈物事〉を共有する」
- コンピュータにデータを入力する ◯ input data into a computer
- コンピュータに情報を記憶させる
  ◯ store information in a computer
- コンピュータでファックスの送受信を行う
  ◯ send and receive faxes on my computer
- アイコンをゴミ箱にドラッグする ◯ drag an icon into the trash
  ☞ drag は「引きずって運ぶ」の意味

▶ ストーリー

We all have to **keep on upgrading our computers**. Also, **the software is often full of bugs**. Then the buyer has to **go to a site and download a patch**. It is as if the maker of your car told that you had to **upgrade** the door, and then had to change the brakes to **make them 'compatible' with the door**. If you bought a car that **was full of bugs**, and were told that you had to **go to a 'site'** to **get a 'patch'**, you would be very surprised.

(我々は皆コンピュータをアップグレードし続けなければならない。また、ソフトウェアはしばしばバグだらけだ。その場合購入者はサイトに行ってパッチをダウンロードせねばならない。これはあたかも自動車のメーカーがあなたに、ドアをアップグレードしたら、その次にブレーキをドアと「互換性のある」よう変えろと言うようなものだ。もしバグだらけの自動車を買わされてから、「パッチ」を得るために「サイト」に行かなければならないと言われたら、あなたは非常に驚くであろう。)

020　COUNTRY / COUNTRYSIDE ・・・ Ⅰ U Ⅰ

> **都**会の生活に疲れた現代人が増える一方で、田舎や田園地帯への回帰や憧れの声も高まりつつある。ここではそのような文脈から 'country' と 'countryside' を用いたさまざまな表現を紹介した。
> ✲ 'country' は「田舎」の意味ではしばしば 'the' と共に用いられ、「地形、土地」の意味では冠詞なしで形容詞をつけて用いられることが多い。
> ✲ 'countryside' は 'the' をつけて用いられることが多い。'countryside' も 'country' も文脈に応じて「田舎」とも「田園地帯」とも訳されるが、前者は特に後者の美しさや外観について述べるとき用いられる。
>
> **>> COUNTRY / NATION; HOLIDAY; SEA / SEASIDE; TRAVEL**

▶ country / countryside から広がるボキャブラリー：名詞表現

❏ 荒れた土地 ○ rough country

❏ ごつごつした土地 ○ rugged country ☞ rugged [rʌ́gid]「起伏のある、岩の多い」

❏ 丘が多い土地 ○ hilly country ☞ hilly「小山の多い、起伏に富んだ」

❏ 山国（山の多い国）○ mountainous country

❏ 雪国（雪の多い国）○ snowy country

❏ 湿地の多い土地 ○ marshy country ☞ < marsh「沼地、湿地帯」

❏ 樹木の多い地方 ○ wooded countryside ☞ wooded「樹木の茂った」

❏ トスカーナ地方の美しい田舎

　○ the beautiful countryside of Tuscany [tʌ́skəni]

❏ 幼年時代を過ごした広々とした田舎

　○ the open countryside of my childhood

❏ 田園地帯の大部分を破壊してしまう新しい道路

　○ a new road which destroys large areas of countryside

❏ 街とその周りの田園地帯

　○ a town and the surrounding countryside

❏ 快適な田園地帯の中に位置した家

　○ a house situated amidst delightful countryside ☞ be situated「(場所に) 位置している」amidst [əmíd] sth「〈物事〉の中に、真ん中に」

❏ 田舎の家より、郊外の家 (がよいということ)

○ a house in the suburbs, rather than in the country
❏ カントリー・ウォークについての提案がいっぱいのガイドブック
　○ a guidebook full of suggestions for country walks
　☞ a country walkは都会の喧噪などを逃れて田園や野道などを散策すること

▶ country / countryside から広がるボキャブラリー：動詞表現

❏ 田舎に平安と静けさを見つける
　○ find peace and quiet in the country
❏ 田舎に家を買う ○ buy a house in the country
❏ 田舎の生活を楽しむ ○ enjoy country life
❏ 昔風の田舎の宿で夜を過ごす
　○ spend the night at an old-fashioned country inn
❏ 田園巡りの旅に出かける ○ set off on a tour of the countryside
　☞ set off「出発する」set off for home「家路につく」
❏ 田園地帯のドライブを楽しむ ○ enjoy a drive in the countryside
❏ 可能な限り多くの田園地帯の保護に努める
　○ try to preserve as much of the countryside as possible
❏ 街が田園地帯の中に広がった。
　○ Towns have spread in to the countryside.
❏ 田舎から都市部に通勤する
　○ commute from the country into town ☞ commute「(遠距離)通勤[通学]する」townは「繁華街、中心地」の意味のときはU扱いとなることに注意

▶ ストーリー

My aunt **has a beautiful house right in the middle of the country**. **The countryside itself was hilly**, and **rather wooded**. This **has now been destroyed** by a new road, which was built so that **more people could come and enjoy the lovely countryside**.

(私の叔母は田舎のど真ん中に美しい家を持っている。その一帯は山がちで、かなり樹木が多かった。これが今では新しい道路によって破壊されてしまった。その道路はより多くの人々が素晴らしい田園地帯を楽しむために訪れることができるよう作られたものだったのだが。)

021 COUNTRY / NATION ⸺ C

> 国を日頃意識することはほとんどないが、対外関係を考える場合にきわめて使用頻度の高い言葉である。ここでも、国対国という文脈から 'country/nation' に関わる頻出表現を紹介する。
>
> ✻ どちらも「国」を意味するが、'country' と言うと、国土としての国に重きがあり、'nation' と言うと、その住民(国民)やその国の社会・経済的な組織(国家)としての側面に重きがある。
>
> ✻ 日本語の「くにに帰る」のような表現に 'country' を用いることはできないことに注意。この場合の「くに」は 'hometown' が適切である。
>
> **>> COUNTRY / COUNTRYSIDE; GOVERNMENT; POLITICS**

▶ country / nation から広がるボキャブラリー:名詞表現

- ❏ 先進国 / 発展途上国 ◯ a developed nation / a developing nation
- ❏ 敵国 / 友好国 ◯ an enemy nation / a friendly nation
- ❏ 同盟国 ◯ an allied nation
- ❏ 国家共同体 ◯ the community of nations
- ❏ 新しい国の誕生 ◯ the birth of a new nation
- ❏ ヨーロッパの主要国 ◯ leading European countries ☞ leading「主要な」
- ❏ 戦争によって引き裂かれた国 ◯ a war-torn country
- ❏ 国全体をつなぐ道路網
    ◯ a road network linking the whole country
- ❏ 国全体の利益になる社会福祉プログラム
    ◯ welfare programmes which benefit the country as a whole
    ☞ benefit sb「〈人〉に利益を与える」 as a whole「(名の後で)全体としての」
- ❏ 国の政府 ◯ the government of a country
- ❏ 国の首都 ◯ a country's capital
- ❏ 我が国の西部で ◯ in the west of our country ☞ 前置詞の違いに注意
- ❏ 我が国の西方に ◯ to the west of our country

▶ country / nation から広がるボキャブラリー:動詞表現

- ❏ 国民を解放する ◯ liberate a nation ☞ liberate [líbərèit] sb「〈人〉を自由にする」 cf. liberty「自由、独立」

組織

- 国民を一つにまとめる ○ unite the nation
- もう一度国を偉大にする ○ make the nation great once more
- 国を滅ぼす ○ destroy a nation
- 大きな危機に瀕して国のために祈る
  ○ <u>pray for</u> the nation <u>in time of</u> great crisis
- ドラッグを国に密輸入する ○ <u>smuggle</u> drugs <u>into</u> a country
  ☞ smuggle *sth*「〈物〉を密輸する」
- 国の地勢を勉強する ○ study the physical geography of a country
- 侵略から自分の国を守る ○ <u>defend</u> <u>my country</u> <u>against</u> invasion
  ☞ 前置詞に注意
- ボブは自分の国に忠誠心がある。 ○ Bob <u>is loyal to</u> his country.
- 自分の国に対して大きな忠誠心を感じる
  ○ <u>feel</u> great <u>loyalty</u> <u>towards</u> my country
- 自分の命を国に捧げる ○ <u>lay down</u> <u>my life</u> <u>for</u> my country
  ☞ lay down *one's* life for *sb/sth*「〈人/事〉のために自分の命を犠牲にする」
- みじめな敗戦の後、国を立て直す
  ○ rebuild a country after a terrible defeat in war
- 国のために新しい憲法を書く
  ○ write a new constitution for the country
- (王様などが) 国を治める ○ <u>rule over</u> a country ☞ rule over *sb*「〈国・国民など〉を支配する」

▶ ストーリー

Probably the idea of '**nation**' and '**country**' has brought the greatest misery to humanity. It is when we **feel excess loyalty to our country** that we **have wars between nations**. We should remember that '**the enemy nation**' is made up of people just like us.

(恐らくは「国家」と「国」という考え方が最大の苦難を人類にもたらしたのだ。国家間で戦争が始まるのは、我々が自分の国に行き過ぎた忠誠心を感じるときである。我々は「敵国」が我々とまったく同じような人々で成り立っていることを忘れてはならない。)

022　DAY / NIGHT　　　　　　　　　C U

> 'day' と 'night' を知らない英語学習者はいないだろうが、これらを適切に用いて時間を表現できる人もまた少ない。ここでは、「時点」と「期間」という視点から 'day' と 'night' を用いた表現を整理した。これらを用いて自分の日常生活を説明できるか試してみよう。
>
> C U ｢～日｣｢～夜｣のように数えるときや、｢～の日｣｢～の夜｣のように一区切りの時間としての 'day' や 'night' について述べる場合 ☞ C
> 自然現象としての 'day' や 'night' について述べる場合 ☞ U
> （EVENING / MORNING の同様の表現も参照のこと）
>
> **>> EVENING / MORNING; TIME**

▶「時点」に関わる表現

- 一昨日 ○ the day before yesterday C
- 一昨日の夜 ○ the night before last
- 先日［先夜］；この間［この間の夜］ ○ the other day [night]
- 二、三日で［二、三夜で］ ○ in two or three days [nights]
- 真っ昼間に［真夜中に］ ○ in the middle of the day [night]
- 日［夜］の始まりに ○ at the beginning of the day [night]
- （昼［夜］の）この時刻に ○ at this time of day [night]
- 一日［隔週の日曜日］ごとに ○ once every other day [Sunday]
- 私の時代は事情が違っていた。
  ○ In my day, things were different. ☞ one's day で「その人がいた［存在した］時期」の意味
- さよならを言わねばならない日が来るだろう。
  ○ The day will come when we will have to say good-bye.
- 夜が突然我々に迫ってきた。
  ○ Night suddenly closed in on us. U ☞ close in on sb/sth「〈人／物〉に迫ってくる」

▶「期間」に関わる表現

- もう一日か二日［一晩か二晩］で ○ in another day [night] or two
- 私たちが初めて会ったその日から ○ since the day we first met

- ❏ 日 [夜] の残った時間 ◐ the rest of the day [night]
- ❏ 一晩中起きている ◐ stay up all night
- ❏ 丸一日 [一晩] 寝る ◐ sleep all day [night]
- ❏ 一日中働く ◐ work for a full day
- ❏ 夜よく休む ◐ get a good night's rest ☞ a good ...で「十分な...」の意味
- ❏ 一日中 [一晩中] 働く ◐ spend the whole day [night] working
  ☞ spend stm doingで「...して〈時間・期間〉を過ごす」
- ❏ その晩をホテルで過ごす ◐ stay the night at a hotel
- ❏ 来る日 [晩] も来る日 [晩] も ◐ day after day [night after night]
- ❏ その日 [夜] は (仕事を) 休む ◐ take the day [night] off ☞ take stm off「〈仕事・学校などを〉(ある期間) 休む」
- ❏ 完全に回復するにはもう一日必要だ
  ◐ need another day to completely recover

▶ day から広がる表現

- ❏ 指定された日 ◐ the appointed day ☞ the appointed place「指定の場所」
- ❏ 運命を決する日 ◐ the fatal [fateful] day
- ❏ 報いを受ける時 ◐ the day of reckoning〈決まり文句〉
- ❏ 結婚式の日 ◐ the wedding day ☞ a wedding (ceremony)「結婚式」
- ❏ 地震が来る日に備える
  ◐ prepare for the day an earthquake will come ☞ the day (when) an earthquake will comeの省略

▶ ストーリー

Yesterday I worked **the whole day** and **most of the night**. **The day before yesterday** was the same. I have been working like this, **day after day** and **night after night**, for a long time now. If I do not **take a few days off**, I will suffer a nervous breakdown.

(昨日私は一日中、そしてほとんど夜通し働いた。一昨日も同じだった。私は今まで長い間、このように来る日も来る日も来る晩も来る晩も働き続けてきた。2、3日休みをとらないと神経をやられてしまうだろう。)

023　DEATH　　　　　　　　　　Ⓒ Ⓤ

> 毎日のように各種メディアで死が報道されている。'death'に関わる表現は 'life' と共に生活空間において知っておくべき頻出項目と言えよう。
>
> 'death' は「死ぬこと」以外に「死に至る直前の状況」に用いられることも多く、特にラベルを設けてまとめておいた。比喩的に用いられているものもあり、すべてマスターしたい。
>
> Ⓒ Ⓤ ┌ 特定の死、あるいはどんな死に方かについて述べる場合 ☞ Ⓒ
> 　　└ 死の概念について述べる場合や死を生と対比する場合 ☞ Ⓤ
>
> **>>ACCIDENT; DISASTER; HOSPITAL; ILLNESS; LIFE**

▶ death から広がるボキャブラリー：名詞表現

- ❏ 偶然の死 [事故死] ◯ an accidental death Ⓒ
- ❏ 急死 [サドンデス] ◯ a sudden death
- ❏ 早過ぎる死；時ならぬ死 ◯ an untimely death
- ❏ 長い病の後の死 ◯ a lingering death ☞「銃撃されてから数時間後に死亡した」ような状況にも用いる。lingering「(名の前で) 長引く、ぐずつく」
- ❏ 溺死 ◯ death by drowning
- ❏ 致死量の注射による死 ◯ death by lethal injection
- ❏ 変死する ◯ meet a violent death ☞ meet *one*'s death「死ぬ」

▶ death から広がるボキャブラリー：動詞表現

- ❏ 家族を最近亡くす ◯ experience a recent death in the family
- ❏ 死因を調査する ◯ investigate the cause of a death
- ❏ 私はボブの死に対して責任がある。
   ◯ I am responsible for Bob's death.
- ❏ メグが死んだという知らせを聞く ◯ hear the news of Meg's death
- ❏ ボブの死に弔辞を表する ◯ express condolences on Bob's death
   ☞ condolences to *sb*「〈人〉に対する哀悼の言葉、弔辞」
- ❏ 親友の死を嘆き悲しむ ◯ mourn a dear friend's death
- ❏ 彼女の命日を覚えている
   ◯ remember the anniversary of her death ☞ anniversary「(毎年の)

記念日」
- 死刑を執行する ◎ carry out a death sentence ☞ carry /sth/ out「〈事〉を実施する、行う」
- 彼は死に直面していた。◎ Death was staring him in the face.
  ☞ stare sb in the face「〈人〉を直視する」
- 彼は酒を飲み過ぎて死んだ。◎ He drank himself to death.
  ☞ drink oneself to のパターンに注意。drink myself to sleep「酔って寝こむ」

▶ 「死の直前」に関わる表現

- 死活問題である。◎ It is a matter of life or death.
- ボブは臨終の床にある。◎ Bob is on his deathbed.
- ボブは死の間際にいる。◎ Bob is on the verge of death. [U]
  ☞ be on the verge of tears「今にも泣きそうだ」
- メグは死にかけている。◎ Meg is at death's door.
  ☞ Meg is dying.「メグは死にかかっている」、Meg is in critical condition.「メグは危篤状態である」
- 九死に一生を得る ◎ cheat death ☞ このcheatは「運良く逃れる」の意味
- 死んだふりをする ◎ feign death ☞ feign [fein] illness「仮病を使う」
- 死者を出さないようにする ◎ prevent a death
- ボブを死ぬほど怖がらせる ◎ almost frighten Bob to death
  ☞ be frightened to death「死ぬほど怖い」

▶ ストーリー

Death is a difficult topic to talk about. This was the last story in this book that I wrote. This is because I **could not bring myself to write about death**. But **there is one sure thing about death**: In the end, we **can never cheat it**. We all hope not to **meet an untimely death**, but **die we must**.

(死は話しづらい話題である。これは私が書いたこの本での最後の話であった。これは私が死について書く気になれなかったからである。しかし、死について一つ確かなことがある。それは、結局私たちは決して死を逃れられないということである。私たちは誰しも早死にしたくないと願う。しかし私たちは死なねばならないのである)

DEATH

024　DEPARTMENT STORE / SUPERMARKET　C

> デパートやスーパー（またはコンビニ 'convenience store'）は最近ではそれらの競合に関わる話題がニュースを賑わせている。ここではその話題も含めて、買い物と生活に関わる表現を紹介した。
> ✱「デパート」の意味で単に 'depart' あるいは 'department' と言わないこと。「デパート」(department store) には、「おもちゃ売り場」(the toy department) や「紳士服売り場」(the menswear department) など多くの 'department' がある。
>
> **>> CLOTHES; FOOD; SHOPPING**

▶ department store /supermarket から広がるボキャブラリー：名詞表現

❏ スーパーマーケット・チェーン ◯ a supermarket chain
❏ 品揃え豊富なスーパーマーケット ◯ a well-stocked supermarket
❏ スーパーマーケットの成長と地元商店街の凋落
　◯ the growth of supermarkets and decline of neighbourhood shops
❏ スーパーマーケット間の激しい競合
　◯ intense competition between supermarkets
❏ デパートの全国チェーン
　◯ a nationwide chain of department stores
❏ デパートの県下［地方］チェーン
　◯ a provincial chain of department stores
❏ 街の大手デパート ◯ the city's major department store
❏ 老舗のデパート ◯ a long-established department store
　☞ established「確立した、定評のある」an established fact「既定の事実」
❏ 洗練された高級志向のデパート
　◯ a smart, upmarket department store ☞ upmarket「高級な、高級志向の」
❏ 大衆向けのデパート ◯ a downmarket department store
❏ 紳士服の品揃えが非常によいデパート
　◯ a department store with a very wide range of men's clothing
　☞ a wide range of sth「広範囲の〈物事〉」
❏ 特売をしているデパート ◯ a department store which has a sale

▶ department store /supermarket から広がるボキャブラリー：動詞表現

❏ ジーンズをデパートではなくアウトレットで安く買う
  ⊙ buy jeans cheaply at an outlet —not a department store
❏ スーパーまで歩いてすぐいける距離に住んでいる
  ⊙ live within easy walking distance of a supermarket
❏ スーパーで毎日の買い物をする
  ⊙ do my daily shopping at the supermarket
❏ スーパーに買い物に行く
  ⊙ go on a shopping trip to the supermarket
❏ スーパーで釣り銭をもらいすぎた。
  ⊙ I was given too much change at the supermarket.
❏ スーパーが販売を中止して回収した品物
  ⊙ an item which has been withdrawn from sale by supermarkets
❏ メグは出来心でスーパーで万引きした。
  ⊙ Meg shoplifted in a supermarket on the spur of the moment.
❏ 一流デパートで新商品を売り出す [発売する]
  ⊙ launch a new product in leading department stores
❏ 二番目の通路を行けば、お茶は右側にあります。
  ⊙ Walk down the second aisle, and the tea is on your right.
  ☞ スーパーでは品物は 'aisle' [áil] に置かれている

▶ ストーリー

I **do not like shopping**. I do not understand people who **go out on shopping expeditions to department stores**, or **spend the whole afternoon window shopping**. The only time I **shop in a department store** is when I **go to the food department** to **buy something a little bit special**.
(私は買い物が好きではない。私はデパートにわざわざ買い物のお出かけをしたり、ウインドーショッピングでまるまる午後を過ごす人たちが理解できない。私がデパートで買い物をするのは、食べ物売り場に行ってちょっと特別な物を買うときくらいである。)

025 DIET .... CU

> ダイエット＝減量、ではない。'diet' は「食事」「食生活」までも指し、日本語の「ダイエット」よりもさらに広く用いられる語である。ここで紹介したさまざまな用例を見れば、この語を含む表現の重要性が理解されるだろう。'diet' =「ダイエット」と考えないこと！
>
> C/U ｛ 特定の食餌療法（ダイエット）や食習慣について述べる場合 ☞ C
> 　　　 日常の食べ物一般、常食について述べる場合 ☞ U
>
> （ただし、この区別がはっきりしない場合もある。下の用例を参照のこと）
>
> **>> FOOD; MEAT / FISH; FITNESS; FRUIT / VEGETABLE**

▶ diet から広がるボキャブラリー：名詞表現

- ❏ すごく流行っているダイエット ◯ a fad diet [C] ☞ fad「一時的なブーム、気まぐれ」
- ❏ 速成ダイエット ◯ a crash diet ☞ crash「（名の前で）応急的な、突貫の」
- ❏ 非常に効果的な減量ダイエット
  ◯ a very effective weight-loss diet
- ❏ ダイエットヨーグルト１パック ◯ a carton of diet yogurt
- ❏ ダイエット高級料理を提供するレストラン
  ◯ a restaurant offering diet haute cuisine [òut kwiziːn] ☞ haute「高級な」
- ❏ ベストセラーのダイエット本 ◯ a best-selling diet book
- ❏ バランスのとれた食生活 ◯ a balanced diet
- ❏ 変化に富んだ食事 ◯ a varied diet
- ❏ 高カロリー食 ◯ a high-calorie diet
- ❏ 高タンパク食 ◯ a high-protein diet
- ❏ 低炭水化物食 ◯ a low-carbohydrate diet
- ❏ 菜食 ◯ a vegetarian diet ☞ a vegetarian「菜食主義者」
- ❏ 食物繊維に富む食事 ◯ a diet high in fibre
- ❏ 飽和脂肪をとらない食事 ◯ a diet without saturated fat
- ❏ たくさんの野菜をとる伝統的な日本の食習慣
  ◯ a traditional Japanese diet with lots of vegetables
- ❏ ここ 30 年の日本の食生活の変遷

◯ changes in the Japanese diet over the last thirty years

▶ diet から広がるボキャブラリー：動詞表現

❏ 数週間で何キロもやせられるダイエットを始める
  ◯ go on a diet that helps me to shed kilogrammes in weeks
❏ 砂糖をとらない食生活をする ◯ adopt a sugar-free diet
❏ ダイエットを根気よく続けられない ◯ cannot stick to my diet
  ☞ stick to *sth*「〈事〉に固執する、専念する」
❏ 結局ダイエットをやめてしまう ◯ finally come off a diet
❏ 栄養士［ダイエティシャン］に日常の食事について助言を求める
  ◯ consult a dietician about my diet
❏ ダイエットと健康のプログラムに従う
  ◯ follow a diet and health programme
❏ 自分にあった食生活［食事］を見つける
  ◯ find a diet that is right for me
❏ 和食はでんぷん質の食べ物が中心となっている。
  ◯ The Japanese diet consists mainly of starchy food.
❏ 環境と食事が要因となって起こった病気
  ◯ illness caused by environmental and dietary factors
❏ 健康を維持するためには食事と運動が重要である。
  ◯ Diet and exercise are important for keeping healthy. ⓤ

▶ ストーリー

We should **keep to a healthy, commonsense diet**. And if we do **put on weight**, there is no point **looking for some magic, painless diet**. **Dieting is like** many things in life: 'No pain, no gain'. Or perhaps, more accurately: 'No pain, no loss'.

(私たちは健康によい常識的な食生活を守るべきだ。もし実際に太ってしまったら、魔法のような、苦労のいらないダイエット法を探してもまったくの無駄である。ダイエットは人生の多くの事柄と似ている。例えば、「働かざる者食うべからず」ということである。あるいはもっと正確に言えば、「働かざる者やせるべからず」となるだろうか。)

DIET 75

026 DIFFICULTY　　　　　　CU

あらゆる困難に直面し、それに対処していくことが生活空間では常に求められる。ここでは、次のCとUの使い分けにもとづき、'difficulty' を用いたさまざまな状況とそれらに対処するための表現を中心に紹介した。

- 特定の問題などに遭遇した場合 ☞ C
- 仕事や課題の性質などについて述べる場合 ☞ U

>> AIM; CHANCE; FAILURE; LUCK; MISTAKE

▶「特定の問題」に関わる表現

- ❏ ささいな困難 ◯ a minor difficulty C
- ❏ 深刻で重大な困難 ◯ a serious and grave difficulty ☞ a serious matter「深刻な問題」 grave danger「重大な危機」
- ❏ 意外な [思いがけない] 難しさ ◯ an unforeseen difficulty
- ❏ 資金難 [お金に困っていること] ◯ financial difficulties
- ❏ 困難を引き起こす ◯ cause a difficulty
- ❏ 困難を作り出す ◯ create a difficulty
- ❏ 困難に遭遇する ◯ encounter a difficulty ☞ encounter Bob「ボブに出くわす」
- ❏ 苦境に陥る ◯ run into difficulties ☞ run into thick fog「濃霧に遭う」
- ❏ 大きな困難が生じた。 ◯ A major difficulty arose. ☞ arise「(問題・危機などが) 生じる」
- ❏ 困難となっている状況 ◯ a situation which presents a difficulty ☞ present [prizént] a serious problem「深刻な問題を引き起こす [となる]」
- ❏ 困難を克服する ◯ overcome a difficulty
- ❏ 難事のもとを見つける ◯ find the source of a difficulty

▶「仕事や課題の性質」に関わる表現

- ❏ だんだん難しくなっていく語学コース
  ◯ a language course which increases in difficulty
- ❏ 読解テキストの難易度 ◯ the level of difficulty of a reading text
- ❏ 人が困っている時に手を貸す ◯ help someone in times of difficulty

☞ in times of antiquity「古代に」

- そのスイマーは溺れかけていた。◯ The swimmer was in difficulty.
- やっと何とか試験に合格する ◯ pass an exam with great difficulty
- 説明が困難である ◯ have difficulty with an explanation[U]
- なかなか妊娠しない ◯ have difficulty in conceiving a baby
  ☞ inは省略可能。下の2例を参照
- 新しい考え方を受け入れるのが難しい
  ◯ have difficulty accepting a new idea
- 新しい仕事に慣れるのに苦労する
  ◯ have difficulty adjusting to a new job ☞ adjust my clock to the correct time「時計を正しい時間に合わせる」

▶決まり文句

- 落ち着いて困難に対処しなさい。
  ◯ Take the difficulties in (your) stride.
  ☞ take something in (my) stride「何かを難なく切り抜ける」
- あなたといると落ち着いた気持ちになれる。
  ◯ I feel at ease with you.
- 私はスーツを着ると落ち着かなかった。
  ◯ I felt ill at ease in a suit.
- この知らせを聞けば心が安まるだろう。
  ◯ This news will help to put your mind at ease.
  ☞ 上の3例における 'at ease' と動詞の結びつきに注意

▶ストーリー

In our lives we **are faced with many difficulties**. And no sooner have we **overcome one difficulty** than we **encounter another one**. Sometimes **these difficulties arise** in an unavoidable manner. At other times we ourselves **create them**.
(私たちは人生で多くの困難に直面する。そして、一つの困難を克服したかと思うと別の困難に遭遇する。これらの困難は起こるのが避けられない場合もあるが、一方、私たちが自らそれらを作り出している場合もあるのだ。)

027 DINNER / LUNCH ･･･････ C U

> 昼食や夕食は朝食 (breakfast) と異なり、外で、あるいは家族以外の人も含めて時間をかけてとる場合が多くなり、それだけ表現の数や使用範囲が増えてくる。その意味でここでは、'dinner/lunch' を用いた対人関係に関わる頻出表現を中心に紹介した。
>
> ✸ 通常、無冠詞で用いられ、C と U の区別がつかない場合が多い。しかし、食事を表す語は前に形容詞がついたり後に関係詞節が続いてそれを説明することが多く、それらの場合は 'a light lunch' のように冠詞を伴い C 扱いになることに注意。以下の用例で確認のこと。
>
> ✸ 'have [eat] lunch'(昼食をとる)の代わりに、'have some lunch'(お昼に何か食べる)と言うのはインフォーマルな表現。
>
> **>> DIET; FRUIT / VEGETABLE; FOOD; MEAT / FISH**

▶ dinner / lunch から広がるボキャブラリー：名詞表現

- ❏ よく調理された夕食 ○ a well-cooked dinner C
- ❏ 調理のされ方がひどい夕食 ○ a badly cooked dinner
- ❏ 早めの昼食 ○ an early lunch
- ❏ ビジネスランチ ○ a business lunch; a working lunch (☞ a business lunch と異なり、商談以外の話し合いも含まれる)
- ❏ 非常に簡単な昼食 ○ a very simple lunch
- ❏ 軽い夕食 ○ a light dinner
- ❏ すごいごちそう ○ a big dinner
- ❏ ディナーをアラカルトで出してくれるレストラン
  ○ a restaurant which serves an à la carte dinner
- ❏ 客のために手の込んだ昼食をこしらえる
  ○ cook an elaborate [ilǽb(ə)rət] lunch for my guests ☞ elaborate patterns「こったパターン」
- ❏ 子供たちのためにお弁当を作る
  ○ make a packed lunch for the kids ☞ a packed train「満員列車」
- ❏ 最高級ワインと共に供されたディナーを楽しむ
  ○ enjoy a dinner served with the finest wines
- ❏ クリスマスに家族で昼食をとる
  ○ have a family lunch on Christmas Day

▶ dinner / lunch から広がるボキャブラリー：動詞表現

- いつも昼食を抜く ◯ always skip lunch
- 昼食は軽い物ですませる ◯ make do with a simple lunch ☞ make do with *sth*「〈物〉で間に合わせる」
- 昼食をかき込む [急いで昼食を食べる] ◯ grab a quick lunch ☞ grab a cup of coffee「コーヒーを大急ぎで飲む」
- 夕食の支度をする ◯ prepare [fix《米》] dinner
- 夕食を出す ◯ serve dinner
- 昼食に友人を招待する ◯ invite a friend for lunch
- ディナーパーティを企画する ◯ organize a dinner party
- ディナーパーティを主催する ◯ host a dinner party
- ディナーパーティを台無しにする ◯ ruin a dinner party
- 昼食に食べ残しを食べる ◯ have leftovers for lunch
- 明晩は友人と一緒に夕食をとる
  ◯ have dinner with a friend tomorrow night ⓤ
- メグを昼食に連れ出す ◯ take Meg out to lunch
- 私はボブの夕食に加わった。◯ I joined Bob for dinner.
- 夕食の残り物を片づける ◯ clear away the remains of the dinner
- 毎年恒例の同窓会の夕食を催す ◯ have an annual reunion dinner
- 昼食時間もぶっ通しで働く ◯ work through the lunch hour
- 昼食休みを2時間とる ◯ have a two-hour break for lunch
- 夕食後の散歩に出かける ◯ go for an after-dinner walk

▶ ストーリー

I **eat quite a substantial lunch**, and then **make do with a simple, light dinner**. Usually, **some leftovers from the day before** are enough. On Sundays, the family usually **has brunch**, and then in the evening we **have a barbeque**.

(私は昼食をたっぷり食べて、夕食は簡単に軽い物ですませる。だいたい前日からの食べ残しがいくらかあれば十分である。我が家は日曜日はだいたいブランチで、夜はバーベキューにしている。)

028 DISASTER .... C U

英語の'disaster'が指すのは重大な災害だけではない。比喩的に用いて「大失敗」程度の軽少な事柄を表すことがある。その意味で'disaster'は我々の生活空間のどこにでも起こりうるものと言えよう。

ここでは、重大な「災害・惨事・災難」などに関わる表現と比喩的に「災難・失敗」などを表すイディオム表現を中心に紹介した。

- どんな災害か特定される場合 ☞ C
- 漠然と「災害」一般について述べる場合 ☞ U

✻この語と結びついてコロケーションを作り、災害の程度を示す形容詞 (major/downright/spectacular/total など) にも注意しよう。

>> ACCIDENT; AMBULANCE / FIRE BRIGADE / POLICE; DEATH; WEATHER

▶重大な「災害・惨事・災難」に関わる表現

- ❏ 自然災害；天災 ◯ a natural disaster C
- ❏ 人災 ◯ a man-made disaster
- ❏ 壮観な大惨事 ◯ a spectacular disaster ☞ a spectacular view「壮観な眺め」
- ❏ 大打撃；大災害 ◯ a major disaster
- ❏ 軍の大惨事 [敗北] ◯ a military disaster
- ❏ 財政上の災難 ◯ a financial disaster
- ❏ いつ終わるとも知れない連続する災難
  ◯ a never-ending series of disasters
- ❏ 災害抑制策 ◯ disaster-control measures
- ❏ 災害に対応する ◯ <u>respond to</u> a disaster
- ❏ 災害に備えて (何をすべきか) 考える ◯ <u>plan for</u> a disaster
- ❏ 国の一部を被災地域であると宣言する
  ◯ declare part of the country a disaster area
  ☞ declare sb/sth (to be) sb/sth「〈人 / 物〉を〈人 / 物〉であると宣言 [表明] する」
- ❏ 政治的な理由のために災害を過小評価して伝える
  ◯ <u>play down</u> a disaster for political reasons
  ☞ play sth down「〈事〉を重要でないように見せる」
- ❏ 被災地域にレスキュー隊を急がせる

rush rescue teams to the disaster area
- 災害のニュースが少しずつ漏れてきた。
  ○ News of the disaster filtered out. ☞ The rumour filtered down to me.「そのうわさは私にも伝わってきた」
- その台風は大惨事をもたらした。○ The typhoon brought disaster. [U]

▶軽少な「災難・失敗」に関わる表現

- まったくの災難 ○ a downright disaster
- 有名なサッカークラブの一連のアンラッキーな出来事
  ○ a catalogue of disasters for a famous football club
  ☞ a catalogue of mistakes「失敗の連続」
- 結婚生活は最初から散々なものだった。
  ○ The marriage was a disaster from the word go.
  ☞ from the word go「初めから、最初から」
- ピクニックはさんざんだった。○ The picnic was a disaster.
- その結果はさんざん[大失敗]だった。○ The result was a disaster.
- パーティはちょっと失敗だった。
  ○ The party turned out to be a bit of a disaster. ☞ turn out to be sth「結局〈事〉であるとわかる」
- その新しい建物は完全な失敗と見なされている。
  ○ The new building is regarded as a total disaster. ☞ regard sb/sth as sth「〈人/物〉を〈事〉とみなす」

▶ストーリー

Natural disasters are a part of life. We hope that none will befall us, but they sometimes do. We should all prepare for disaster in order to protect ourselves. In Japan, all households should plan for what to do in the case of (an) earthquake.
(自然の災害は生活の一部である。私たちは、一つも自分に降りかかってほしくないと願うが、時に自分に降りかかる。私たちは皆自分の身を守るため災害に備えるべきである。日本では、すべての家庭は地震の場合に何をすべきか考えておくべきである。)

DISASTER

029 DREAM　C

> 夢は眠っているときだけでなく、起きているときの生活にも大きな影響を与えるという意味で生活空間の一部と言えよう。そこから派生してさらに未来の希望に関して「夢」(dream)を用いるのは日英語共通の発想であり、これに関わる表現もマスターしたい。
> ✲ 'dream'と最もよく結びつく動詞は'have'である。さらに、英語では、「夢を見る」(×see a dream)のではなく、「夢で何かを見る」(see something in a dream)と表現することに注意。
> ✲「悪夢」は'a bad dream'とも言えるが、さらにひどい夢(a very bad dream)を一語で表す'a nightmare'という言葉がある。
>
> **>> AIM; SLEEP**

▶「睡眠」に関わる表現

- ❏ 昨夜の夢 ◯ last night's dream
- ❏ 悪夢(のようなこと) ◯ a bad dream
- ❏ ありありとした夢；生々しい夢 ◯ a vivid dream
- ❏ 不安な夢を見てひどくうなされる
  ◯ have troubled dreams and terrible nightmares ☞ troubled「問題の多い」
- ❏ 夢を思い出す ◯ recall a dream
- ❏ 夢の最中に目を覚ます ◯ wake up in the middle of a dream
- ❏ 夢を分析する ◯ analyze a dream
- ❏ 繰り返し見る夢を解釈する ◯ interpret a recurring dream I have

▶「希望」に関わる表現

- ❏ うまくいかなかった夢 ◯ a dream which turned sour
- ❏ 一生懸命働いて、自分の夢を実現させる
  ◯ work hard and make my dream come true
- ❏ 百万長者になるという自分の夢を実現する
  ◯ realize my dream of becoming a millionaire
- ❏ 夢はもう少しで実現しそうだった。
  ◯ The dream came near to realization. ☞ be near to crying / death

「泣き出さんばかりだ / 死と隣り合わせだ」
- ❏ 自分の夢の家を買う ◯ buy my dream home ☞ buy a new home「新しい家を買う」
- ❏ それは私が夢に見たドレスだった。
  ◯ It was the dress of my dreams.
- ❏ 私は自分の夢を達成できればよいと思う。
  ◯ I hope to be able to achieve my dream.
- ❏ ボブは夢心地で暮らしている。◯ Bob lives in a dream.
- ❏ 結局それはすべて夢だった。◯ It all turned out to be a dream.
- ❏ 彼と結婚できたのはまるで夢みたいだった。
  ◯ Marrying him was like a dream come true.

▶決まり文句

- ❏ メグはうっとりとした表情を浮かべている。
  ◯ Meg has a dreamy expression on her face.
- ❏ 私の考えは空想にすぎない。
  ◯ My idea is nothing more than (= only) a daydream.
- ❏ 私が宝くじに当たるなど夢のまた夢だった。
  ◯ That I would win the lottery was beyond my wildest dreams.
  ☞ beyond my wildest dreams「自分の予想もしないほどよく」
- ❏ 私は彼に金を貸してくれと頼もうとは夢にも思わない。《動詞》
  ◯ I would never dream of asking him to lend me money.

▶ストーリー

Quite often I **get confused between dreams and reality**. I feel quite sure that something happened. I later **find out that it was a dream**. At other times, I **think something was a dream**, and only later do I **find out it was a real occurrence**.

(私は夢と現実の区別がつかなくなることが少なからずある。私は何かが起きたと確かに感じても、後でそれが夢だったことがわかるのだ。一方、夢だと思っても、後になって初めて、それが実際に起こった出来事だとわかったりするのだ。)

030 DRINK（酒類） · · · · · · · · · · · · C U

> 酒は社交の場に欠かせない潤滑油であるが、「飲み過ぎ」の悪影響も取りざたされる昨今である。ここではアルコール飲料の 'drink' をもとに、社交に関わる表現（☞〈動詞〉）や「酒の影響」に関わる表現を整理した。（清涼飲料の 'drink' は次項参照）
>
> ✱ 'Would you like a drink?'（何か飲みますか）と言えば、普通、アルコール飲料を勧めることに注意。飲み物の性質を問わない場合は 'Would you like something to drink?'（何か飲み物を召し上がりますか）と言う。
>
> 酒以外も含めて「飲み物」を意味する場合 ☞ C
> 物質としての「アルコール」を意味する場合 ☞ U

>> DINNER / LUNCH; DRINK（清涼飲料）; FOOD

▶ drink（酒類）から広がるボキャブラリー

- 酒類；アルコール飲料 ○ an alcoholic drink
- カクテル；混合酒 ○ a mixed drink
- （アルコール度数の高い）強い飲み物 ○ a strong drink
- ぐっとくる（きつい）酒 ○ a good stiff drink
- 薄い酒 ○ a weak drink ☞ 以上4例はそれらの飲料が器に入った一杯分を表す

▶「酒の影響」に関わる表現

- １、２杯飲んだ後、頭がふらふらしているように感じる
  ○ feel light-headed after a drink or two
- メグはぐでんぐでんに酔っている［飲み過ぎて泥酔している］。
  ○ Meg is befuddled with too much drink.
- ボブは飲んでも酔わない［酒に強い］。○ Bob can hold his drink.
- 飲み過ぎは健康［身体］によくない。
  ○ Too much drink is bad for you. U
- アルコールの効果で涙もろくなる人もいる。
  ○ Drink can make some people sentimental.
- 一杯ひっかければ温まるよ。○ A quick drink will warm you up.
  ☞ have a quick drink of water「水を１杯ぐっと飲む」
- その酒を飲んだらくらくらした。○ The drink made me feel dizzy.

▶ drink から広がるボキャブラリー：動詞表現

- 一杯やりたくてたまりません。◐ I <u>am dying for</u> a drink. ⓒ ☞ be dying for sth「〈物〉がほしくてたまらない」
- （酒を）2、3杯飲む ◐ have a couple of drinks
- つらい一日の仕事が終わった後にぐっと一杯やりたい
  ◐ need a quick drink after a hard day's work
- 何も考えずぐいぐい飲む ◐ <u>toss back a drink</u> <u>without hesitation</u>
  ☞ toss my head back「頭をつんと後ろにそらす」
- 飲み物を味わう ◐ savour the taste of a drink ☞ savour sth「〈飲食物〉をゆっくり味わう、賞味する」
- できるだけ長い間ちびりちびり飲む
  ◐ nurse a drink for <u>as long as possible</u> ☞ nurse
- お客に飲み物を注ぐ ◐ <u>pour a drink for</u> my guest
- 訪問者に飲み物を出す ◐ <u>serve drinks to</u> the visitors
- つき合いですすめられた飲み物を受ける
  ◐ accept a drink <u>for the sake of politeness</u>
- 一杯やろうとボブを誘う ◐ <u>invite Bob out for</u> a drink
- バーにいる全員に酒をふるまう［おごる］
  ◐ <u>buy a round of drinks for</u> everyone in the bar ☞ a roundは「酒をふるまうこと、居合わせた一同へのひと渡り分」
- メグに飲み物を飲んでしまう時間を与える
  ◐ give Meg time to finish her drink

▶ ストーリー

Drink should always be taken in moderation. If you find yourself **dying for a drink** every night, or if you boast that you **can hold your drink**, this is a sign that something is wrong. In such a case it may be necessary to get professional help.

（アルコールは常に適度にとられるべきである。もしあなたが毎晩飲まずにはいられなかったり、自分は酒に強いと豪語しているのなら、これは何か問題があるという信号である。このような場合、専門家の手助けを受けることが必要になるだろう。）

031 DRINK（清涼飲料） C

'**D**rink' は酒類のほか、水や嗜好品としての飲料も意味し、生活空間の中で我々をリラックスさせてくれる存在である。〈関連表現〉として多数紹介した「のどの渇き」に関わる表現と共に、この語を通して飲み物に関わるさまざまな表現をマスターしよう。

✱「水を飲みたい」と英語で表現する場合、日本人は 'I want to drink some water.' と言いがちだが、ネイティブスピーカーは 'I want to have a drink of water.' と言う場合が多いので要注意！

>> DRINK（酒類）; FOOD

▶ drink（清涼飲料）から広がるボキャブラリー：名詞表現

- ❏ 清涼飲料；ソフトドリンク ◯ a soft drink
- ❏ 炭酸飲料（気泡性の飲み物） ◯ a fizzy drink
- ❏ 栄養ドリンク ◯ a nutritional [n(j)uːtríʃ(ə)nəl] drink
- ❏ のどの渇きをいやす飲み物 ◯ a thirst-quenching drink
- ❏ お茶あるいはコーヒーのような熱い［温かい］飲み物
  ◯ a hot drink like tea or coffee
- ❏ 気が抜けている飲み物 ◯ a drink that has gone flat ☞ go flat には「パンクする」の意味もある
- ❏ 氷のように冷たい飲み物 ◯ an ice-cold drink
- ❏ 味が薄すぎる飲み物 ◯ a drink that is too weak
  ☞ 上の3例は前項同様、それらの飲料が器に入った具体的な形を意味する

▶ drink から広がるボキャブラリー：動詞表現

- ❏ 飲み物をかき混ぜる ◯ stir a drink
- ❏ 飲み物に甘味料を加える ◯ add sweetener to a drink
- ❏ 水で飲み物を薄める ◯ dilute a drink with water
- ❏ 飲み物に角氷を2つ入れる
  ◯ put a couple of ice cubes into a drink
- ❏ 背の高いコップで飲み物を出す ◯ serve a drink in a tall glass
- ❏ メグに元気になってもらおうと温かい飲み物を与える
  ◯ give Meg a hot drink to revive her

モノ

- 飲み物をぐいと飲み干す ○ gulp down a drink
- 飲み物を一気に飲み干す ○ take a swig of a drink ☞ from the bottle をつけると「ラッパ飲みする」の意味になる
- 熱い飲み物をゆっくりとすする ○ slowly sip a hot drink
- コーラを一杯飲んだら気分爽快となった。
  ○ A drink of Coke refreshed me.
- 一杯おごらせていただきます。○ I'd like to buy you a drink.

▶「のどの渇き」に関わる表現

- ボブに飲み物をすすめる ○ offer Bob something to drink
- 本当に何か飲みたい ○ really want something to drink
- 本当にのどが渇いている。○ I am really thirsty.
- のどが渇いて死にそうだ。○ I am dying of thirst.
- のどが渇いて、お腹もすいている。○ I am thirsty and hungry.
- コーラ1缶でのどの渇きをいやす
  ○ quench my thirst with a can of cola
- 三日間何も飲まずに過ごす
  ○ go without anything to drink for three days ☞ go without sth 「〈物〉をなしですます」

▶ ストーリー

I **was really thirsty** when I got home; I **was almost dying of thirst**. I was looking forward to **having a nice cold drink**—perhaps **a nice glass of iced tea**. But when I opened the fridge, there was nothing there. I then thought that I **could have a drink of ice water**. When I opened the freezer there was no ice there. Finally I just **had a drink of water**.

(家に帰ったとき私は本当にのどが渇いていた。のどが渇いて死にそうだったのだ。私はおいしい冷たい飲み物、多分おいしいアイスティーを1杯飲むのを楽しみにしていた。しかし私が冷蔵庫を開けると中には何もなかった。そこで私は冷たい水でも飲めればと思った。私がフリーザーを開けると、そこに氷はなかった。結局、水を一杯飲んだだけだった。)

DRINK (清涼飲料)

032 ECONOMY ... C U

「経済」と聞くと、実体がなくとらえどころのない印象があるが、英語の 'economy' は C 扱いで具体的な制度や組織などを表す場合が多い。このことに注意して以下の用例を見ていこう。特に 'economy' と結びつく動詞をよくマスターすること。

- 経済制度や経済組織を指す場合 ☞ C
- 国や社会の経済を指す場合 ☞ U (the をつけて用いることが多い)

✲ 'economy' は複数形で用いられ「倹約、節約、経済性」の意味もある。
  例 make various economies いろいろと節約をする
     economies of scale 規模の経済性

>> AGRICULTURE / INDUSTRY; CHANGE; COMPANY

▶ economy から広がるボキャブラリー：名詞表現

- ❏ 計画経済 ◯ a planned economy C
- ❏ 自由市場経済 ◯ a free-market economy
- ❏ 健全な経済 ◯ a sound economy ☞ sound management「堅実な経営」
- ❏ 安定した経済 ◯ a stable economy ☞ a stable peace「永続的な平和」
- ❏ 急速に拡大を続ける経済 ◯ a rapidly expanding economy
- ❏ 緩慢な経済 ◯ a sluggish economy ☞ feel sluggish「身体がだるく感じる」
- ❏ 弱体化した [不安定な] 経済 ◯ a shaky economy ☞ be shaky on my legs「足元がよろめく」
- ❏ 崩壊しつつある経済 ◯ a collapsing economy
- ❏ 深い景気後退 ◯ an economy in deep recession
- ❏ 回復しつつある経済 ◯ an economy that is recovering
- ❏ サービスベースの経済 ◯ a service-based economy
- ❏ 世界四番目の経済大国 ◯ the world's fourth largest economy

▶ economy から広がるボキャブラリー：名詞表現

- ❏ 経済制裁 [通商停止] で国の経済を破壊する
    ◯ destroy a country's economy with an economic embargo
    ☞ an embargo「通商停止、貿易禁止」 lift an embargo「通商 [貿易] 禁止を解除する」
- ❏ 経済成長が非常にゆっくりな国

- ◎ a country whose economy is growing very slowly
❏ 経済のサービス部門を拡大する
    - ◎ expand the service sector of the economy
❏ 政府の景気浮揚計画 ◎ government plans to boost the economy
    ☞ boost *sth*「(値段)をつりあげる、〈経済〉を発展させる」
❏ いくつかの国の経済力の低下
    - ◎ the deteriorating performance of some countries' economies
❏ 経済の自由化 ◎ the liberalization of the economy [U]
❏ 経済全体に (助成金や税金引き下げなどの) 刺激策を導入する
    - ◎ introduce incentives throughout the economy ☞ an incentive to *sth*「〈物事〉に対する刺激、誘因、動機」
❏ 海外からの投資に経済を開放する
    - ◎ open the economy to foreign investment
❏ 地元経済に大きく寄与するホテル
    - ◎ a hotel which makes a major contribution to the local economy
    ☞ make a contribution to *sth*「〈物事〉に寄与 [貢献] する」

▶ 関連表現

❏ 生活水準 ◎ the standard of living
❏ 国民総生産 ◎ the gross national product [GNP]
❏ 消費者物価指数 ◎ the consumer price index
❏ 年間200パーセントのインフレ ◎ inflation of 200 percent a year
❏ ミクロ経済の専門家 ◎ an expert in microeconomics
❏ 経済モデル作りの専門家 ◎ an expert in economic modelling

▶ ストーリー

The Japanese economy has been in difficulties for a number of years now. From time to time we hear that **there are signs of an economic recovery**, but **unemployment continues to rise** and **the manufacturing sector continues to shrink**.
(日本経済はこれまで何年もの間苦境にあった。景気回復の兆しがあると時折耳にするが、失業率は上昇し続け、製造部門は縮小し続ける。)

033 EDUCATION · · · · · · · · · · · · C U

教育は現代社会の諸問題と密接な関係があると言えよう。その意味で、ここでは特に家庭と教育の関係、社会的制度としての教育という視点から、'education' を用いたさまざまな表現を紹介した。
- 人が受ける特定のタイプの教育について述べる場合 ☞ C
- 制度としての教育について述べる場合 ☞ U

>> CHILD; HOLIDAY

▶ education から広がるボキャブラリー：名詞表現

- ❏ 初等教育 ◯ primary education; elementary education Ⓤ
- ❏ 中等教育 ◯ secondary education
- ❏ 高等教育（大学での教育）◯ higher education
- ❏ 義務教育 ◯ compulsory education ☞ compulsory measures「強制手段」
- ❏ 特殊教育 ◯ special education ☞ （身体障害者やろうあ者に対する）制度としての特殊教育を指す
- ❏ （普通の教育と対照させて）特別な教育 ◯ a special education ☞ 特定の教育のタイプを指す
- ❏ 体育 ◯ physical education [PE]
- ❏ 正規の / 非公式の学校教育 ◯ formal / informal education
- ❏ 教育学部 ◯ the Faculty of Education

▶ education から広がるボキャブラリー：動詞表現

- ❏ 子供の私学の教育費を払う
  ◯ <u>pay for</u> private education for my child
- ❏ 多くの費用がかかった教育
  ◯ an education which cost a lot of money Ⓒ
- ❏ 宗教教育には利点があると信じる
  ◯ <u>believe in</u> the advantages of a religious education ☞ believe in *sth*「〈事〉の存在を信じる」
- ❏ 現代教育の恩恵を受ける
  ◯ receive the benefits of a modern education

組織

- 私は幸運にも良い教育を受けた。
    - ◎ I was fortunate enough to have got a good education.
    - ☞ be fortunate enough to *do*「幸運にも…する」

▶「教育制度」に関わる表現

- 公教育に多くの金を使う
    - ◎ spend a lot of money on public education ☞ spend *sth* on *sb/sth*「〈金〉を〈人/事〉に費やす」
- 教育制度を改善する ◎ improve the education system
- 教育に対する投資不足を批判する
    - ◎ criticize the lack of investment in education
- 教育水準を向上させる ◎ improve standards of education
- 現代社会における教育の役割を強調する
    - ◎ stress the role of education in modern society
- 読み書きそろばんを重んじる教育
    - ◎ education which emphasizes the three R's [reading, writing, arithmetic]
- 「ゆとり教育」を考える
    - ◎ consider the advantages of 'relaxed education'

▶ ストーリー

In Japan, **there are not enough places for everyone who wishes to go to public high schools**. In many countries, anyone who wants to, **can go to public high schools**. The Japanese argument is that **high school is not part of compulsory education**. This means that some parents have to **spend a lot of money on education at private high schools.**

(日本では、公立高校への進学希望者が全員入学できるだけの定員数がない。多くの国では、希望者の誰もが公立高校に行くことができる。日本の考え方では、高校は義務教育の一部ではないのである。ということは、親たちの中には私立高校での教育に多額の金を費やさなければならない場合があるということになる。)

EDUCATION

034 ELECTRICITY / GAS / WATER ・・・ U

電気、ガス、水道なしでは我々の生活は成り立たず、これらを習慣的に扱う行為に関わる定型表現はきわめて多い。ここでは特にこれらと動詞とのコロケーションでカギとなる 'off' と 'on' の用法をマスターすること。'off' と 'on' はセットで考えよう。

✱ これらの語はすべて U であるが、建物内（家の中など）で用いられる際は 'the' を伴うことに注意。以下の用例で確認のこと。

>> ECONOMY; HOME

▶ electricity から広がるボキャブラリー

❏ 電気料金の値上がり ◯ a rise in electricity prices ☞ a rise in unemployment「失業率の増加」
❏ 発電する ◯ generate electricity ☞ generate suspicion「疑惑を招く」
❏ 地域に電気を供給する ◯ supply electricity to an area
❏ 原子力によって作られた電気
  ◯ electricity generated by nuclear power
❏ 水力発電をする ◯ produce hydroelectricity
❏ 電気を消費する ◯ consume electricity
❏ 安い夜間料金で電気を使う
  ◯ use electricity at the cheap night-rate
❏ 夏の電力消費の増加
  ◯ an increase in electricity consumption in the summer
❏ 美しい景観を損ねる高圧線の鉄塔
  ◯ electricity pylons that destroy the beauty of the view
❏ 高圧線配電網のダウンが停電を起こした。
  ◯ A failure in the electricity grid caused a blackout. ☞ a blackoutは電気が消えること。電力供給の停止はa power failureという

▶ gas から広がるボキャブラリー

❏ ガスをつける ◯ turn the gas on ☞ turn /sth/ onの形。次も同じ
❏ ガス（の元栓）を止める ◯ turn the gas off (at the mains)
❏ ガス（による）暖房 ◯ heating by gas

- 火事を起こしたガス漏れ ○ a gas leak that caused a fire
- 地域にガスをひく ○ <u>lay on</u> gas to an area ☞ lay on water「水道をひく」
- ガス料金を支払う ○ pay the gas bill
- 石油とガスのパイプラインを作る ○ build oil and gas pipelines
- 天然ガスを探してボーリングを行う ○ <u>drill for</u> natural gas ☞ drill for *sth*「〈物〉を求めて穴を掘る」
- ガス料金が6パーセント上がった。
  ○ The price of gas has <u>gone up</u> 6 percent. ☞ Taxi fares have gone up.「タクシー料金が上がった」

▶ water から広がるボキャブラリー

- うっかり水を流しっぱなしにしておく
  ○ carelessly leave the water running ☞ leave *sth* doing「〈事〉を...するままにしておく」
- 水道の蛇口をしめるのを忘れる ○ <u>forget to turn the water off</u>
- 貯水池の貯蔵量が非常に少ないため給水制限を実施する
  ○ introduce water rationing because the reservoirs are very low
- 新鮮な飲料水を供給する ○ supply fresh drinking water
- 上水道は汚染された。○ The water supply was contaminated.
- うちのガス、電気、水道はすべて止められた。
  ○ My gas, electricity, and water <u>were all cut off</u>.

▶ ストーリー

After I leave home, I often wonder if I **have turned the gas and electricity off**. **Leaving the lights on** does not really matter. But **forgetting to turn off the gas in the kitchen** is dangerous. Now I have a checklist in the hallway. I always **check that nothing is left on** before I leave home.

(私は家を出た後、ガスと電気を止めたかなと思うことがよくある。電灯をつけっぱなしにしておくのはそれほど問題ではない。しかし台所のガスを止め忘れるのは危険である。現在私は玄関にチェックリストを貼ってある。家を出る前に、私は消し忘れがないかを常にチェックしている。)

ELECTRICITY / GAS / WATER

035 EMOTION C U

感情を内に抑える日本文化に対して、ストレートに外に出す英語圏ではその表現はきわめて重要で 'emotion' は生活空間の核の一つと言えよう。以下のように、「目に見える感情」と「目に見えない感情」に整理して考えると、実際の使用に有用であろう。

✱ 'emotion' は主に U 扱いだが以下のような区別に注意。

- C 特定の感情のタイプ (喜怒哀楽) について述べる場合 ☞ C
- U 感動や感激、興奮などの強い感情を表す場合 ☞ U

>> BEHAVIOUR; CHARACTER; KINDNESS; LOVE

▶「見える感情」に関わる表現

- ❏ 感情の爆発 ◯ an outburst of emotion
- ❏ 感情の発露 ◯ a release of emotion ☞ a feeling of release「解放感」
- ❏ 制御できない感情 ◯ an uncontrollable emotion
- ❏ 感動を露わにする ◯ express emotion U
- ❏ 聴衆の感動を呼び起こす ◯ arouse the emotion of the audience
- ❏ 感動の気持ちを外に見せる ◯ outwardly show emotion
- ❏ 感情をこめて何かを言う ◯ say something with emotion
- ❏ 視聴者の感情につけ込むドラマ

  ◯ a drama which plays on the emotions of the audience
  ☞ play on sth「(気持ちなど) につけ込む」

- ❏ 感情ではなく理性に基づいた結論

  ◯ a conclusion based on reason, not emotion

▶「見えない感情」に関わる表現

- ❏ うっ積した感情 ◯ pent-up emotion ☞ pent-up rage「うっ憤」
- ❏ 感情を抑える ◯ suppress an emotion C
- ❏ 自分の激情を抑えようとする ◯ try to control my emotions
- ❏ 自分の感情を隠す話し方

  ◯ a way of speaking that hides my emotions

- ❏ 感情の制御を取り戻す ◯ regain control over my emotions
- ❏ 感情をこめずに話す ◯ speak without emotion

- メグの胸には何の感動も起こらなかった。
  - ○ Meg felt absolutely no emotion.
- 感情のかけらも示さない ○ show not a flicker of emotion ☞ show a flicker of surprise「驚きの色を見せる」
- 感情に欠ける小説の登場人物
  - ○ characters in a novel who lack emotion
- 彼の声には感情がこもっていなかった。
  - ○ There was no emotion in his voice.

▶ 関連表現

- メグは興奮のるつぼである。 ○ Meg is full of excitement.
- 自分の成功に満足を感じる ○ feel satisfaction at my success
- その知らせを聞いて深い悲しみを経験する
  - ○ experience great grief at hearing the news
- ボブは自分がしたことを思うと恥ずかしくてたまらない。
  - ○ Bob is filled with shame for what he has done.
- 彼の言葉に対する自分の怒りを抑える
  - ○ control my anger at his words
- 不正に対し怒りに震える ○ be overcome by rage at an injustice
  ☞ be overcome with shyness「恥ずかしく何も言えない」(be overcomeは「打ちのめされる」の意味)
- 彼女に対する愛情をなくす
  - ○ lose my feeling of affection towards her

▶ ストーリー

It is very easy for us to **be ruled by our emotions**. If you **are involved in some kind of emotional issue**, it is very important to **let reason, rather than emotion, be your guide**. You **must control any outbursts of emotion**.

(私たちは感情に非常に支配されやすい。もしあなたが何らかの感情面での問題に関わっているのなら、感情よりはむしろ理性に従うことが非常に重要である。あなたは感情のいかなる爆発もコントロールしなくてはならないから。)

036　E-MAIL ··· CU / INTERNET

ひと昔前には我々の生活空間にその名前さえ存在しなかったこの2つなしには、今や仕事はもとより日常生活さえも機能しないことが少なくない。これらは'computer'と密接な関係があることから、ここでも同じコンセプト（手こずる/使いこなす）で表現を整理して紹介する。
✻ e-mailは単に'mail'と略す場合も多い。また、'e-mail'に対して「普通の郵便」を'p-mail'（p = physical）あるいは'snail mail'（カタツムリ郵便）と呼ぶこともある。

CU ｛ 個別のメッセージについて述べる場合 ☞ C
システムとしてのEメールについて述べる場合 ☞ U
✻ Internetは通常'the Internet'の形で用いる。

>> **CELLPHONE; COMPUTER; TECHNOLOGY**

▶「手こずる状況」に関わる表現

❏ インターネットに接続しようとしてエラーメッセージが繰り返し出る
　◯ <u>keep on</u> getting an error message when <u>trying to</u> <u>connect to</u> the Internet

❏ メールの添付書類が開けない
　◯ cannot open an e-mail attachment

❏ インターネット接続の設定の仕方がわからない
　◯ have no idea how to configure my internet connection

❏ メールのありがたみ[便利さ]がわかる
　◯ appreciate the advantages of e-mail U ☞ appreciateは「真価を認める、理解する」こと。I really appreciate it.「本当に感謝します」（丁寧な感謝）

❏ 一日に500通のメールを受け取る
　◯ receive 500 e-mails in one day C

❏ メグから受け取ったメールはまた文字化けしていた。
　◯ The e-mail I got from Meg was garbled again. ☞ a garbled phone message「よく聞き取れない留守電話」

❏ メグの受信箱はジャンクメールであふれている。
　◯ Meg's mailbox is overflowing with junk mail.

❏ 添付書類をうっかり解凍してコンピュータウイルスに感染した。
　◯ I got a computer virus when I carelessly extracted the

attached document.
- そのメールは開かずに捨てた。🟢 I threw away the mail unopened.
- ハードディスクを消去してしまったコンピュータウイルス

  🟢 a computer virus that wiped my hard disk clean ☞ wipe the desk clean「机をふいてきれいにする」

▶「使いこなす状況」に関わる表現

- スパムメールをフィルタリングするコンピュータ・プログラム

  🟢 a computer program that filters spam from my e-mail
- インターネット上で何かがどこにあるか探すのに役立つ素晴らしいアプリケーション

  🟢 a great application which helps you locate stuff on the Internet ☞ locate sth「〈物事の所在〉を突き止める」
- 情報を探してSafari [Chrome]でネットをブラウズする

  🟢 browse the Internet with Safari [Chrome] searching for the information ☞ search the Internet for sth「〈物事〉を求めてネットを探す」
- ネットで買いたい品物を探すのにイーベイのサイトを使う

  🟢 use the eBay site to search for goods you want to purchase on the Internet
- インターネットで音声や画像のストリーミング放送を楽しむ

  🟢 enjoy audio and video streaming over the Internet

▶ ストーリー

The Internet is an information superhighway. If you **are not connected to the Internet**, it is as if you are on the outside looking in. If you do not **have access to the Internet**, it means that you do not know that there is **a window to the world of information**.

(インターネットは情報のスーパーハイウェイだ。インターネットに接続していなければ、まるで家の外にいて中をのぞき込んでいるようなものである。インターネットにアクセスすることができなければ、情報の世界に通じる窓があるということを知らないことになる。)

037 ENJOYMENT ... U

楽しむこと、楽しく過ごすことは文化的生活の一部であり、その対象や方法・手段も多様化している。それらの表現をここでは楽しみの「追求」と「妨害」の両面から 'enjoyment' を用いて整理した。〈関連表現〉では動詞や形容詞と前置詞の結びつきに注意したい。

>> HAPPINESS; HOBBY

▶「楽しさの追求」に関わる表現

- 食の楽しみ ◯ enjoyment of food
- 自分の楽しみの主な源 ◯ my main source of enjoyment
- その映画を心ゆくまで楽しむこと
  ◯ my thorough enjoyment of the movie ☞ thorough [θə́ːroʊ | θʌ́rə]「徹底的な、完全な」a thorough investigation「徹底的な調査」
- 人生の本当の楽しみ ◯ the sheer enjoyment of life ☞ sheer「(名の前で) まったくの」by sheer luck「まったくの幸運で」
- 人生の楽しみを増やす ◯ increase my enjoyment of life
- 音楽から大きな喜びと楽しみを得る
  ◯ gain great pleasure and enjoyment from music
- 知らない人々と会うことにより多大な楽しみを得る
  ◯ get immense enjoyment from meeting new people
- ほかのみんなと一緒に歌うことに楽しみを見出す
  ◯ find enjoyment in singing with everyone else
- 楽しさを露わにしながら部屋に入る
  ◯ enter a room with evident enjoyment
- 音楽によってその映画をいっそう楽しむことができた。
  ◯ The music added to my enjoyment of the film. ☞ add to sth「〈感情や量など〉を増す」
- そのワインで食事がいっそうおいしくなった。
  ◯ The wine stimulated my enjoyment of the meal. ☞ stimulate sth「〈物事〉を刺激する」stimulate my curiosity「好奇心を刺激する」

▶「楽しさの妨害」に関わる表現

❏ テレビを楽しく観るのを妨げる騒音
  ○ a noise which affects my enjoyment of watching television
❏ 大声で話をして皆が映画を楽しむのを台無しにする
  ○ spoil everyone's enjoyment of the movie by talking in a loud voice
❏ 彼の不用意な発言でその小説を読む楽しみが半減した。
  ○ His thoughtless comments limited my enjoyment of the novel.
❏ 少数の行動によって多数の楽しみが損なわれた。
  ○ The behaviour of a minority ruined the enjoyment of the majority.

▶さまざまな「楽しみ」を表す関連表現

❏ 丁寧に自分の仕事をすることに喜びを感じる
  ○ take pleasure in doing my job with care
❏ いたずらして喜ぶ子供
  ○ a child who takes delight in being naughty
❏ その知らせを聞いて大いに満足する
  ○ feel great satisfaction at hearing the news
❏ 私は幸福な気持ちに包まれた。
  ○ A feeling of happiness came over me. ☞ come over sb「(病気・感情などが)〈人〉を襲う」

▶ストーリー

In the last twenty years '**having fun**' has become a major part of our culture. It seems that if we are not '**having a great time**' or '**really enjoying ourselves**', then we are not **living a full life**. No longer do people **find enjoyment in the simple pleasures of life**.

(これまでの20年で「楽しむ」ことは私たちの文化で重要な部分をしめるようになった。もし私たちが「愉快に過ごしてい」ないか、「心から楽しく」ないなら、充実した生活を送っていないと思われる。もはや私たちは人生の単純な快楽の中に楽しみを見出すことはないのである。)

038 ENVIRONMENT ・・・・・・・・ C U

近年、「地球温暖化」(global warming)、「オゾン層の破壊」(the destruction of the ozone layer)、「森林破壊」(deforestation)、「砂漠化」(desertification)、「魚乱獲」(overfishing) など、環境とその保護に対する関心が高まりつつあり、それらに関する話題が各種メディアを賑わせている。ここでは環境の「保護」と「破壊」、さらに自分がおかれている「境遇」としての環境という視点から 'environment' と結びつくさまざまな表現をマスターしよう。

✱ C U の区別よりも以下のような違いに注意するとよい。
- 生態系を意味する場合 ☞ 通常theを伴う
- 自分のおかれている境遇や事情を意味する場合 ☞ 通常anを伴う
(以下の用例中で典型的な表現にそれぞれ*と**のマークで示した)

>> AGRICULTURE/INDUSTRY; ECONOMY; COUNTRY/COUNTRYSIDE; SEA/SEASIDE

▶「環境保護」に関わる表現

- 環境保護 [保全] ◯ conservation of the environment
- 環境を保護 [保全] する ◯ preserve the environment*
- 海の環境を守る ◯ protect the marine environment
- 過激な環境保護論者 ◯ a radical environmentalist
- 生き物とそれらの自然環境
  ◯ living creatures and their natural environment
- 政府の賢明な環境政策
  ◯ an enlightened government policy on the environment

▶「環境破壊」に関わる表現

- 環境を害する化学物質
  ◯ a chemical substance that harms the environment
- 環境によくない開発プロジェクト
  ◯ a development project that is bad for the environment
- 今にも起こりそうな環境災害
  ◯ an environmental disaster waiting to happen
- 環境を汚染する ◯ contaminate the environment
- 環境を破壊する ◯ destroy the environment

- 酸性雨により北欧の環境が損われた。
  - Acid rain hurt the environment in northern Europe.
- 未処理の下水で海の環境を汚す
  - pollute the marine environment with untreated sewage
- 環境を損ねる危険を覚悟で食物の生産を増やす
  - increase food production at the risk of damaging the environment
- 無力な環境省 ○ a Ministry of the Environment that is powerless
- 二酸化炭素ではなく、メタンが環境に脅威であるという見方
  - the view that methane, and not CO_2 [carbon dioxide], is a danger to the environment

▶「境遇・事情」に関わる関連表現

- 我々の社会環境 ○ our social environment
- 企業をとりまく環境 ○ the corporate environment
- 競争の激しいビジネス環境 ○ a competitive business environment
- 自分が働いて楽しい環境
  - an environment that I can enjoy working in**
- 急速に劣悪になっていく都市環境
  - a rapidly deteriorating urban environment

▶ ストーリー

Governments are developing an international policy on **global warming** (or **climate change**). Some people say that CO_2 is **damaging the environment** by, for example, causing **a rise in sea levels**. However, **the Climategate scandals**, and the very cold winter of 2009-2010 have caused many people to **doubt global warming**.

（各国の政府は地球温暖化（あるいは気候変動）についての国際政策を練りあげつつある。二酸化炭素は例えば海面の上昇を引き起こすことにより環境を破壊するという人たちもいる。しかし、クライメートゲート事件、そして2009年から2010年にかけての非常に寒い冬は、多くの人々に地球温暖化に対する疑惑を起こさせているのである。）

ENVIRONMENT

039 EVENING / MORNING ····· [C][U]

> 'Evening/morning' は 'day/night' と共に時間の区切りを表すのに用いられる重要な語である。これらを用いてスケジュールを自由に表現できるようになろう。また、これらは名詞以外に形容詞として用いられる場合もあり、特にラベルを設けて用例をあげた。
> 　数えたり、「〜の朝/晩」のように呼んだりする場合 ☞ [C]
> 　自然現象としての 'evening/morning' について述べる場合 ☞ [U]
>
> **>> DAY/NIGHT ; TIME**

▶「時点」に関わる表現

- 先週のうすら寒い朝に ○ on a chilly morning last week [C]
- 毎朝6時発の列車 ○ a train which leaves at six every morning
- 3月15日の晩に ○ on the evening of 15th March
- 明晩人に会う約束がある
  ○ have an appointment tomorrow evening
- 昨日の朝ボブに会った。○ I saw Bob yesterday morning.

▶「期間」に関わる表現

- 午前2時に起床する ○ get up at two in the morning
- 午前中の大半を働く ○ work for most of the morning
- 午前中をだらだら過ごす ○ idle away the morning ☞ idle /stm/ away
  「(何もしないで) ゆったりと〈時〉を過ごす」
- 午前中のほとんどを寝て過ごす
  ○ spend most of my morning sleeping
- 夜遅く家に戻る ○ return home in the late evening
- 夜早い時間にメグと会う ○ see Meg earlier in the evening
- 素晴らしい夕べを過ごす ○ have a wonderful evening
- メグと一緒に楽しい夜を過ごす
  ○ spend an enjoyable evening with Meg
- 夜の終わりが近づいた。○ The end of the evening approached.
- 朝は一日のうちで私の大好きな時である。
  ○ Morning is my favourite time of the day. [U]

▶ 形容詞としての用法

- 夕日の斜めに差す光 ◯ the slanting rays of the evening sun
  - ☞ slanting「傾いた、斜めの」＜ slant「傾く、斜めになる」
- 午前半ばにコーヒーブレイクをとる
  ◯ have a mid-morning coffee break
- 早朝の日差しを楽しむ ◯ enjoy the early morning light
- 夕食の席につく ◯ sit down to the evening meal
- 夕刊を今か今かと待つ ◯ wait anxiously for the evening paper
  - ☞ anxiously「切望して、心配して」
- フランス語を上達させるために夜間のクラスに通う
  ◯ go to evening classes to improve my French
- イブニングドレス[夜会服]を着る ◯ put on an evening dress

▶決まり文句

- 私は朝から晩まで働いた。
  ◯ I worked from morning to [till] night.
  - ☞ I was on duty morning, noon, and night.「一日中勤務だった」
- 私は朝型人間ではない。◯ I am not a morning person.
  - ☞「夜型人間」は a night person と言う
- (今晩は) これでお開きにしましょう。◯ Let's call it an evening.
  - ☞ call it a day「(1日の) 仕事を切り上げる」

▶ ストーリー

Yesterday I **got up late in the morning**, and **started my day with a morning cup of tea**. Then I **spent the rest of the morning reading the paper**. I worked in my study **from midday until the early evening**. I then watched TV for a bit, **had my evening meal**, and went to bed.

(昨日、私は朝遅く起床すると朝のお茶一杯でその日をスタートさせた。それから午前中の残りの時間は新聞を読んで過ごした。正午から晩早くまで書斎で仕事をした。それから少しテレビを見て、夕食を食べると就寝した。)

040　FACE　　　　　　　　　　　　　C

> **顔**は身体の一部としての役割の他、「表情」を現す重要な役割がある。ここでも、まず基本的な顔の形を紹介し、さらに 'face' を用いた表現を「見せること」（主に自分の顔・表情）と「見ること」（主に他人の顔・表情）という2つのグループに分けて整理した。
> ✱ 日本語の「顔」が英語で 'head' になる場合があることにも注意。
> 例 「窓から顔を出す」→ stick my head out of the window
>
> **>> CHARACTER; HAIR**

▶ face から広がるボキャブラリー：名詞表現

- 丸顔 ● a round face ☞ He has a round face.「彼は丸顔だ」
- 長細い顔；うかぬ顔［憂うつな顔］● a long face
- 角張った顔 ● a square face
- うりざね顔 ● an oval face ☞ oval「楕円形の」
- 真顔；しかめっ面 ● a serious face
- まじめな顔 ● an earnest face
- しわが寄った顔 ● a wrinkled face
- いかつい顔 ● a craggy face
- ニキビ面（づら） ● a face with a lot of pimples
- 青白い顔 ● a pale face ☞ look pale「顔色が悪い」
- 顔が真っ赤になる ● be red in the face

▶「表情を見せること」に関わる表現

- 空に向かって顔を上げる ● raise my face to the sky
- 仰向けに横たわる ● lie face upwards ☞「顔を上に向けて」ということ
- うつぶせでぐっすり眠っている ● lie on my face, sound asleep
   ☞ lie on my stomach「うつぶせになる」
- （笑わずに）真顔でいる ● keep a straight face
- おどけた表情を見せる ● make a funny face
- ボブの顔は喜びで輝いた。● Bob's face lit up in delight.
- ボブは顔に喜びの表情を浮かべていた。
   ● Bob had a pleased expression on his face.

- メグは顔に微笑を浮かべていた。 ◯ Meg had a smile on her face.
- 失望が彼女の顔をよぎった。 ◯ Disappointment crossed her face.
  - ☞ A good idea crossed my mind.「よい考えがふと心に浮かんだ」
- 自分の顔を見せる勇気がない ◯ do not dare to show my face
- ボブを面と向かって笑う ◯ laugh in Bob's face
- 私は顔面を殴打された。 ◯ I was hit in the face. ☞ be hit on the head「頭を殴られる」
- 何とか体面を繕う ◯ manage to save face
- 上司は面目を失うのを恐れている。
  ◯ The boss is afraid of losing face.
- 私の顔はこの地域でよく知られている。
  ◯ My face is well known in this area.

▶「表情を見ること」に関わる表現

- メグの顔をまっすぐ見つめる ◯ stare directly into Meg's face
- 振り返ってボブを見る ◯ turn my face to look at Bob
- メグと顔をつきあわせて座る ◯ sit face-to-face with Meg
- ボブの顔に怒りの表情が見える ◯ see a look of anger in Bob's face
- メグの表情に返事をうかがう ◯ search Meg's face for an answer
- メグの顔つきから彼女の心を読む ◯ read Meg's face
- 顔を見てボブだとわかる ◯ recognize Bob's face
- 死に直面する ◯ stare death in the face
  - ☞ このin the faceは「目前に(迫って)」の意

▶ ストーリー

My head is rather large. I have a large forehead and slightly bushy eyebrows. My eyelashes are very long. My cheeks tend to be slightly red. I have a weak chin, so I hide it with a beard.

(私の頭はどちらかというと大きい。額は大きく、眉は少しふさふさしている。まつげは非常に長い。ほおは少し赤みがかっている。あごが貧弱なので、あごひげで隠している。)

FACE

041　FAILURE　　　　　　　　　　　C U

英語の'failure'が意味するのは「失敗」だけではない。「(するのを)怠ること(怠慢)」「しないこと(不履行)」をも意味し、マイナスの行動を表す場面で広く用いられる語である。

ここでも、'failure'を用いた「大きな失敗」に相当する表現、「人間の行動」や「物事」に関わるマイナスの表現を紹介した。

- 特定の失敗・不履行やそのタイプについて述べる場合 ☞ C
- 失敗一般(人生の経験としての失敗など)について述べる場合 ☞ U

>> APOLOGY; CHANCE; DIFFICULTY; LUCK; SUCCESS

▶「大きな失敗」に関わる表現

- まったくの失敗 ◎ a total failure ᶜ
- 救いようのない失敗 ◎ a hopeless failure
- みじめな失敗 ◎ a miserable failure
- 完全な失敗 ◎ an outright failure ☞ an outright majority「絶対多数」
- 非常に高い不合格率[失敗の割合] ◎ a very high failure rate

▶「人間の行動」に関わるマイナスの表現

- 提案の不履行 ◎ the failure of a proposal
- 病気を直すことができないこと ◎ a failure to cure a disease
- 事実に立ち向かわないこと ◎ a failure to face the facts
- 運転中に注意を怠ること
   ◎ a failure to pay attention when driving
- 十分な時間をかけて行動を起こさないこと
   ◎ a failure to take action in sufficient time
- テロに対する軍事的な解決策の失敗
   ◎ the failure of the military solution to terrorism
- 失敗に終わった計画 ◎ a plan that ended in failure ☞ end in success「成功裡に終わる」
- ボブは失敗を恐れて冒険をしなかった。
   ◎ Bob is afraid of failure, so took no chances. ☞ take a chance [chances]「思い切ってやってみる」

- 人生で何度も失敗を経験する
    - ○ experience failure many times in my life ⓤ
- 私の計画は結局失敗する運命だ。○ My plan is doomed to failure.
    - ☞ We are all doomed to die in the end.「我々は結局皆死ぬ運命にある」
- 失敗の原因がわかる ○ identify the cause of a failure
- 成功か失敗はあなたにかかっている。
    - ○ Success or failure depends on you.

▶「物事」に関わるマイナスの表現

- 肝機能の低下 ○ liver failure
- 彼の健康が徐々に悪化していくこと
    - ○ a gradual failure of his health
- 停電 ○ a power failure ☞ a blackout (No.034)
- バッテリーのダウン ○ battery failure
- 政治上の失敗 ○ political failure
- 経済上の失敗 ○ economic failure
- 農作物の不作 ○ a failure of the crops
- 試験に落ちること ○ failure in an exam
- 交渉の失敗 ○ the failure of negotiations
- エンストで立ち往生する ○ suffer engine failure ☞ suffer great losses
「大損害を受ける」

▶ ストーリー

I have no space to tell you the story of the Scottish hero, Robert the Bruce. But what Robert learnt was that **however many times we fail**, if we **continue trying, never giving up**, we **will eventually succeed**. So if you **experience failure, do not be disheartened**.

(スコットランドの英雄、ロバート・ザ・ブルースのお話をするスペースはありません。しかしロバートが学んだことは、何度失敗しても、決して諦めないで努力を続ければ、最後には成功するものであるということでした。だから失敗を経験しても気落ちしてはいけません。)

042 FAMILY C

> 家族は生活の中心であり、最小の社会的な単位である。自己紹介そして人間関係に必要な 'family' に関わる表現をマスターしておきたい。
>
> ✻ 英語では、家族を一つの集合体ととらえて 'the family is' とも、あるいは成員を重視して 'the family are' とも言うことができる。もちろん複数の家族について述べる場合は 'the families are' と言う。
>
> **>> CHILD; HOME; HUSBAND / WIFE**

▶ family から広がるボキャブラリー：名詞表現

- ❏ 自分の家柄 ○ my family background
- ❏ 自分の肉親 ○ my immediate family ☞「いちばん近い親族」の意味
- ❏ 10人からなる大家族 ○ a large family of ten people
- ❏ 片親しかいない家庭 ○ a single-parent family
- ❏ 平均的な家庭 ○ an average family
- ❏ 裕福な家庭 ○ a well-off family
- ❏ 幸福な家庭 ○ a happy family
- ❏ 労働者階級の家族 ○ a working-class family
- ❏ 多くの問題を抱える家族 ○ a family with a lot of problems

▶ family から広がるボキャブラリー：動詞表現

- ❏ 著名な家柄の出である ○ come of a distinguished family
   ☞ a distinguished school「名門校」
- ❏ 子供を育てる ○ raise a family
- ❏ 居を構えて長子をもうける ○ settle down and start a family
- ❏ 幸せな家庭で大きくなる ○ grow up in a happy family
- ❏ メグは有名な家柄の子孫である［の血を引いている］。
   ○ Meg is descended from a famous family.
- ❏ 自分の家族を養うことができない ○ cannot support my family
- ❏ 家族のコネを通して職を得る
   ○ get a job through family connections
- ❏ 同族経営の会社で働く ○ work for the family company

▶「成員」に関わる表現

- スミス一家 ◎ the Smith family
- 大家族の全員 ◎ all the members of a large family
- 家長 ◎ the head of the family
- 家族の5人の息子たちの長男
    ◎ the eldest of five sons in the family
- 家族の集まり ◎ a family gathering
- かかりつけの医者 ◎ the family doctor
- うちは四人家族です。◎ There are four (people) in my family.

▶決まり文句

- 彼女は一家の大黒柱［稼ぎ手］である。
    ◎ She is <u>the main breadwinner</u> in the family.
- うちは禿(はげ)の家系である。◎ Baldness <u>runs in</u> our family.
    ☞ このrunは「(血筋・特徴などが)伝わる、流れる」の意
- どんな家にも外聞をはばかる内輪の秘密がある。
    ◎ Every family <u>has a skeleton in the closet [cupboard]</u>.

▶ ストーリー

When people refer to 'my family', they usually mean **their nuclear family**. The idea of **one large, extended family — the 'traditional family'**, **all living under one roof**, is not very attractive to modern young people. The pattern now is for a couple to **get married in their thirties, settle down, and have one child**.

(一般に「私の家族は…」という場合、たいてい核家族を意味する。大家族や拡大家族、すなわち一つ屋根の下に全員が生活する昔ながらの家族、という考え方は現代の若い人たちにとってあまり魅力的ではない。現在のパターンは、カップルが30代で結婚し、居を構え、子供を一人つくるというものである。)

043 FASHION ... C U

ファッション（流行）が今や一時的な流れでなく、生活空間の重要部分をしめていることは間違いない。この項だけでなく以下の参照項目の表現を合わせてマスターすれば、あなたは「イケてる」人っぽく (like a 'with-it' person) 英語を話せるようになるだろう。

- 特定のファッションやスタイルについて述べる場合 ☞ C
- トレンドや生活における役割について述べる場合 ☞ U

>> CLOTHES; HAIR; SHOPPING

▶「社会のしくみ」に関わる表現

- ファッションの世界［ファッション界］ ○ the fashion world
- ファッションデザイナー ○ a fashion designer
- ファッションデザインを勉強する ○ study fashion design
- attend a fashion show ○ ファッションショーに行く
- ブティックで買い物をする ○ shop at fashion boutiques
- ファッション雑誌 ○ a fashion magazine

▶「流行を追うこと」に関わる表現

- 度肝を抜くファッション ○ a stunning fashion [C] ☞ a stunning view「息をのむような眺め」
- 現代ファッションの傾向 ○ trends in modern fashion [U]
- 若者の間で流行る ○ come into fashion among young people
- 非常に早く廃れる ○ go out of fashion very quickly
- 流行を作り出す映画スター
  ○ a movie star who sets the fashion
- 流行の頻繁な変化について行く
  ○ keep up with frequent changes in fashion ☞ keep up with the times「時代に遅れずについていく」
- 若い女性向けの最新ファッションに追随する
  ○ follow the latest fashions for young women
- 今流行っている一番新しい服を着る
  ○ wear the latest in current fashions

❏ ボブは流行を追ってばかりいる。◯ Bob is a slave to fashion.
　☞ She is a slave to money.「彼女は金の亡者だ」
❏ メグは優れたファッション感覚を持っている。
　◯ Meg has an excellent fashion sense.　☞ have a sense of humour
「ユーモアの感覚がある」

▶ 関連表現

❏ 非常にファッショナブルな服を着る
　◯ wear very fashionable clothes
❏ メグは非常にトレンディな人間である。
　◯ Meg is a very trendy person.
❏ (一時的に) 大流行している靴
　◯ shoes that are all the rage
❏ 短いスカートが大流行だ。
　◯ Short skirts are all the vogue.
❏ 幅広のベルトは流行の最先端である。
　◯ Wide belts are the latest thing.
❏ 後ろ向きに帽子をかぶることが若い男性の間で「旬」だ。
　◯ Wearing a cap backwards is 'in' among young men.

▶ ストーリー

I used to **keep up with the latest fashions**. Whenever something **came into fashion**, I bought it. If I did not, it meant I **was hopelessly out of fashion**. **Fashions were changing so quickly** that I had to throw away almost new clothes. Now I have stopped **being a slave to fashion**. Now, I just **wear ordinary, sensible clothes**.

(私は昔は最新のファッションに遅れまいとしていた。何か流行り出すと、それを買った。そうしないと、私は救いようがないくらい時代遅れだということになったからだ。ファッションの移り変わりはあまりに速く、私は買ったばかりの服を捨てざるをえなかったほどだ。現在私はファッションに憂き身をやつすのはやめた。私は今では普通のまともな服を着ているだけである。)

044　FISH / MEAT　　　　　　　　　　　U

動物から人へ感染する病気の存在が明らかになり、肉類に関する意識が高まりつつある。ここでは魚・肉類と我々の食生活に関わる頻出表現はもちろんのこと、時事的な話題も合わせて紹介した。
✻ 'fish' や 'meat' を食べ物や物質として述べる場合は U 扱いになる。数えるには 'a piece of 〜' などを用いなければならない (☞*)。
✻魚を「食べ物」でなく「生き物」として数える場合は 'two fish' とも 'two fishes' とも言える。

>> DIET; DINNER / LUNCH; FOOD; FRUIT / VEGETABLE

▶ 魚に関わる表現

- ❏ 新鮮な魚 ⊙ fresh fish
- ❏ 冷凍の魚 ⊙ frozen fish
- ❏ 生の魚；刺身 ⊙ raw fish
- ❏ 魚の干物一枚 ⊙ a piece of dried fish*
- ❏ 魚の薫製二切れ ⊙ two slices of smoked fish*
- ❏ 魚を三枚におろす ⊙ fillet a fish ☞ fillet [fílit] は名では「(骨なしの)切り身、ヒレ (肉)」
- ❏ メインコースに魚を食べる ⊙ have fish as the main course
- ❏ 魚料理に合わせて辛口の白ワインを出す
  ⊙ serve a dry white wine with the fish ☞ a ...はワインの種類・タイプを意味する。sweet wine「甘口のワイン」
- ❏ 大漁 ⊙ a large catch of fish ☞ fish catches「漁獲量」
- ❏ 国の魚類総消費量 ⊙ a country's total fish consumption
- ❏ 貝を食べて食中毒になる ⊙ get food poisoning from shellfish

▶ 肉に関わる表現

- ❏ 肉、鳥肉、魚貝類 ⊙ meat, poultry, and seafood
- ❏ 肉200グラム ⊙ 200 grammes of meat
- ❏ 脂身が少ない肉 ⊙ lean meat
- ❏ 脂身が多い肉 ⊙ fatty meat
- ❏ 霜降り肉 ⊙ well-marbled meat

- ミンチ ○ minced meat
- オーブンで肉を焼く ○ roast the meat in the oven
- 肉をソーセージと一緒にバーベキューにする

    barbeque the meat with the sausages
- 肉をサイコロ状に切る、あるいはぶつ切りにする

    ○ cut meat into cubes, or small blocks
- 肉を柔らかくするために茹でる

    ○ boil some meat to make it tender
- 肉の汚染を避ける ○ avoid contamination of meat
- 人が食べるには向かない肉

    ○ meat that is unfit for human consumption
- 狂牛病にかかっている牛からとった肉

    ○ meat from a cow that has BSE ['mad cow disease']
- 鳥インフルエンザに感染した鶏の肉

    ○ chicken meat from a bird infected with avian influenza ['bird flu'] ☞ His flu infected his wife. 「彼の流感が妻にうつった」

▶決まり文句

- ビルはいつも大酒を食らっている。○ Bill drinks like a fish.
- 甲の薬は乙の毒。《諺》

    ○ One man's meat is another man's poison. ☞ 好き嫌いは人によって異なるということ

▶ストーリー

In English, **fish is often called 'brain food'**. This is perhaps an example of folk wisdom and science reaching the same conclusion. It seems that **eating fish is good for the brain**. So, **stay away from meat**, especially **fatty meat**, and **eat plenty of fish**.

(英語では魚はしばしば「脳の食べ物」と呼ばれる。これはおそらく民間の知恵と科学が同じ結論に達した例である。魚を食べることは脳のために良いように思われる。だから、肉、特に脂身が多い肉を避けて魚をたくさん食べなさい。)

045 FITNESS [U]

> 健康の増進とその管理はブームを過ぎ、我々の生活の一部として定着した感がある。「フィットネス」はカタカナ語としても定着した。生活の中で 'fitness' がどのように使われているか、'diet' や似たような意味を持つ 'health' と合わせてマスターしておきたい。
>
> 'fitness' は 'health' よりも体調面・体力的な健康状態に重きがあることにも注意して以下の用例を見ていってほしい。
>
> **>> DIET; HEALTH**

▶「ライフスタイルとしての健康」に関わる表現

- (身体的な) 健康状態 ◯ fitness
- (気持ちの面も含めた) 総合的な健康状態 ◯ general well-being
- 健康不足 ◯ a lack of fitness
- 個人的なフィットネス・トレーニング
  ◯ personal fitness training
- 生涯を通して良好な健康状態を維持すること
  ◯ the maintenance of physical fitness throughout life
- 良好な健康レベルに達する ◯ reach a good level of fitness
- 運動選手にフィットネステストを行う
  ◯ give an athlete a fitness test
- 厳しい健康管理に従う ◯ follow a strict fitness regime ☞ a regime [riʒi:m]「管理方法、制度」 a dietary regime「食生活の管理」
- １年を通して身体全体の健康状態を維持する
  ◯ maintain my year-round general fitness ☞ all (the) year round「1年中」(副詞句)
- 新しい従業員の健康と体調検査
  ◯ a health and fitness check of new employees
- そのフットボール [サッカー] チームの全体的な健康状態の水準は非常に高かった。
  ◯ The overall standard of fitness of the football team was very high. ☞ the overall result「総合成績、総合的な結果」

▶「設備」に関わる表現

❏ 屋内プールとフィットネス・ルームを備えたホテル
　◯ <u>a hotel with</u> an indoor swimming pool and a fitness room
❏ フィットネス施設とエアロビック教室
　◯ fitness facilities and aerobic classes

▶ 関連表現

❏ 毎朝1時間の運動をする
　◯ do a one-hour workout every morning
❏ ジムでウェートトレーニングをする
　◯ do my weight training in the gym
❏ 運動のしすぎで体が凝っている
　◯ feel stiff <u>from</u> too much exercise ☞ be tired from overwork「残業で疲れている」
❏ 私は体調が良い。◯ I <u>am in good condition</u>.
❏ メグは体調が良い。◯ Meg <u>is in shape</u>.
❏ ボブは体調が良くない。◯ Bob <u>is out of shape</u>.
❏ 私はすこぶる調子が良い。◯ I feel <u>as fit as a fiddle</u>. ☞ くだけた表現

▶ ストーリー

I am certainly not **a fitness fanatic**, but I do **try to keep in shape**. I **do not like doing exercise**, but nevertheless, every morning I **go for a twenty-minute walk**. By doing this I **can maintain a reasonable level of fitness**. As well as **the fitness benefits of this**, there are psychological benefits as well. After the walk, I **feel relaxed and mentally alert**.
(私は健康マニアなどではない。しかし私は確かに体調の維持に努めている。私は運動をすることが好きではないが、それにもかかわらず、毎朝20分間散歩に出かける。こうすることによって私は満足のいく健康状態を維持することができる。これは健康状態の維持によいだけでなく精神衛生の面でもよい。散歩の後はリラックスして頭の働きも活発になるのだ。)

046 FOOD C U

食に関わる行為を英語で表すことは意外と難しい。それと意識しないで無意識に行っているものが多いからである。ここでは、食べ物自体の味と調理法に関する表現、さらに食べる行為のバリエーションを紹介した。いずれも毎日のように口にするもの、行っている行為を表す用例ばかりである。すべて確実にマスターしたい。

C {特定の食べ物やそのタイプについて述べる場合 ☞ C
U 食べ物について全般的に、特に栄養の見地から述べる場合 ☞ U

✻下記のように 'food' の表す意味は広く、状況によって日本語では「食(べ)物」「食品」「食料」などと訳し分けられることにも注意。

>> DIET; DINNER / LUNCH; FISH / MEAT; FRUIT / VEGETABLE; HEALTH

▶ food から広がるボキャブラリー：名詞表現

❏ 脂っこく精製糖が多い食べ物
  ○ foods rich in fat and refined sugar C ☞ refined「精製された」 raw sugar「粗糖」 low sugar「微糖」
❏ スパイス [香辛料] がきいた食べ物 ○ spicy food
❏ 塩辛い [しょっぱい] 食べ物 ○ salty food
❏ おいしそうな / 味気ない食べ物 ○ appetizing / tasteless food
❏ 味気ない食べ物 ○ bland food ☞ bland comments「当たり障りのない発言」
❏ 菜食主義者に適した食べ物 ○ food suitable for vegetarians
❏ 適切に (加熱) 調理した食品 ○ properly cooked food
❏ 生煮え [生焼け] の料理 ○ undercooked food
❏ 煮すぎた [焼きすぎた] 料理 ○ overcooked food
❏ 非常に食欲をそそる食べ物 ○ food that is very tempting ☞ a tempting offer「魅力的なオファー」
❏ 誕生パーティのための特別料理 ○ special food for a birthday party

▶ food から広がるボキャブラリー：動詞表現

❏ 食べ物を少しずつかじる ○ nibble at my food
❏ 食べ物を飲み込む ○ swallow my food ☞ drink my beer in one swallow「ビールを一気飲みする」

モノ

- 食べ物を無理に飲み込む ◯ gulp down my food
- 1杯のミルクと一緒に食べ物を胃に流し込む
  ◯ wash down my food with a glass of milk
- 食べ物を料理するのに丸1時間かける
  ◯ take a whole hour to cook the food
- 食べ物を網焼きバーベキューにする ◯ barbeque the food on a grill
- 食べ物をしっかりかむ ◯ chew my food properly
- 食べ物をきちんと消化する ◯ digest food properly [U]
- 栄養があって健康に良い食べ物以外食べない
  ◯ eat nothing but nourishing, wholesome food
- 体に良くない食べ物ばかりに夢中になる
  ◯ overindulge in all the wrong foods
- おかわりをする ◯ take [have] a second helping of food
- 私の大好きな食べ物は焼き魚である。
  ◯ My favourite food is grilled fish.
- 私はこの食べ物を食べるとあたる [この食べ物は私に合わない]。
  ◯ This food does not agree with me.
- 低カロリー食品限定の食生活をする
  ◯ limit your diet to low-calorie foods
- 購入する食品すべての表示をチェックする
  ◯ check the labelling on all the foods you buy

▶ ストーリー

I **was starving**, so I **put some leftover food in the microwave** to **heat it up**. I **ate it quickly, swallowing it without really chewing**. Then I rushed out to work. I **must stop eating like this: leftovers, frozen food, instant food, junk food**! **My digestion is very bad** and I **suffer from constipation**.

(私はすごくお腹がすいていたので、電子レンジに料理の残りを入れて加熱した。ちゃんとかもうともせず、飲み込むように素早くそれを食べた。それから私はあわてて仕事に出かけた。食べ残し、冷凍食品、インスタント食品、ジャンクフード！──私はこのような食べ方をやめなくてはならない。消化は非常に悪く、便秘に悩まされている。)

FOOD

047　FRIENDSHIP　　　　　　　 C U

友情や友好関係は個人的なつき合いだけのものではない。会社や外交においても 'friendship' は非常に重要である。ここに紹介した用例は公私どちらにもあてはまるものであり、状況に合わせて使い分けてみよう。

C 何らかの友情や友好関係を表す場合 ☞ C
U 「友情というもの」について述べる場合 ☞ U

✲ 'friendship' の反対語は 'enmity' である（例 feel enmity towards *sb* 人に敵意を抱く）が、幸いこの語はCore Nounsには入っていない。

>>FAMILY; KINDNESS; LOVE

▶ friendship から広がるボキャブラリー：名詞表現

❏ 親交 ◯ a close [klóus] friendship
❏ 固い友情 ◯ a firm friendship ☞ a firm decision「固い決意」
❏ （異性との）親密な交際 ◯ an intimate friendship ☞ 性的な関係を暗示する場合があるので、通常は上の2例を用いる
❏ 長く不変の友情 ◯ a long-lasting friendship
❏ 末永き交誼 ◯ an enduring friendship ☞ an enduring peace「恒久的平和」
❏ 二人の間の特別な友情
　◯ a special friendship between two people C
❏ 深くいつまでも変わらない友情
　◯ a deep and permanent friendship
❏ 二国間の友好条約 ◯ a treaty of friendship between two nations
❏ 本当の友情は見つけにくい。
　◯ Genuine friendship is hard to find. ☞ Bob is hard to please.「ボブは気難しい」

▶ friendship から広がるボキャブラリー：名詞表現

❏ 誰かと新たに友好関係を築く
　◯ form a new friendship with someone
❏ 見知らぬ人と交友を結ぶ
　◯ strike up a friendship with a stranger ☞ strike /*sth*/ up「〈関係・会

話など〉を開始する」 strike up a conversation「会話を始める」
- ❏ 友情から何かをする ○ do something <u>out of friendship</u>
- ❏ 何年もたってからメグと私の旧交を温める
  ○ renew my friendship with Meg after many years
- ❏ ボブの支援と友情に感謝する
  ○ appreciate Bob's support and friendship ⓤ
- ❏ メグとボブの友情を壊す
  ○ destroy the friendship between Meg and Bob

▶ 関連表現

- ❏ 友達と親類 ○ friends and relatives
- ❏ 家族の親友 ○ a close friend of the family
- ❏ 親しい友人 ○ a dear friend
- ❏ 信頼できる友人 ○ a trusted friend
- ❏ 誠実な友人 ○ a faithful friend
- ❏ 自分の一番の友達 ○ my best friend
- ❏ ボブと私は一番の親友だ。 ○ Bob and I are the best of friends.
- ❏ 隣人と友達になる ○ <u>make friends with</u> the neighbours ☞ friends と複数形であることに注意
- ❏ 敵に友好的な身振りをする
  ○ make a friendly gesture to the enemy
- ❏ メグは誰にでもとても親切だ。
  ○ Meg is very friendly to everyone.

▶ ストーリー

My grandmother **has a very wide circle of friends**. Wherever she goes, she soon **makes friends with new people**. She has the ability to **strike up a friendship with a complete stranger**, and she will **help people out of friendship**.

(私の祖母は友達の輪がすごく広い。どこに行っても初めて会う人たちとすぐ友達になる。彼女にはまったく見知らぬ人と友達になれる能力があるのだ。そして、友情から人に手を貸すのも習慣になっている。)

048 FRUIT Ⓒ Ⓤ / VEGETABLE Ⓒ

果物や野菜は、料理はもちろん見た目にも我々の生活空間を豊かにしてくれる。ここでは、これらを用いた行動に関わる表現と共に、意外と英語が知られていない果物・野菜も紹介した。

- 個々の果物を指したり、果物のタイプについて述べる場合 ☞ Ⓒ
- 果物全体を指したり、食べ物としての果物を意味する場合 ☞ Ⓤ

>> DIET; DINNER / LUNCH; FISH / MEAT; FOOD

▶ fruit / vegetable から広がるボキャブラリー

- 緑色野菜 ◯ green vegetables
- 葉菜 ◯ leafy vegetables ☞ a leafy area「緑豊かな地域」
- 根菜 ◯ root vegetables ☞ the root「(問題の) 根源、根本」
- 新鮮な果実 ◯ fresh fruit Ⓤ
- 多種多様な野菜と果物 ◯ a wide variety of vegetables and fruit
  ☞ a variety of sth「いろいろな〈物〉」
- 冷凍果物/ドライフルーツ ◯ frozen / dried fruit
- 生野菜 ◯ raw vegetables ☞ an raw egg「生卵」
- (加熱)調理した野菜 ◯ cooked vegetables
- 害虫に強い種類の果物を栽培する
  ◯ grow pest-resistant varieties of fruit ☞ -resistant「〜に抵抗力のある」
- 化学肥料を使わないで栽培された果物
  ◯ fruit that has been grown without the use of chemical fertilizers
- 一年中手に入れられる果物と野菜
  ◯ fruit and vegetables which are available all the year round
- 世界各地から輸入された山のような珍しい果物
  ◯ a pile of exotic fruits from different parts of the world
  ☞ a pile of books「山積みの本」

▶ 果物や野菜に関わる動作

- 瓶詰めして果物を保存する ◯ preserve fruit by bottling
- 野菜を洗って調理する ◯ wash and prepare vegetables ☞ prepare は手の込んだ料理をする場合に用いる

- 果物の皮をむく ○ peel fruit
- リンゴを四等分に切り分ける ○ cut an apple into quarters
- カボチャをさいの目に切る ○ dice a pumpkin
- キュウリを薄く切る ○ slice a cucumber
- ジャガイモをつぶす ○ mash potatoes ☞ mashed potato「マッシュポテト」
- レモンを絞る ○ squeeze a lemon
- 材料を混ぜ合わせる ○ blend the ingredients
- 混ぜ合わせたものに刻んだ玉ねぎを加える
  ○ add the chopped onions to the mixture

▶ 意外と知らない果物と野菜

- キンカン ○ a kumquat [kʌ́mkwɔt]
- ビワ ○ a loquat [lóukwɔt]
- 柿 ○ a persimmon [pərsímən]
- ザクロ ○ a pomegranate [pɔ́m(ə)grænət]
- パッションフルーツ ○ a passion fruit
- ナス ○ an aubergine [óubərʒiːn] (= an eggplant)
- カブ ○ a turnip [tə́ːrnip]
- ズッキーニ ○ a courgette [kuərʒét|kɔː-] (= a zucchini)
- 芽キャベツ ○ Brussels sprouts
- インゲン豆 ○ haricot [hǽrikòu] beans (= navy beans)

▶ ストーリー

'Dai wa shoo o kaneru' is a good principle for carpentry, but **not for cooking**. In making a curry, I always **add too much chopped onion**, for example, and then have to 'balance it' with **more potatoes and meat**. This process continues till I **have a curry for a dozen people**.

(「大は小を兼ねる」は大工仕事の鉄則であるが、料理には当てはまらない。カレーを作るとき、私はいつも、例えば、刻み玉ねぎを加えすぎてしまい、ジャガイモと肉を多く入れて「バランスをとら」なければならない。こんな手順を繰り返して、結局10人分ほどのカレーを作ってしまうのである。)

049 GOVERNMENT ･････････ CU

政府が生活空間の核であるかどうかは議論の余地があるところだが、我々の生活を大きく左右する存在であることは間違いない。その意味で 'government' に関するさまざまな表現をぜひ押さえておきたい。いずれも新聞などで頻出のものばかりである。

- 特定の政府や統治する人々を指す場合 ☞ C
- 社会をまとめる制度としての政府について述べる場合 ☞ U

(〈決まり文句〉のリンカーンの言葉を参照)

>> COUNTRY/NATION; ECONOMY; POLITICS

▶ government から広がるボキャブラリー

- ❏ 組閣する ○ form a government C
- ❏ 政府を率いる [政府の長となる] ○ head the government
- ❏ 現在の政府を支持する ○ support the present government
- ❏ 新政府でポストを求める
  ○ seek a position in the new government
- ❏ 政府を辞める ○ resign from a government
- ❏ 内閣不信任案を可決する/提出する
  ○ pass / move a no-confidence motion in the government
- ❏ 倒閣する ○ overthrow the government ☞ overthrow old systems「古い制度を撤廃する」
- ❏ 政府を攻撃する ○ attack the government
- ❏ 傀儡政府を樹立する ○ set up a puppet government
- ❏ 政権交代 ○ a change of government
- ❏ 連立政権 ○ a coalition government

▶「政策」に関わる表現

- ❏ 政府による推薦 ○ a recommendation by the government
- ❏ 政策の変更 ○ a change in government policy
- ❏ 増税しないという政府の約束
  ○ a government promise not to raise taxes
- ❏ 財政支出の増加 ○ an increase in government spending

- 政府によって設立された委員会
  a committee set up by the government
- 税政改革を通して政府財政を改善する
  ○ improve government finances through tax reform
- 野党は政府の経済政策の誤りを非難した。
  ○ The opposition party blamed the government for its mistakes in economic policy.

▶ 関連表現

- 総理大臣；首相 ○ the Prime Minister
- 外務大臣 ○ the Minister of Foreign Affairs
- 財務大臣 ○ the Minister of Finance
- 文科大臣 ○ the Minister of Education (Culture, Sports, Science and Technology) ☞ 括弧内は通例省略される
- 保健大臣 ○ the Minister of Health
- 厚生大臣 ○ the Minister of Health, Labour and Welfare
- 農業大臣 ○ the Minister of Agriculture
- 国防大臣 ○ the Minister of Defence

▶ 決まり文句

- 人民の、人民による、人民のための政府 (Abraham Lincoln)
  ○ government of the people, by the people, for the people [U]

▶ ストーリー

Do governments exist for the people, or **do the people exist for the government**? In **democratic countries**, the answer is obvious. It is **the electorate who vote the government in** and **vote it out**. **Politicians** are nothing more than **representatives of the people**.

(政府が人々のために存在するのか、あるいは人々が政府のために存在するのか？　民主主義の国では答えは明らかである。政府を当選させるのも落とすのも有権者なのである。政治家は国民の代表にすぎないのである。)

050 GROWTH .... C U

成長するのは形あるものだけではない。文化や経済など社会におけるさまざまな現象の広がりも「成長」という考え方でとらえる機会は多い。ここでも、'growth' を用いた一般的な表現に加え、特に最近話題となる「経済の成長」に関わる表現を多数紹介した。

- C 有形の物の成長や成長のタイプについて述べる場合 ☞ C
- U 現象の拡大や割合・スピードの増大などについて述べる場合 ☞ U

(特に U の場合に結びつく語句や用法に注意すること)

>> CHANGE; ECONOMY; TECHNOLOGY

▶ growth から広がるボキャブラリー:動詞表現

- ❏ 成長を促す ○ encourage growth
- ❏ 経済成長を促進する ○ foster economic growth ☞ foster a child「子供を育てる」
- ❏ 産業の成長を促進する ○ promote the growth of an industry
- ❏ 技術の進歩を遅らせる ○ retard the growth in technology ☞ retard the growth of plants「植物の成長を遅らせる」
- ❏ 人口増加の速度を遅める家族計画のプログラム
    ○ a family planning programme which <u>slows down</u> population growth
- ❏ 寒い天候により植物の成長が妨げられた。
    ○ The growth of the plant was stunted by the cold weather. C
    ☞ stunt sth「〈成長・発達など〉を妨げる、阻む」

▶「成長」に関わる一般的な表現

- ❏ 都市の広がり ○ the growth of cities
- ❏ 人口の増大 ○ growth in the population
- ❏ 数の増加 ○ growth in numbers
- ❏ 一週間伸びたあごひげ ○ a week's growth of beard
- ❏ 木の成長率の低下 ○ a reduction in the rate of growth of trees
- ❏ 植物が丈夫に育つために必要な諸条件
    ○ the conditions necessary for the vigorous growth of a plant

- ❏ 子供の知性の成長と発達
  - ◯ the growth and development of a child's intellect

▶「経済の成長」に関わる表現

- ❏ 経済成長の鈍り ◯ weak growth in the economy [U]
- ❏ 健全な経済成長 ◯ sound economic growth
- ❏ サービス部門の拡大 ◯ the growth of the service sector
- ❏ 過去一年における収益の35％の増大
  - ◯ a 35% growth of incomes in the last year
- ❏ 経済成長率 ◯ the rate of economic growth
- ❏ 平均17％の総合成長率 ◯ overall growth rates averaging 17%
- ❏ 国の輸出品の増加 ◯ the growth of exports of a country
- ❏ 経済のマイナス成長を予測する
  - ◯ forecast negative economic growth
- ❏ 経済成長の目標を定める ◯ <u>set a target for</u> economic growth
- ❏ 経済成長を妨げる状況
  - ◯ conditions which check economic growth ☞ このcheckは「急に止める、阻止する」の意味。check myself「思いとどまる」
- ❏ 人口増加が引き続き経済成長を上回る。
  - ◯ Population growth <u>continues to</u> outstrip economic growth.
- ❏ 観光事業はこの町の成長産業の一つである。
  - ◯ Tourism is <u>a growth industry</u> in this town.

▶ ストーリー

Our lives centre around **the concept of economic growth**. Every day, we read about **the growth of employment, growth in consumer spending**, and so on. **The more growth**, the better. There is no discussion on where **all this growth** will finally lead us all, though.

(私たちの生活は経済成長という考え方が中心になっている。毎日私たちは雇用の拡大、消費者支出の増大などについて書かれたものを目にする。成長は大きければ大きいほど良い。このすべての成長が最終的に私たち全員をどこに導くのかについての論議はないのだが。)

051 HAIR ・・・・・・・・・・・・・・・ C U

> **髪**が我々の生活空間の中心部にあることは、CMや広告に目を向ければ一目瞭然である。特に「髪の手入れ (hair care)」は今や男女共通の話題であり、少なくとも若い(?)男性読者はこれについてもマスターしておこう！また、髪の色のバリエーションは英語圏では日本よりもその重要性が高く、ここでも各種紹介した。
>
> 髪の毛一本一本について述べる場合 ☞ C
> 髪の毛全体を指す場合 ☞ U
>
> **>> CLOTHES; FACE; FASHION**

▶ hair から広がるボキャブラリー

❏ 赤いストレートヘアの女性 ● a woman with straight red hair ⓤ
  ☞ with の用い方に注意。以下の例でも同様
❏ 肩までかかる白髪の女性
  ● a woman with shoulder-length grey hair
❏ ウエーブのかかった長い髪の男性 ● a man with long wavy hair
❏ とても不自然に見えるブリーチヘア
  ● bleached hair which looks very unnatural
❏ 色黒/色白でふさふさした黒髪をしている
  ● have a dark / fair complexion and thick black hair
  ☞ a complexion は「顔色、血色、肌の色つや」の意味
❏ 繊細な顔立ちと柔らかな金髪をしている
  ● have delicate features and soft golden hair
❏ 短く黒い髪と整った顔立ちをしている
  ● have short dark hair and regular features

▶ 「手入れ」に関わる表現

❏ ドライヘア用のシャンプー ● a shampoo for dry hair
❏ オイリーヘア用のヘアコンディショナー
  ● a hair conditioner for oily hair
❏ 整えやすい髪 ● hair that is manageable
❏ ヘアドライヤーで猫を乾かす ● blow-dry the cat with a hair drier

- 自分で髪をセットする ◯ set my hair myself
- 美容室でパーマをかけてもらう
    ◯ have my hair permed at the hairdresser's
- 母親を説得して髪の毛を染めるのを許可してもらう
    ◯ persuade my mother to let me dye my hair
- 携帯用の化粧鏡を出して髪の毛を整える
    ◯ take a vanity mirror and adjust my hair
- わずかな髪でハゲたところを隠そうとする
    ◯ try to hide a bald patch with a few hairs ©
- 私の髪はめちゃくちゃだ！ ◯ My hair is all messed up! ☞ My room is a mess.「私の部屋はめちゃくちゃだ」(名)
- その髪の毛はどうしたの!? ◯ What have you done to your hair!?

▶決まり文句

- ボブはそのひどい光景を目にしても落ち着き払っていた。
    ◯ Bob did not turn a hair at the terrible sight.
- 髪の毛を逆立たせる光景
    ◯ a sight which makes my hair stand on end
- 怒り狂って髪の毛をかきむしる
    ◯ tear my hair out in exasperation
- よしよし、落ち着いて！ ◯ Okay, okay. Keep your hair on!

▶ストーリー

So many Japanese people **have nice thick black hair**, and yet so many people **dye it**. One of my favourite Japanese expressions is 'midori no kurokami'(**glossy black hair**). Unfortunately we **see little of that these days**. English has a similar expression: '**Her hair is so black that it is blue**'.
（非常に多くの日本人がきれいなふさふさした黒髪をしているのに髪の毛を染めている。私の大好きな日本語の一つに「緑の黒髪」があるが、残念なことに最近ではそれを見ることはあまりない。英語にも似たような表現がある：「彼女の髪は非常に黒くて青いほどだ」。）

052 HAPPINESS 〔U〕

> **幸**福か否かが最終的に人生の指標になることは間違いなく、文学やドラマのテーマはこれに尽きると言えるだろう。ここでは「幸福であること」に加えて「幸福でないこと」に関わる表現も紹介した。場合に応じて使い分けてほしい。
>
> ✻ 英語の 'happiness' は日本語の「幸福、幸運、幸せ」などをカバーしていることに注意。用例に則して確認しておこう。
>
> **>> EMOTION; ENJOYMENT; HOBBY**

▶「幸福であること」に関わる表現

- ❏ 個人的な幸福 ◯ personal happiness
- ❏ これ以上ない幸福感 ◯ a feeling of sheer happiness
- ❏ 希望と幸福の時 ◯ a time of hope and happiness
- ❏ 至福の瞬間 ◯ a moment of supreme happiness
- ❏ 最大多数の最大幸福 (Jeremy Bentham の言葉)
  ◯ the greatest happiness of the greatest number
- ❏ 幸福の可能性を見出す ◯ find a chance of happiness
- ❏ 人生からほんの一握りの幸せをかすめとる
  ◯ snatch <u>a little bit of</u> happiness from life ☞ snatch the knife from the burglar「泥棒からナイフを奪いとる」 with a bit of luck「うまくいけば」
- ❏ 田舎暮らしで静かな幸せを求める
  ◯ seek quiet happiness in the country life
- ❏ 自分の中に暖かい幸福を感じる
  ◯ feel <u>a warm glow of</u> happiness inside me ☞ feel a glow of pleasure「熱烈な喜びを感じる」
- ❏ 幸福と悲しみをないまぜに経験する
  ◯ experience a mixture of happiness and sadness
- ❏ 新婚夫婦の健康と幸せに乾杯する
  ◯ <u>drink to</u> the health and happiness of the newly married couple ☞ drink to the success of sb「〈人〉の成功を祝して乾杯する」
- ❏ お二人に幸多かれとお祈りします。
  ◯ I wish you both every happiness.

- 幸せの表情が彼女の顔に広がった。
    - A look of happiness grew on her face.
- 愛する人が私の幸福の源である。
    - The person I love is the source of my happiness.
- 子供たちによって永遠の幸福がもたらされるのである。
    - Children are a cause of long-lasting happiness.

▶「幸福でないこと」に関わる表現

- 長続きしない幸福 ○ happiness which never lasts
- はかない幸福 ○ fragile happiness ☞ a fragile peace「つかの間の平和」
- 幸福になる唯一の機会を失う/得る
    - lose / gain my only chance of happiness
- メグの幸せになりたい気持ちを壊す
    - destroy Meg's hopes of happiness
- 国のために自分自身の幸せを犠牲にする
    - sacrifice my own happiness for the sake of my country
- 幸せは金では買えない。○ Money cannot bring happiness.
- 父の急死によって私の幸せに暗雲が広がった。
    - My father's sudden death clouded my happiness.
- 私は幸せに見放された。○ Happiness deserted me. ☞ Meg was deserted by her parents.「メグは両親に捨てられた」

▶ ストーリー

The novelist Jane Austen wrote that 'A large income is **the best recipe for happiness**'. **Does money really bring happiness?** Some very rich people are **miserable**. There is also someone who said, '**Money does not bring happiness**, but it certainly **makes unhappiness more comfortable**'.

(小説家ジェーン・オースチンは「高所得は幸福への最良の秘訣である」と書いた。しかし金が本当に幸福をもたらすか? 金持ちの中にもみじめな人たちがいる。同じく「金は幸福をもたらさない。しかしそれは不幸であることを楽にしてくれることは確かだ」と言った人もいる。)

HAPPINESS

053　HEALTH　　　　　　　　　　　　　Ⓤ

> 自分の健康状態をきちんと説明できることは日常生活での必須事項である。ここでも 'health' を用いて「健康であること/ないこと」を表す表現を整理し、さらに社会と健康との関わり（健康制度）も扱った（☞〈「社会のしくみ」に関わる表現〉）。参照項目、特に 'diet' や 'fitness' と合わせてマスターすれば、より効果的である。
>
> **>> DEATH; DIET; FITNESS; HOSPITAL; ILLNESS**

▶「健康であること」に関わる表現

❏ よい健康状態を維持する ◯ maintain my good health
❏ ボブは健康で顔が輝いている。◯ Bob is glowing with health.
❏ 私は幸いにも健康を享受することができた。
　◯ I was lucky enough to enjoy good health.
❏ 私は着実に快方に向かっている。
　◯ My health is steadily improving.
❏ メグは常に心身ともに健康である。
　◯ Meg is always in good physical and mental health.
❏ 彼女は長い療養期間をへて健康を取り戻した。
　◯ She regained her health after a long convalescence.
　☞ convalescence [kɑ̀nvəlés(ə)ns | kɔ̀n-]「(病後・手術後の) 回復期、静養期」

▶「健康でないこと」に関わる表現

❏ 健康に害のあるものだらけの仕事 ◯ a job full of health hazards
❏ ボブは非常に病弱である。◯ Bob has very delicate health.
❏ このところの健康状態の悪化
　◯ a recent deterioration in my health ☞ a deterioration in the quality「質の低下」
❏ 健康上の理由で引退する ◯ retire for health reasons
❏ 過労のため健康を損なう ◯ ruin my health because of overwork
❏ 私はストレスのために健康を害した。
　◯ My health has suffered because of stress.
❏ 飲み過ぎると体をこわしますよ。

- ○ Too much alcohol will ruin your health.
- ❏ 喫煙は健康に良くない。○ Smoking is not good for your health.

▶「社会のしくみ」に関わる表現

- ❏ 世界保健機構 ○ the World Health Organization [WHO]
- ❏ 厚生労働省 ○ the Ministry of Health, Labour and Welfare
- ❏ 保健大臣 ○ the Minister of Health
- ❏ 健康政策 ○ a health policy
- ❏ 厳しい健康および安全条例 ○ strict health and safety regulations
- ❏ 共同社会における健康管理の問題
  ○ problems of health care in the community
- ❏ 福祉と健康管理の問題に関する議会での討論
  ○ a parliamentary debate on welfare and health-care issues
- ❏ 治療よりむしろ予防に関わる医療サービスを強調する
  ○ stress preventive, rather than curative, health services
  ☞ preventive measures「予防策」
- ❏ 健康保険に多くの金を支払う
  ○ pay a lot of money for my health insurance

▶ 関連表現

- ❏ 健康によい気候 ○ a healthy [healthful《米》] climate
- ❏ 健康的なライフスタイルを持つ ○ have a healthy lifestyle
- ❏ 子供たちはとても健康そうだ。○ The children look very healthy.

▶ ストーリー

You must try to **keep in good health**. You can do this by **eating a balanced diet, taking a reasonable amount of exercise, not drinking too much alcohol**, and **not neglecting to go for regular health checks**.
(私たちは良い健康状態を保つよう努めなければならない。このためにはバランスのとれた食事をとり、適切な量の運動をし、飲み過ぎないようにして、定期的な健康診断を受けるのを怠らないことである。)

HEALTH

054　HOBBY　　C

> オタクという言葉に代表されるように、趣味は日本人の生活空間において、実に幅広いレベルで取り組まれるテーマである。以下の表現をマスターして自分の趣味や関心について紹介してみよう。
>
> そのさい、'hobby' を扱ういろいろな動詞句と共に、〈自分の興味を表す表現〉であげた各種イディオムの前置詞の使い方 ('have an interest in' 'be keen on' 'be crazy about' など) に注意すること。
>
> **>> ENJOYMENT; HOLIDAY; INTEREST; TIME**

▶ hobby から広がるボキャブラリー：名詞表現

- 週末の趣味 ◯ a weekend hobby
- 貝殻を集める趣味 ◯ a hobby of collecting shells
- お年寄りにより適した趣味 ◯ a hobby more suitable for old people
- 魅力的で変わった趣味 ◯ a fascinating and unusual hobby
- 夢中にさせる趣味 ◯ an absorbing hobby ☞ be absorbed in thought「物思いにふける」
- 楽しい趣味 ◯ a pleasant hobby ☞ a pleasant surprise「楽しい驚き」

▶ hobby から広がるボキャブラリー：動詞表現

- 新しい趣味を始める ◯ take up a new hobby ☞ take up jogging「(趣味として) ジョギングを始める」
- 定年後自分の趣味に専念する
  ◯ concentrate on my hobby after retirement
- 趣味に多くの時間を費やす ◯ spend a lot of time on my hobby
- 切手収集の趣味に熱中する
  ◯ go in for the hobby of stamp collecting
- 一種の趣味として中古自動車を修理する
  ◯ repair old cars as a kind of hobby ☞ a kind of sth「一種の〈物〉」
- 自分の趣味を追求する時間を見つける
  ◯ find time to pursue my hobby ☞ pursueは目的などを長期にわたって追求すること
- 金になる [割に合う] 趣味を持つ ◯ have a paying hobby ☞ Honesty

doesn't pay.「正直者はばかをみる（割に合わない）」
- 趣味を仕事に変える ◯ turn my hobby into a business
- 趣味を通じてたくさんの知らない人たちと出会う
  ◯ meet a lot of new people through my hobby
- 私は趣味にとりつかれた。◯ My hobby became an obsession.

▶自分の興味を表す表現

- 私はほとんどのスポーツがやるのも観るのも大好きだ。
  ◯ I am keen on both watching and playing most sports.
- 模型列車を夢中になって集めている。
  ◯ I am an enthusiastic collector of model trains.
- ベイブ・ルースに関することなら何にでも夢中になる。
  ◯ I am crazy about anything to do with Babe Ruth. ☞ something [nothing] to do with sth「何かに関係のあること[ないこと]」
- 野鳥観察に魅せられている。◯ I am fascinated in birdwatching.
- 花瓶にとりつかれている。◯ I have an obsession about vases.
- 模型飛行機作りに関心がある。
  ◯ I have an interest in making model planes.
- アニメオタク ◯ an animation freak
- 鉄道オタク ◯ a train spotter ☞ 機関車の型式やナンバーを当てる
- コンピュータオタク ◯ a computer nerd [geek; weenie]

▶ ストーリー

After retiring, Granpa **took up carpentry**. He **is very keen on this hobby**. He makes tables and chairs, and sells them. He **spends more time on his 'hobby'**, and makes more money, than when he had 'a real job'. So, he **has turned his hobby into a real business.**

(定年後おじいちゃんは大工仕事を始めた。おじいちゃんはこの趣味にすごく凝っている。テーブルと椅子を作って売るのだ。おじいちゃんは以前持っていた「本職」よりも「趣味」に多くの時間を割き、しかももっと儲けるようになった。それで、おじいちゃんは趣味を本当のビジネスに変えたのだ。)

055 HOLIDAY　　　　　　　　　　C

休暇の取り方・過ごし方は人それぞれであり、休日に対する考え方も国や文化により異なる。ここでは'holiday'に関する以下の一般的な表現をマスターしながら、自分の休暇の過ごし方を考えてみよう。
✼通常 C であるが、無冠詞で用いられる定型表現 (☞*) に注意したい。一定の期間がある休日は複数形で用いられる (☞**) ことも多い。

>>COUNTRY / COUNTRYSIDE; HOTEL; SEA / SEASIDE; TRAVEL; WEEKEND; WORK

▶ holiday から広がるボキャブラリー：名詞表現

- （旅行代理店が斡旋する）パッケージホリデー ◯ a package holiday
- くつろげる休日 ◯ a relaxing holiday ☞ a relaxing place「気の置けない場所」
- a camping holiday ◯ キャンプして過ごす休日
- 野鳥観察をして過ごす休日 ◯ a birdwatching holiday
- 10日間の休日 ◯ a ten-day holiday
- 祝祭日 ◯ a public holiday
- 一般公休日《英》；銀行業務休止日《米》◯ a bank holiday
- 宗教上の休日 ◯ a religious holiday
- またとない（最高の）休日 ◯ the holiday of my lifetime ☞ the chance of a lifetime「またとない好機」
- 天候のため台無しになった休日 ◯ a holiday ruined by the weather

▶ holiday から広がるボキャブラリー：動詞表現

- 休暇で外国に行く ◯ go abroad on holiday *
- メグは休暇で不在である。◯ Meg is away on holiday. *
- タヒチで休日を過ごす ◯ spend a holiday in Tahiti
- 休暇から戻る ◯ return from holiday *
- 夏期休暇を楽しみにする
   ◯ look forward to the summer holidays **
- クリスマス休みの間はただのんびりする
   ◯ just relax over the Christmas holidays ** ☞ over the holidays は「休暇中ずっと」の意味

- ❏ 外国で休暇をとる余裕がない
  - ◯ cannot afford a holiday abroad ☞ cannot afford a car「車を買う余裕がない」
- ❏ 休暇をキャンセルして払い戻しをしてもらう
  - ◯ cancel a holiday and get a refund

▶「時と場所」に関わる表現

- ❏ 休暇月 ◯ the holiday months
- ❏ ホリデーシーズン ◯ the holiday season
- ❏ 学校が休みの期間 ◯ the period of the school holidays ※※
- ❏ 休日を過ごす別荘 ◯ a holiday cottage
- ❏ 休日を過ごす別宅 ◯ a holiday home
- ❏ 高級ホリデーリゾート ◯ an exclusive holiday resort ☞ exclusiveは「排他的な、閉鎖的な」から「高級な、上流の」の意味。an exclusive club「(会員制の) 高級クラブ」
- ❏ 海辺で休日をとる ◯ take a holiday by the sea
- ❏ 山で休日を楽しむ ◯ enjoy a holiday in the mountains

▶ ストーリー

In America, the word '**vacation**' is used to refer to **several days off work or school**. In Britain, the usual word is '**holiday**'. In America one '**goes on vacation**', but in Britain one '**goes on holiday**'. In Britain '**vacation**' is used to refer to '**university vacation**'. For **one day off**, in both countries the usual word is 'holiday', as in, '**Tomorrow I will take a holiday**'.

(アメリカでは、'vacation' という単語は仕事あるいは学校から離れる数日を指して使われる。英国では、これにあたる言葉はふつう 'holiday' である。アメリカでは「休暇に出かける」を 'go on vacation' というが、英国では 'go on holiday' という。英国では 'vacation' は 'university vacation' という場合に使われる。一日の休日には、例えば 'Tomorrow I will take a holiday'(明日休みを取ります)のように、両国ともふつう 'holiday' が使われる。)

HOLIDAY

056 HOME · C U

建物としての 'house' と比べて 'home' は暖かみを感じさせる「家庭としての存在」が強く意識される。〈決まり文句〉にあげたイディオム的な表現や名詞以外の用法 (☞*) にも注意。

C U { 家のタイプや建物としての家 ('house' と同じような意味) ☞ C
家庭や故郷、自分の住む地域など感情面を強調する場合 ☞ U

>> FAMILY; HUSBAND / WIFE

▶ home から広がるボキャブラリー：名詞表現

- 現在の家 ◯ my present home
- 前の家 ◯ my former home
- 仮住まいしている家 ◯ my temporary home
- 留守宅 [空き家] ◯ an empty home
- 移動住宅 ◯ a mobile home
- 空調設備付きの家 ◯ an air-conditioned home
- 田舎の家 ◯ a home in the country C
- 養家 ◯ a foster home
- 特別養護老人ホーム ◯ a nursing home ☞ a nursing mother「乳母、養母」
- 退職者向け住宅 [施設] ◯ a retirement home

▶ home から広がるボキャブラリー：名詞表現

- マイホームを買う ◯ buy a home
- 家を出る；故郷や国を離れる ◯ leave home
- 家庭 [故国] を恋しく思う（ホームシックなど）◯ long for home U
- 家庭料理をなつかしがる ◯ miss home cooking* ☞ I'll miss you.「君がいないと寂しくなる」
- 実家にいる家族と連絡を欠かさない
  ◯ keep in touch with the family back home* ☞ keep / get in touch with sb「〈人〉と連絡を取り続ける/取る」
- 私の夫は家からはるか遠くの支店に配属された。
  ◯ My husband was posted to a branch far away from home.
- 在宅勤務をする ◯ work from home

- 週末にだけ家に帰る ◎ go home only <u>at weekends</u>*

▶ 関連表現

- 素敵な風通しがよい台所 ◎ a nice, airy kitchen
- 南向きの寝室 ◎ a south-facing bedroom
- 快適な居間 ◎ a comfortable living room
- 変わった趣向の装飾がなされたダイニング
  ◎ a dining room decorated <u>in strange taste</u> ☞ in good taste「上品な」
- 子供たちの寝室はいつもひどく散らかっている。
  ◎ The kids' bedroom is always <u>in a terrible mess</u>.

▶決まり文句

- ホーム、スイートホーム（愛情あふれる家庭を憧れる言葉）
  ◎ Home, Sweet Home.
- 我が家に勝る場所はない。◎ There is no place like home.《諺》
- 楽にしてください。◎ <u>Make yourself at home</u>.
- メグといると本当にくつろいだ気分になった。
  ◎ Meg really <u>made me feel at home</u>.
  ☞ この2例のat homeは「気楽に、くつろいで」の意
- その事件は私に真実を話すことの大切さを痛切に感じさせた。
  ◎ The incident <u>brought home to</u> me the importance of telling the truth.* ☞ このhomeは「深く、十分に」という副詞。drive sth home to sb「〈事〉を〈人〉に納得させる」

▶ ストーリー

I do not like being away from home for too long. When I **am away from home for quite a long time**, more than anything else, I find that I soon begin to **miss my mother's home cooking**.

（私はあまり長く家をあけるのが好きではない。長期間家にいないと、何よりもまず母の家庭料理が恋しくなり始めるのだ。）

HOME

057 HOSPITAL C

病院は自分自身が世話にならなくとも、普段の生活でこれに関連した表現にふれる機会は意外に多くCore Nounsに含めた。下記には多少専門的と思える表現もあるが、テレビ、新聞などでよく見聞きするものであり覚えておきたい。

✱ 英国では医学の場としての 'hospital' には冠詞をつけない ('school' や 'church' や 'market' と同じ用法) が、米国では通常 'the' をつけて用いる。'hospital' を建物として述べる場合は両国とも 'the' をつける。

>> ACCIDENT; AMBULANCE / FIRE BRIGADE / POLICE; DEATH; DIET; HEALTH; ILLNESS

▶ hospital から広がるボキャブラリー:名詞表現

- ❏ 総合病院 ○ a general hospital
- ❏ 救急病院 ○ an emergency hospital
- ❏ (医科大学の付属病院などの) 教育研究病院 ○ a teaching hospital
- ❏ 精神病院 ○ a mental hospital
- ❏ 産科病院 ○ a maternity hospital
- ❏ 隔離病院 ○ an isolation hospital
- ❏ その土地の [地元の] 病院 ○ the local hospital

▶ hospital から広がるボキャブラリー:動詞表現

- ❏ 入院する / 退院する ○ enter / leave hospital
- ❏ ボブは入院した。○ Bob was admitted to hospital. ☞ be admitted to *sth*「〈物〉へ入る [仲間になる] ことを許される」
- ❏ 彼は病院で回復しつつある。○ He is recovering in hospital.
- ❏ メグは救急車で病院に運ばれた。
   ○ Meg was taken to hospital by ambulance.
- ❏ 私は病院に緊急移送された。○ I was rushed to hospital.
- ❏ 目を覚ましたら病院で寝ていた。
   ○ I woke up to find myself in hospital. ☞ wake up to find myself in *spl*「目が覚めたら〈場所〉にいる」
- ❏ ボブは入院して容態は予断を許さないが安定している。
   ○ Bob is in critical, but stable, condition in hospital.

- ❏ 間もなく病院からの（一時）帰宅を許可されるだろう。
  - ○ I will soon be allowed home from hospital.
- ❏ 明日退院する。○ I will be discharged from hospital tomorrow.

▶ 関連表現

- ❏ 末期疾患 ○ a terminal illness
- ❏ 心臓移植を受ける ○ undergo a heart transplant
- ❏ 重症の脳卒中を患う ○ suffer a serious stroke ☞ 一時的な状態 *cf.* suffer from constant headaches「慢性的な頭痛を患う」
- ❏ 緊急手術をしてメグの視力を救う
  - ○ save Meg's sight after an emergency operation

▶ さまざまな「科」

- ❏ 産婦人科 ○ the Department of Obstetrics [əbstétriks] and Gynecology [gàinikɔ́lədʒi]
- ❏ 小児科 ○ the Department of Pediatrics [pìːdiǽtriks]
- ❏ 整形外科 ○ the Department of Orthopedics [ɔ̀ːrθəpíːdiks]
- ❏ 耳鼻咽喉科 ○ the Department of Otolaryngology [òutoulæringɔ́lədʒi]
- ❏ 泌尿器科 ○ the Department of Urology [ju(ə)rɔ́lədʒi]
- ❏ 心臓病科 ○ the Department of Cardiology [kὰːrdiɔ́lədʒi]
- ❏ 胃腸科 ○ the Department of Gastro-Enterology [gæ̀strə-entərɔ́lədʒi]
- ❏ 眼科 ○ the Department of Ophthalmology [ɔ̀fθəlmɔ́lədʒi]

▶ ストーリー

I **have been in hospital** only once in my life. I was there for about a week or so **for a minor operation**. Before I **was admitted to hospital** I was very nervous. But everyone was very kind and nice, and I **did not mind my stay in hospital**.

（私は生まれてこのかた一度しか入院したことがない。私はちょっとした手術のためにおよそ1週間ほど入院した。私は入院する前はとても不安であった。しかしみんなが非常に親切でよくしてくれて、入院していても気に障ることがなかった。）

HOSPITAL

058 HOTEL C

> ホテルは余暇や休暇の長期化に伴い、生活空間の中で使用頻度・有用性が高まりつつある。ここではその「設備」も含め、'hotel' の種類、滞在時に使うことが多いと思われる表現を中心に紹介した。
>
> ✱ 類義語として 'inn' があるが、これは小規模の特に田舎にある家族経営の宿泊所を指す場合が多い。
>
> 例「旅館」→ a Japanese-style inn
> 　「民宿」→ a private home that takes in paying guests
>
> >> **COUNTRY / COUNTRYSIDE; HOLIDAY; SEA / SEASIDE; TRAVEL; WEEKEND**

▶ hotel から広がるボキャブラリー:名詞表現

- 海辺のホテル ○ a seaside hotel
- 湖畔のホテル ○ a lakeside hotel
- 山のホテル ○ a hotel in the mountains
- 空港のホテル ○ an airport hotel
- 線路を見晴らすホテル ○ a hotel overlooking the railway tracks
  ☞ The window overlooked the sea.「窓から海が見渡せた」
- 街の真ん中に位置するホテル

  ○ a hotel situated in the middle of town　☞ be situated at/in/on *spl*
  「〈場所〉に位置している、ある」
- 快適な四つ星のホテル ○ a comfortable four-star hotel
- 優れたサービスのホテル ○ a hotel with excellent service
- 一流の設備のあるホテル ○ a hotel with first-class facilities
- 豪華なホテル ○ a luxurious hotel
- 空調設備の完備したホテル ○ a fully air-conditioned hotel
- 家族経営のホテル ○ a family-run hotel
- 非常に親しみのある雰囲気のホテル

  ○ a hotel with a very friendly atmosphere
  ☞ 以上の用例中、a hotel with *sth*（〈物〉を備えたホテル）の頻出パターンに注意

▶ hotel から広がるボキャブラリー:動詞表現

- ホテルの部屋を予約する ○ book [reserve (米)] a room in a hotel

組織

- ❏ ホテルに部屋を取る ◯ take a room at a hotel
- ❏ ホテルにチェックインする ◯ <u>check in to</u> a hotel
- ❏ ホテルをチェックアウトする ◯ <u>check out of</u> a hotel
- ❏ ホテルに滞在するが食事は外でする ◯ stay in the hotel, but <u>eat out</u>
    ☞ eat in「(外食せずに) 家で食事をする、店内で食べる (↔ take out [away])」
- ❏ すてきなホテルで週末を過ごす
    ◯ spend the weekend at a nice hotel
- ❏ 自分の家をホテルに作りかえる ◯ <u>convert</u> <u>our house</u> <u>into</u> a hotel
- ❏ ホテルのマネージャーに会うことを要求する
    ◯ <u>demand to</u> see the manager of the hotel

▶「設備」に関わる表現

- ❏ ホテルの表玄関 ◯ the main entrance of a hotel
- ❏ ホテルのロビー ◯ the foyer of a hotel
- ❏ ホテルのスイートルーム ◯ a hotel suite ☞ 居間と寝室の続いた部屋
- ❏ 2つのシングルベッドがある (ホテルの) 部屋；ツインルーム
    ◯ a hotel room with two single beds
- ❏ 夕食の後にホテルのバーで会う
    ◯ meet in the hotel bar after dinner

▶ ストーリー

Our company **runs many kinds of hotels**: **small hotels with thirty or so bedrooms**, **medium-sized hotels with up to two-hundred rooms**, **large hotels with several hundred rooms**, **airport hotels**, and so on. In all our hotels, our motto is: '**The guest comes first**'.

(我が社はさまざまなタイプのホテルを経営している。約30部屋がある小さいホテル、200部屋をも有する中型のホテル、何百もの部屋を有する大ホテル、空港のホテルなどである。すべてのホテルで我が社のモットーは「お客様第一」である。)

059 HOUSEWORK　U

家事は現在（少なくとも米国では）、もはや 'housewives'（主婦）の仕事ではなく、'homemakers'（家政担当者：性別、既婚未婚に関係なし）のする仕事になっている。ここでも、'housework' をもとにして、家事を行うことに関わる表現の他、家事に対する考え方に関わる表現を多く紹介した。
✻ 'housework' は C と間違いやすいので要注意。

>> FAMILY; HOME; DEPARTMENT STORE / SUPERMARKET; SHOPPING

▶ housework から広がるボキャブラリー：名詞表現

❏ 簡単な家事しかできない年配の婦人
　➲ an old lady who can do only light housework

❏ 家事を手伝えるようになった年頃の子供
　➲ a child who is old enough to help out with housework
　☞ help outは「（困ったときに）手伝う、助けてあげる」こと。help /*sb*/ out「〈人〉を手伝う」の型もある

❏ 家事を分担しない夫
　➲ a husband who does not share housework

❏ 家事をすべて午前中に片づけようとする
　➲ try to get all my housework done in the morning　☞ get *sth* done「〈事〉を仕上げてしまう」

❏ 今日すべき家事がたくさんある
　➲ have a lot of housework to do today

❏ 買い物と家事のような日々の雑用をする
　➲ do the everyday chores, like shopping and housework

❏ 家事をもっと楽にしてくれる省力装置をたくさん持っている
　➲ have many labour-saving devices that make housework easier

❏ 家事を単調で退屈なものだと考える
　➲ regard housework as dull and boring

❏ 家事が好きではない ➲ do not like housework

❏ 家事をひどく嫌う ➲ intensely dislike housework

- ❏ 家事のイライラに耐えられない
  - ◯ cannot stand the frustration of housework

▶ 関連表現

- ❏ 年に一度の大掃除をする ◯ do the spring cleaning
- ❏ 洗濯物をする ◯ do the laundry
- ❏ (食後の) 食器洗いをする ◯ do the washing up
  - ☞ ここまでのdo the -ingの形に注意。すべて日課に関わる表現。*cf.* do the shopping「(毎日の) 買い物をする」do the cleaning「(毎日の) 掃除をする」
- ❏ 窓掃除をする ◯ wash the windows
- ❏ 新しいドレスを縫う ◯ sew [sóu] a new dress
- ❏ 棚のほこりをはらう ◯ dust the shelves
- ❏ 床にモップをかける ◯ mop the floor
- ❏ カーペットに掃除機をかける
  - ◯ run a vacuum cleaner over the carpet ☞ a Mac running Windows ウィンドウズの動くマック
- ❏ 家具を磨く ◯ polish the furniture
- ❏ 洗濯物を外に干して乾かす ◯ hang the laundry out to dry
- ❏ 布団を外に干す ◯ put the futons out to air
- ❏ 服にアイロンをかける ◯ iron [áiərn] the clothes
- ❏ 靴下を繕う ◯ mend a sock

▶ ストーリー

The two sexes might be equal, and 'modern husbands' **might help in the house**, but it is still women who **do most of the housework**. These days there are more **pre-prepared foods**, and **household machines and equipment**, and **labour-saving devices**, and so on, but many women still **spend most of the time doing the housework**.
(両性は平等だろうし、「今時の夫」は家事を手伝ってくれるだろう。しかし家事の大半を行うのはまだ女性たちである。最近では、事前に調理された即席食品や家庭用の機器や省力装置などが以前よりも増えている。しかし家事に大半の時間を費やす女性はまだまだ多い。)

060　HUSBAND / WIFE　　　　Ⓒ

> 家庭内不和の問題が各種メディアを賑わせることが多くなってきた。'husband' と 'wife' に関する表現を押さえておくことも実用英語学習の重要テーマとなりつつある。
>
> 一方、結婚しないで一緒に住むカップルも増えつつあり、このような場合 'husband' や 'wife' の代わりに 'partner' という語がよく用いられる（例 I would like to introduce my partner. 私のパートナーをご紹介します）。それと共に、'spouse'（配偶者）は以前は官僚的で堅苦しい語であったが、今では多く用いられるようになっている。
>
> **>> CHILD; FAMILY; HOME; HOUSEWORK; LOVE; MAN / WOMAN; MARRIAGE**

▶ husband / wife から広がるボキャブラリー：名詞表現

- ❏ 支えてくれる［協力的な］妻 ◯ a supportive wife ☞ Meg is supportive of her husband.「メグは夫にやさしく接している」
- ❏ 理解のある［ものわかりのよい］夫 ◯ an understanding husband
- ❏ 前妻 ◯ my ex-wife
- ❏ 内縁の夫 ◯ a common-law husband
- ❏ （仲違いして）別居中の妻 ◯ my estranged wife ☞ become estranged「疎遠になる」
- ❏ 将来の夫候補 ◯ a prospective husband ☞ a prospective buyer「見込み客（買ってくれそうな客）」
- ❏ 二度目の妻；後妻 ◯ my second wife
- ❏ 家族の大黒柱である妻
  ◯ a wife who is the main breadwinner in the family
- ❏ 不貞な夫 ◯ an unfaithful husband
- ❏ 不倫をする妻 ◯ a wife who plays around with other men

▶ husband / wife から広がるボキャブラリー：動詞表現

- ❏ 夫をガンで失う ◯ lose my husband to cancer
- ❏ 妻を捨てる ◯ leave my wife ☞ 他の女性に走ること
- ❏ 夫を見捨てる ◯ desert [dizə́ːrt] my husband
- ❏ 妻や子供たちと別居する ◯ live apart from my wife and children

- 私は妻を深く愛している。 ◯ I am deeply in love with my wife.
- 妻をなおざりにしている ◯ neglect my wife
- 夫や子供たちとの家族生活を楽しむ
  ◯ enjoy family life with my husband and children
- 子供の養育を妻に任せる
  ◯ leave my wife in charge of bringing up the kids
- 最初の夫との間に二人の子供をもうける
  ◯ have two children by my first husband
- ボブの奥さんは近々子供が生まれる予定だ。
  ◯ Bob's wife is expecting.

▶ 関連表現

- 配偶者 ◯ a spouse [spáos, spáoz]
- 新婚カップル ◯ a newly married couple
- 結婚50周年を祝う夫婦
  ◯ a couple who are celebrating their fiftieth wedding anniversary
- 義理の父 / 母 ◯ a father-in-law / a mother-in-law
- 姻族；義理の親 ◯ the in-laws

▶ ストーリー

Many **family dramas** on Japanese TV revolve around miso soup. **The couple get married** and **live with the in-laws**. Soon **the mother-in-law** starts to complain that Taro likes his miso soup this way—and not that way. Taro **does not support his wife**, but just sits at the table saying nothing. After that, **things go from bad to worse**.

（日本のテレビの家族ドラマは多くがみそ汁を中心に展開する。カップルは結婚すると姻戚と同居する。まもなく姑が、太郎の好きなみそ汁はこういう風であって、そんな風ではないと不平を言い始める。太郎は妻をかばってあげず、何も言わないで食卓に座っているだけだ。その後自体はさらに悪化していく。）

061　IDEA　　　　　　　　　　　　　C

> 「思いつき」「考え」「見当」「提案」「アイディア」—これらはすべて英語の 'idea' がカバーする範囲である。この語が我々の思考活動の素であることがわかるだろう。ここでは、'idea' を用いた思考活動に関わる表現をプラス・マイナスの視点で整理し、一般的な表現も加えて紹介した。特に一緒に使われる形容詞と動詞に注意したい。
> **>> AIM; INTEREST**

▶プラスの idea に関わる表現

- 良い考え ○ a good idea
- 素晴らしい思いつき ○ a brilliant idea
- 気の利いた [巧妙な、独創的な] 考え ○ an ingenious idea
- うまい考え ○ a successful idea
- 考えを発展させる [ふくらませる] ○ develop an idea ☞ develop muscles「筋肉を鍛える」
- アイディアを頭の中ではっきりさせる
  ○ get an idea clear in my mind
- メグから提案されたアイディアが気に入る
  ○ like an idea suggested by Meg
- ブレーンストーミングを行うことによってアイディアを生み出す
  ○ generate ideas by brainstorming
- そのプロジェクトを続けるという考え方を支持する
  ○ support the idea of continuing with the project ☞ continue with sth は「(中断した後で) 続行する」という意味
- 物事の意味をはっきりわかっている
  ○ have a clear idea of what something means
- たくさんの新しいアイディアが出された。(会議などで)
  ○ A lot of new ideas have come up.

▶マイナスの idea に関わる表現

- 愚かな考え ○ a stupid idea
- 途方もない考え ○ a crazy idea

- ばかばかしい考え ○ an absurd idea
- こじつけた考え ○ a farfetched idea
- 次に何をすべきかわからない ○ <u>have no idea</u> what to do next
- ボブが何を話をしているかまったく見当もつかない
  ○ <u>do not have the faintest idea</u> what Bob is talking about
- 考えを批判する；アイディアにけちをつける ○ criticize an idea
- メグのアイディアを盗む ○ steal Meg's idea

▶一般的な表現

- ありふれた考え ○ a familiar idea
- 主な考え方；中心思想 ○ the main idea
- ボブの意見に同意する ○ <u>fall in with</u> Bob's idea ☞ fall in with *sth*「(考え・計画など) に同意する」
- プロジェクトのアイディアがある ○ have an idea for a project
- 考えを試す ○ test an idea
- 他の人々と意見を交換する ○ <u>exchange</u> ideas <u>with</u> other people
- その場の思いつきの [突拍子もない] 意見を出す
  ○ produce <u>an off-the-top-of-the-head idea</u> ☞ produce my passport「パスポートを提示する」

▶ストーリー

As the chemist August Kekulé **was dozing off, the solution to the structure of the benzene molecule suddenly occurred to him**. I often **find new ideas** in the area between wakefulness and sleep. In this area, many **farfetched and absurd ideas have occurred to me**. Nevertheless, they usually **contain some useful element**.

(化学者アウグスト・ケクレがまどろんでいると、ベンゼン分子の構造を解く方法が突然頭に浮かんだ。私は覚醒と睡眠の間の領域に新しいアイディアを見つけることがしばしばある。これまでこの領域に浮かんできたのは、数多くのこじつけたアイディアや、ばかばかしいアイディアだった。それにも関わらず、それらのアイディアにはたいてい何らかの有用な要素が含まれている。)

062 ILLNESS ・・・・・・・・・・ C U

病気も病院と並んで、近寄りたくないが避けて通れない生活空間の核と言えよう。特に「病気である/にかかる/が治る」表現に注意したい。よく話題に上る病名や症状についても各種紹介した。

- 特定の病気やそのタイプについて述べる場合 ☞ C
- 病気について一般的に述べる場合 ☞ U

✲ 同義語に 'sickness' があるが、こちらはそれほど重病でなく、早く治りそうな病気について用いられる。'disease' は普通、病気が具体的な症状を伴う文脈で用いられ、重病を示唆する。

  例 have a liver disease 肝臓病がある
  　 suffer from an unknown disease 不明の病気を患う

>> DEATH; DIET; FITNESS; HEALTH; HOSPITAL

▶ illness から広がるボキャブラリー

- ❏ ひどい病気にかかる ◯ get a terrible illness C
- ❏ 病気にかかる ◯ come down with an illness
- ❏ 生命に関わる病気にかかっている
  ◯ have a life-threatening illness ☞ -threatening は「～を脅かすような」
- ❏ 病気から立ち直る ◯ get over an illness ☞ get over the difficulty「その問題を克服する」
- ❏ 重病が回復する ◯ recover from a serious illness
- ❏ 仮病をつかう ◯ feign [pretend] illness
- ❏ ボブが病気の間ずっと看護する ◯ nurse Bob through an illness
- ❏ 私は長く病いと闘っている。◯ I am coping with my long illness.
  ☞ cope with sth「〈困難な事など〉をうまく処理する、何とか切り抜ける」
- ❏ 病気の症状を述べる ◯ describe the symptoms of an illness
- ❏ 病気の原因を見つける ◯ find out the cause of an illness
- ❏ 自分の「病気」を運動不足と診断する
  ◯ diagnose [dáiəgnòus] my 'illness' as lack of exercise
- ❏ 病気のため欠勤する/学校を休む
  ◯ miss work / school because of illness U

▶ 関連表現（動詞にも注意）

- 糖尿病を患う ◯ <u>suffer from</u> diabetes [dàiəbíːtiːz]
- ぜんそくを患う ◯ <u>suffer from</u> asthma [ǽzmə]
- 気管支炎にかかっている ◯ have bronchitis [brɔnkáitis]
- 高血圧である ◯ have high blood pressure
- 水虫ができている ◯ have athlete's foot
- 胃かいようができている ◯ have a stomach ulcer [ʌ́lsər]
- ひどくのどが痛い ◯ have a terrible sore throat
- 腫れ物ができている ◯ have a boil
- ニキビができている ◯ have acne [ǽkni]
- 関節炎がある ◯ have arthritis [ɑːrθráitis]
- リューマチにかかっている ◯ have rheumatism [rúːmətizm]
- 肩[首]がこっている ◯ have a stiff neck
- 花粉症にかかっている ◯ have hay fever
- 性病(性行為感染症)をうつされる
  ◯ catch a sexually transmitted disease
- 水ぼうそうにかかる ◯ catch chicken pox
- ハシカにかかる ◯ catch measles [míːzlz]
- おたふくかぜにかかる ◯ get mumps [mʌ́mps]
- 風邪がなかなか抜けない ◯ cannot <u>get rid of</u> my cold
- ひどい偏頭痛を治す ◯ cure a terrible migraine [máigrein]
- A型肝炎の治療を受ける
  ◯ receive treatment for hepatitis [hèpətáitis] A

▶ ストーリー

My friend Harry **has been in hospital** for a month. He **was always getting tired and feeling run down**. The doctors **have not been able to diagnose any particular illness**, but say he **has some kind of syndrome** (something with **a long medical name**).

(私の友人ハリーは入院してひと月になる。彼は常に疲れて体が参っていた。医者の診断では病気を特定することができなかったが、彼には何らかの症候群(長い医学名をもったもの)があると言う。)

063 INTEREST ······ C U

> 興味・関心は我々の知的生活と切り離せないものである。ここでも 'interest' を用いて知的興味・関心を述べる表現を紹介した。
> - 特定の興味・関心やそのタイプについて述べる場合 ☞ C
> - 興味・関心について一般的に述べる場合 ☞ U
>
> また、「興味・関心を表す形容詞」には重要な文法的使い分けのポイントがあり、これを〈関連表現〉と〈ストーリー〉にまとめておいた。セットで覚えて間違えないようにしたい。
>
> **>> AIM; ENJOYMENT; HOBBY; IDEA**

▶ interest から広がるボキャブラリー：動詞表現

- 人生［生活］に興味を持つ ◯ take an interest in life C
- 自分の英語学習に対する興味を維持する
  ◯ maintain interest in my study of English ☞ maintain life「生命を維持する」
- 学業に対する興味を取り戻す
  ◯ regain interest in schoolwork ☞ regain consciousness「意識を取り戻す」
- 音楽に対する子供の興味を刺激する
  ◯ stimulate a child's interest in music ☞ stimulate economic growth「経済成長を刺激する、促す」
- 自分の学生の興味とモチベーションを伸ばしてあげる
  ◯ develop interest and motivation in my students
- 自分に関係のないことに対して興味を示す
  ◯ display an interest in something that does not concern me
- 常に学生の興味を引きつけておける教授
  ◯ a professor who can always hold the students' interest
- 選挙への関心を失う ◯ lose interest in the elections U

表現（-ed 形と -ing 形の使い分けは非常に重要）

- 面白い映画に興味を引きつけられる
  ◯ be interested by an interesting movie

- 意外な進展に驚く
  - ○ be surprised by a surprising development
- 満足な食事に満足する
  - ○ be satisfied by a satisfying meal
- 魅惑的な俳優に夢中になる
  - ○ be captivated by a captivating actor
- 面白いゲームに興奮する
  - ○ be excited by an exciting game
- スリル満点のレースにわくわくする
  - ○ be thrilled by a thrilling race
- 面白い物語を楽しむ
  - ○ be amused by an amusing story
- 間の悪いコメントに恥ずかしい思いをする
  - ○ be embarrassed by an embarrassing comment
- わけのわからない問題に当惑する
  - ○ be puzzled by a puzzling problem
- 恐ろしいホラー映画におびえる
  - ○ be frightened by a frightening horror film

▶ ストーリー

Learners of English have difficulty with **pairs like 'interested' vs. 'interesting'**. The '-ed' words are related to how I feel about someone or something. Thus I **am amused by a joke**. I **am amused** because **the joke is amusing**. So, remember, '**I am -ed**'; '**the stimulus is -ing**'. **The movie was boring, so I was bored by it**.

(英語の学習者は 'interested' と 'interesting' のようなペアに苦労します。'-ed' がつく語は自分が人や物についてどのように感じるかに関わるものです。ですから、'I am amused by a joke.'（私は冗談を面白がる）のように用います。冗談が面白い（amusing）から、私は面白がらされている（amused）のです。ですからこのように覚えてください。自分が主語のときは 'I am -ed'、刺激するものが主語のときは 'Is -ing'。映画は退屈であった（boring）。それで私は映画に退屈した（bored）。)

064 KINDNESS ･････････････ C U

> 親切は人間関係を円滑にする意味で生活空間の中の欠かせない要素である。「親切にする/される」両方の視点から 'kindness' に関わる表現を紹介した。
> - 個別の親切な行為について述べる場合 ☞ C
> - 親切さについて一般的に述べる場合 ☞ U
>
> 特に、'kindness' と 'friendship' と 'love' は生活空間における重要な組み合わせなので、これらは合わせてマスターしよう。
>
> **>> EMOTION; FRIENDSHIP; LOVE**

▶「親切にすること」に関わる表現

- ボブに大変親切にしてあげる ◯ show Bob great kindness ᵁ
- 親切心から何かをする ◯ do something out of kindness ☞ out of curiosity「好奇心から」
- ボブの親切に報いる ◯ repay Bob's kindness ☞ repay a loan「ローンを返済する」
- ボブの親切を無視する ◯ disregard Bob's kindness
- 同情と思いやりをもって彼女に悪い知らせを打ち明ける
  ◯ break the bad news to her with sympathy and kindness

▶「親切にされること」に関わる表現

- メグからの親切をありがたく受け取る
  ◯ accept Meg's kindness with gratitude
- 皆様にお目をかけて頂き誠に有り難うございます。
  ◯ I appreciate the kindness everyone showed me.
- あなたに親切にしてもらう筋合いではない
  ◯ do not deserve your kindness
- ボブの親切のおかげである ◯ benefit from Bob's kindness ☞ benefit from sth「〈物事〉から利益を得る」
- 他人に親切にしてもらって成功する
  ◯ succeed through the kindness of others
- 見知らぬ人からこれ以上ないほど親切にしてもらう

- ○ experience every kindness from strangers
- ❏ 決してメグの親切を忘れはしない ○ never forget Meg's kindness
- ❏ メグの親切につけ込む［甘える］ ○ presume on Meg's kindness
    - ☞ presume on *sth*「〈善意・友情など〉につけ込む」 *cf.* take advantage of her weakness「彼女の弱みにつけ込む」
- ❏ 彼の親切に私は心を打たれた。 ○ His kindness touched me.
- ❏ 私はあなたから受けた多くの親切が忘れられない。
    - ○ I cannot forget your many kindnesses. ©
- ❏ あなたのご親切にはお礼の言葉もありません。
    - ○ I cannot thank you enough for your kindness.
- ❏ メグは親切にも私に本当のことを教えてくれた。
    - ○ Meg did me the kindness to tell me the truth.

▶ kindness を用いた対句（まとめて覚えておくと便利）

- ❏ 親切と援助 ○ kindness and help
- ❏ 親切と寛容 ○ kindness and generosity
- ❏ 親切と理解 ○ kindness and understanding
- ❏ 親切と許容 ○ kindness and tolerance
- ❏ 親切と同情 ○ kindness and compassion
- ❏ 親切と誠実さ ○ kindness and sincerity
- ❏ 丁重さと親切 ○ courtesy and kindness
- ❏ 慈善と人情 ○ charity and human kindness
- ❏ 世話と親切 ○ care and kindness

▶ ストーリー

I think that **kindness** includes many other feelings, such as **generosity**, **understanding**, **sympathy** and **sincerity**. By **showing kindness to others**, it is likely that they will **repay our kindness**.

（私は親切には、寛容、理解、同情そして誠実さのような、多くの他の感情が含まれると思う。他の人たちに親切にしてあげることによって、彼らが私たちの親切に報いてくれる場合も多いだろう。）

065 LANGUAGE ... C U

言葉はコミュニケーションの中心的手段であるが、一方で外国語の場合は学習すべき対象としての性格を帯びてくる。ここでは 'language' を用いた「言葉遣い」に関わる表現として主に前者を、動詞関連および決まり文句として主に後者を紹介した。

※ 以下の C と U の区別に即して、「言語」「言葉」と訳し分けられる場合が多いことにも注意。

C 特定の言語について（学問的に）述べる場合 ☞ C
U 言葉遣いや言葉を話す能力について述べる場合 ☞ U

>> APOLOGY; LIE / TRUTH; THANKS

▶「言葉遣い」に関わる表現

❏ 書き言葉 ◯ written language (↔ colloquial language 口語)
❏ くだけた言葉 ◯ informal language
❏ 専門用語；術語 ◯ technical language ☞ a technical book「専門書」
❏ はしたない[みだらな]言葉 ◯ dirty language ☞ dirty jokes「みだらな冗談」
❏ 下品な言葉 ◯ vulgar language U ☞ vulgar manners「無作法」
❏ 口汚い言葉；暴言 ◯ abusive language ☞ become abusive「乱暴にふるまう」
❏ 乱暴な言葉 ◯ rough language
❏ 優雅な[気品のある]言葉 ◯ elegant language
❏ 丁寧な言葉 ◯ polite language
❏ お役所言葉 ◯ bureaucratic [bjù(ə)rəkrǽtik] language

▶ language から広がるボキャブラリー：動詞表現

❏ 言語の起源を研究する ◯ study the origins of language U
❏ 国語を標準化する ◯ standardize the national language
❏ エスペラント語のような人工的な言語を創り出す
  ◯ create an artificial language like Esperanto
❏ 死語を解読する ◯ decipher [disáifər] a dead language C
❏ 外国語と格闘する ◯ struggle with a foreign language
❏ つかえながら[たどたどしく]言葉を話す

○ speak a language haltingly ☞ haltingly ＜ halt「立ち止まる」
❏ 流ちょうに言葉を話す ○ speak a language fluently
❏ 私は5、6か国語が使いこなせる。
　○ I am comfortable in five or six languages. ☞ be comfortable with English「英語を使いこなせる」
❏ 私は数か国語で用を足すことができる。
　○ I can get by in several languages.
❏ 自分の子供を二か国語が話せるように育てる
　○ bring up my child to speak two languages
❏ 言葉を正しく使わないことを批判する
　○ criticize incorrect use of the language

▶決まり文句

❏ 少し言葉を知っていればすごく役に立つ。
　○ A little language goes a long way.
　☞ go some way towards sth「〈事〉に少し役に立つ」
❏ 私たちは考え方がよく似ている［うまが合う、気持ちが通じる］。
　○ We speak the same language.
❏ 言葉遣いに気をつけなさい！ ○ Watch your language!
❏ あなたはその言葉を自由に使いこなせますね！
　○ Your command of the language is excellent!

▶ストーリー

Learning a language presents great difficulty to a lot of people. Even after years of study, **many learners can only speak the target language haltingly**, and **write it very incorrectly**. There must surely be **quicker ways of mastering a foreign language** than the methods currently used.

（言語を学習することは多くの人々に大きな困難となっている。何年も勉強しても、目標の言語をつっかえながらでしか話せなかったり、書くのも不正確な学習者が多い。現在用いられている方法よりも速く外国語をマスターするやり方がきっとあるに違いない。）

066 LIE ・・・ C / TRUTH ・・・ U

嘘と真実は表裏一体の存在である。真実がある限り嘘もなくならない。この2つに関わる表現は同時にマスターしておきたい。

✲ 'truth' は通常 U 扱いだが、まれに「真理（とされるもの）」(a belief that is accepted to be true) という意味では C となる。

例 We hold these truths to be self-evident, that all men are created equal, ... (我々はすべての人間が等しく創造されていること…というこれらの真理が自明のことであると考え…)　［米国の独立宣言より］

>> APOLOGY; LANGUAGE

▶「嘘をつくこと」に関わる表現

❏ 嘘をつく ➲ tell a lie

❏ 嘘を口にする ➲ utter a lie ☞ not utter a word「ひとことも言わない」

❏ 嘘をついて赤面する ➲ blush when I tell a lie ☞ blush for shame「恥ずかしくて顔が赤くなる」

❏ 嘘をつき続ける ➲ persist with a lie
☞ persist with *sth*「〈事〉に固執する」

❏ 嘘をつくよりむしろ真実に尾ひれを付ける
➲ embroider the truth, rather than tell a lie ☞ embroider the dress with flowers「ドレスに花柄の刺繍を縫い込む」

❏ 嘘を見破られる；嘘のぼろが出る ➲ be caught out in a lie

❏ 嘘だとわかる ➲ detect a lie

❏ 嘘を見破る ➲ see through a lie ☞ see through Meg「メグの本心を見破る」

❏ 見え透いた嘘を明らかにする ➲ reveal a blatant lie

❏ 嘘だらけ［嘘八百］の話をする ➲ tell a story that is pack of lies

❏ 彼女が言ったことはすべて嘘のかたまり［嘘八百］だった。
➲ Everything she said was a tissue of lies.

❏（性格的に）メグは嘘がつけない。➲ Meg is incapable of telling a lie.

▶「真実・真相を語ること」に関わる表現

❏ 真相を突き止める ➲ find out the truth

❏ 真実を発見する ➲ discover the truth

- 真実は明らかになるだろう。◯ The truth will come out.
- 真実の抑圧 ◯ the suppression of the truth
- 真実からかけ離れた陳述
  ◯ a statement which is nowhere near the truth ☞ nowhere near ...「...には程遠い、とても...ではない」
- 真実がこれっぽっちも含まれていない話
  ◯ a story which does not possess one ounce of truth
  ☞ not ... one ounce of something「これっぽっちもない」
- 自分の主張は真実だと他の人に納得させる
  ◯ convince others of the truth of my claim
- このうわさには真実がない。◯ There is no truth in this rumour.

▶決まり文句

- 私は嘘をついていない。真実をすべて語っていなかっただけだ。
  ◯ I did not tell a lie. I was being economical with the truth.
  ☞ be economical with *sth*「〈物〉を節約して使う」
- 真実は二者の供述の間のどこかにある。
  ◯ The truth lies somewhere between the statements of the two parties.
  ☞ この lie は動詞で「ある」の意味

▶ストーリー

Parents teach children that they must **always tell the truth**, and **never tell lies.** But we can imagine situations in which **telling a convincing lie**, or **telling a lie skilfully**, might save a human life. Perhaps we should teach children the difference between **moral and immoral lies**.

（親は子供たちに、常に真実を話し、決して嘘をついてはならないと教える。しかし私たちは説得力がある嘘をつくことや巧みに嘘をつくことで人間の生命が救われるような状況を思い浮かべることができる。ひょっとしたら私たちは子供たちに悪意のない嘘とある嘘の違いを教えるべきなのかもしれない。）

067 LIFE CU

「生活空間」(the lifespace) が示すように「生」(life) は我々の生活そのものである。'life' は場合に応じて何通りも訳語があり、この語に関わる表現は具体的なものから比喩的なものまで幅広い。ここでは、'life' が表す「期間」と「死」をテーマに用例を多数紹介した。「生活を送る」表現に関わる動詞のバリエーションにも注意したい。

C { ほとんどの場合 ☞ C
U { 死と対比されて概念的に用いられたり、「生命を持った存在」を意味する場合 ☞ U

>> DEATH; HEALTH; ILLNESS

▶ life から広がるボキャブラリー

- 楽な [豊かな] 生活を送る ◯ live a life of ease C
- 不安のない生活を送る ◯ live a life without care
- 贅沢三昧の生活を送る ◯ lead a life of luxury
- 充実した生活を送る ◯ lead a full life
- 非常に幸せな家庭生活を送る ◯ have a very happy home life
- 退屈な生活を送る ◯ live a dull life
- 退屈な生活を送る ◯ have a boring life
- 自分の学生生活を回想する ◯ look back on my school life ☞ look back on sth「〈事〉を思い出す」
- 興味ある社交生活を送る ◯ have an interesting social life
- 上流社会の生活を楽しむ ◯ enjoy the high life
- 田舎と都会の両方の生活を楽しむ
  ◯ enjoy both rural and urban life
- 火星には生命が存在するか。 ◯ Is there life on Mars? U

▶「期間」に関わる表現

- 人生で最悪の病気を経験する
  ◯ experience the worst illness in my life
- 私は死ぬまでに一度でいいからオーロラを見たい。
  ◯ I want to see the aurora [ərɔ́ːrə] once in my life.

- ボブは人生の終わりに近づいている［臨終間際である］。
  - ◎ Bob is near the end of his life.
- 私は自分の生涯の仕事を誇りに思う。◎ I am proud of my life work.
- 離婚の後、人生をやり直す
  - ◎ put my life together again after a divorce ☞ put *sth* together「〈物事〉を元通りにする、組み立てる」
- メアリー女王の生涯についての本を書く
  - ◎ write a book on the life of Queen Mary
- 彼女は今まで何もかもつらい人生だった。
  - ◎ Her whole life has been terrible.

▶「死」に関わる表現

- 命からがら逃げる ◎ flee for my life ☞ for *one's* life「必死で、命がけで」
- 生死をかけた争いに勝つ ◎ win a life-and-death struggle
- 溺れかけた人の命を救う ◎ save the life of a drowning person
  - ☞ He is almost drowned.「彼はおぼれかけた」
- 不必要に人の寿命を長くする ◎ needlessly prolong a person's life

▶決まり文句

- それが人生だ［仕方がない］！ ◎ That's life!
- 彼は気楽で贅沢な生活を送っている。
  - ◎ He leads the life of Reilly [Riley].《英》

▶ストーリー

What do people want to **get out of life**? Some people want to **lead ordinary, everyday lives**. Others want **lives that are full of excitement**. Others never want to **work in their lives**, but want to **lead a life of luxury and ease**.

（人は人生から何を得たいと思うのか？ 普通に毎日の生活を送ることを望む人もいる。一方で興奮に満ちた人生を望む人もいる。また、一生決して働きたいと思わず、気楽に贅沢な生活をただ送りたいと考える人もいる。）

LIFE 159

068 LOVE C U

愛という言葉は男女間のものだけでない。英語の影響か、日本でも親族関係などに広く用いられるようになってきた。ここでも 'love' のバリエーションと交際に関わる表現を多く紹介した。

- 愛情や恋愛の気持ちを表す場合 ☞ U
- 強い好みや嗜好を表す場合 ☞ U または 'a ～ love' の形

* 'She/He's my lover.' などと軽々しく言わないこと。これは婚外の性的関係を強く示唆する表現である。ノーマルな交際を言いたい場合は「関連表現」の2つの文（☞ *）を用いればよい。

>> FAMILY; FRIENDSHIP; HUSBAND / WIFE; KINDNESS; MAN / WOMAN

▶ love から広がるボキャブラリー：動詞表現

- ❏ 激しく愛し合う（セックスをする）◯ make passionate love
- ❏ 彼女に恋を打ち明ける ◯ declare my love to her ☞ declare war「宣戦布告する」
- ❏ 愛を言葉で表現する ◯ express my love in words ☞ in a word「要するに」
- ❏ 私はメグにすっかり惚れこんでいる。
  ◯ I am hopelessly in love with Meg. ☞ hopelessly「絶望的なほどに」
- ❏ 真実の愛を経験する ◯ experience true love
- ❏ 永遠の愛を誓う ◯ vow undying love ☞ vow to learn English「英語をものにすることを誓う」
- ❏ メグの愛を大切にする ◯ cherish Meg's love
- ❏ betray Bob's love ◯ ボブの愛を裏切る
- ❏ 精神的な愛［プラトニック・ラブ］の意味を理解する
  ◯ understand the meaning of platonic love
- ❏ 人類を深く愛する ◯ have a deep love of humanity C
- ❏ 博愛を感じる ◯ feel brotherly love U
- ❏ 母国を愛する ◯ have a love for my country
- ❏ 自然を深く愛する ◯ have a great love of nature

▶ 関連表現

- ❏ 愛と憎しみ ◯ love and hate
- ❏ 愛と情熱と性欲の入り混じった感情

- ○ a feeling that is a mixture of love, passion, and sex
- ❏ 恋に夢中の若者 ○ a love-struck young man
- ❏ わくわくするような情事をもつ ○ have an exciting love affair
  - ☞ My husband is having an affair.「夫は浮気をしている」
- ❏ 自分の先生に熱を上げる ○ have a crush on my teacher ☞ have a crush on sb「〈人〉に夢中になる」
- ❏ 心からボブを愛する ○ love Bob with all my heart
- ❏ 初恋の人を懐かしく思い出す ○ fondly remember my first love
- ❏ 彼はのぼせあがることと愛することの区別がつかない。
  - ○ He cannot distinguish between infatuation and love.
  - ☞ infatuationは一次的に夢中になること
- ❏ メグとボブはつき合っている。
  - ○ Meg and Bob are seeing each other.* / Meg and Bob are going out.*
- ❏ ボブはメグと適切でない関係 [不倫関係] を持った。
  - ○ Bob had a relationship with Meg that was not appropriate.

▶決まり文句

- ❏ 愛は盲目。○ Love is blind.
- ❏ メグが私の生き甲斐だ。○ Meg is the love of my life.
- ❏ それは一目惚れだった。○ It was a case of love at first sight.
- ❏ 二人はお互いにぞっこんだった。
  - ○ The two of them fell head-over-heels in love.

▶ ストーリー

Paul and Mary **fell in love—love at first sight**! They promised to **love each other with all their heart**. But **the path of true love** is seldom an easy one. This story has an unhappy ending—an ending about **betraying another's love**.

(ポールとメアリーは恋に落ちた。しかも一目惚れ！彼らは心の底からお互いを愛し合うことを約束した。しかし真実の愛の道のりはめったに容易なものではない。この物語は不幸な終わりを迎えた。相手の愛を裏切るという終わりを。)

069 LUCK   U

運の良し悪しはどうにもならないものである。しかし我々は何かにつけ運が良いか悪いかを気にかける。生活空間での心の持ち方を左右する 'luck' に関わるさまざまな表現を確認しておきたい。
✼ 'luck' が単なる中間的な「運」だけでなく、それだけで「幸運」を意味する場合もあるのは日本語と同じである。

>> AIM; CHANCE; HAPPINESS

▶「幸運」に関わる表現

- ❏ 初心者の幸運 [ビギナーズラック] ◯ beginner's luck
- ❏ まったくの幸運 ◯ pure good luck
- ❏ 幸運を信じる ◯ believe in good luck ☞ believe in *sth* は「〈物事〉の存在を信じる」という意味
- ❏ ボブのために幸運を祈る ◯ wish Bob (the best of) luck
- ❏ 彼女の幸運をうれしく思う ◯ rejoice in her luck
- ❏ ボブは運がよい [ついている]。◯ Bob is in luck.
- ❏ (自分自身の) ツキを育てる ◯ make my own luck
- ❏ あなたは運に恵まれている。◯ You are blessed with luck.
- ❏ 自分の運を信じることができない ◯ cannot believe my luck
- ❏ あわよくば私たちはうまくいくはずだ。
  ◯ With any [a bit of] luck we should succeed.

▶「悪運」に関わる表現

- ❏ 私はついていない [不運である]。◯ I am out of luck.
- ❏ 不運を冷静に受け入れること
  ◯ a philosophical acceptance of bad luck ☞ be philosophical about *sth*「〈事〉を冷静に受け止める」
- ❏ 自分たちの敗北をまったく運がなかったと意に介さない
  ◯ dismiss our defeat as pure bad luck ☞ dismiss *sth* as ...「〈事〉を...として退ける、否定する」
- ❏ 彼の運はついに尽きた。◯ His luck finally ran out. ☞ Time is running out.「そろそろ時間切れだ」

出来事

- 私は魚釣りに行ったがついていなかった。
  - I went fishing, but did not have any luck.
- このところ災難続きだ。 ○ I have had a run of bad luck recently.

▶決まり文句

- 運命の巡り合わせ、単なる偶然の結果 ○ the luck of the draw
- 運良く［運悪く］；偶然 ○ as luck would have it
- 実力より運で勝つ ○ win more by luck than by ability
- 調子に乗って危険を冒す ○ push my luck
- 運試しをする ○ try my luck
- 俺の運なんてこんなもんさ！ ○ That's just my luck!
- （残念ながら）だめだった！ ○ No such luck! ☞ そううまくはいかなかったということ
- お気の毒に！ ○ Hard luck!
- ついてないね！ ○ Tough luck!《英》
- 私は不運続きでお金に困っている。 ○ I am down on my luck.
- 運が向いてきた。 ○ My luck is in.
- ついていなかった／ついていた。 ○ Luck was against us / with us.
- この次はがんばってね！ ○ Better luck next time!
- やっと最後に運がまわってきた。
  - We finally lucked out in the end. (動詞)《米》

▶ ストーリー

Napoleon said that the great generals were **the lucky ones**, not the good ones. I think he meant that skill is not as important as **being blessed with luck**. Some people always seem to **have all the luck**. For me, it is always a case of '**Tough luck!**', or '**Better luck next time!**'

（ナポレオンは言った。偉大な将官とはよい将官ではなく運がよい将官であると。彼の意味するところは、技能は運に恵まれていることに比べればさほど重要ではないということだと思う。いつも運を独り占めにしているように思われる人もいる。私の場合はいつも「ついてなかった」あるいは「次はがんばれ」なのである。）

070 MAN / WOMAN C

> 男女に関わる表現は、昨今のジェンダーフリー (gender-free) の考え方の伸張に伴いデリケートなものになってきた。性差別を助長するような表現は避けるべきだが、伝統的な固定観念に基づく表現は、日本はもとより英語圏でもまだまだ多く見られる。
> ✱ 以下の用例、特に「男女関係」は 'man' と 'woman' を交換可能である。「社会のしくみ」に関わる表現は日本での状況はどうだろうか。
> **>> HUSBAND / WIFE; LOVE; MARRIAGE;**

▶「男女関係」に関わる表現

- 既婚女性 ◯ a married woman
- 離婚した男性 ◯ a divorced man ☞ We got divorced.「私たちは離婚した」
- 独身女性 ◯ a single woman
- やもめ男 [独身男性] ◯ an unattached man ☞ Bob is still unattached.「ボブはまだ独身だ」
- 30代前半の女性 ◯ a woman in her early thirties
- 60代中盤の男性 ◯ a man in his mid-sixties
- 女性といちゃつく ◯ <u>flirt with</u> a woman ☞ flirt with the idea of getting a job「就職してみようかと考えてみる」
- 男性と一緒に住む [同棲する] ◯ <u>live with</u> a man

▶「男性」に関わる表現

- きれいに髭を剃った男性 ◯ a clean-shaven man
- ハンサムな中年男性 ◯ a handsome middle-aged man
- 私の右腕 ◯ my right-hand man
- 自分の腕一本でたたき上げた男 ◯ a self-made man
- すけべなやつ [男] ◯ a dirty old man
- 活動家 ◯ a man of action
- 世慣れした男 [俗人] ◯ a man of the world

▶「女性」に関わる表現

- かわいい女性 ◯ a pretty woman

- 美しい女性 ◯ a beautiful woman
- スタイルのよい女性 ◯ a woman with a nice figure
- 女性作家 ◯ a woman writer
- 女性宰相 ◯ a woman prime minister
- 子供をたくさん生んだ女性
  ◯ a woman who has borne a lot of children

▶「社会のしくみ」に関わる表現

- 女性への(男性と比較しての)薄給 ◯ lower pay for women
- 女性を差別する ◯ discriminate against women
- 多くの上級職で女性のしめる割合が少ないこと
  ◯ the under-representation of women in many senior posts
- 女性に有利にはたらく逆差別
  ◯ reverse discrimination which favours women ☞ favour men over women「女性よりも男性を優遇する」
- 部長は自分の部下に酒を飲め飲めと無理矢理勧めた。
  ◯ The boss urged drinks on his men. ☞ urge Bob not to go「ボブに行かないよう強く勧めた[説得した]」

▶ ストーリー

Sexual prejudice is a part of language. Many people still say '**a career woman**', or '**a working woman**' because these are seen as exceptions to **the traditional view that a woman's place is in the home**. It would be strange to say 'a career man'. And '**working man**' does not mean 'a man who works', but 'a man who works in a non-office job, probably **doing manual labour**'.

(性的な偏見は言語の一部である。「キャリアウーマン」とか「働く女性」などと言う人はいまだに多い。なぜなら、これらの発言は女性のいる場所は家庭だという伝統的な見解の例外だと考えられているからだ。「キャリアマン」と言うとおかしく聞こえるだろう。さらに「働く男性」と言うと「職業を持っている男性」ではなく、「オフィスワークではなく、恐らく肉体労働をしている男性」を意味するのである。)

071 MARRIAGE C U

結婚は人生最高の慶事であるが、最近では逆の文脈で話題になる場合も多い(同性間の結婚の話題も)。ここではそのような表現も多く紹介した。これらを見れば、なぜ 'marriage' が Core Nouns に選ばれたかわかるだろう。'marriage' は「結婚」のほか、文脈によって「結婚生活」まで意味することに注意。

- 個別の結婚やそのタイプについて述べる場合 ☞ C
- 社会制度としての結婚について述べる場合 ☞ U

>> CHILD; HOME; HOUSEWORK; HUSBAND / WIFE; LOVE; MAN/WOMAN

▶「よい結婚」に関わる表現

- ❑ 幸福な結婚 ◯ a happy marriage C
- ❑ お互いの敬意に基づいた結婚
  ◯ a marriage based on mutual respect
- ❑ 順風満帆な結婚生活 ◯ a marriage made in heaven ☞ 決まり文句
- ❑ 円満な結婚生活の秘訣 ◯ the secret of a successful marriage

▶「だめな結婚」に関わる表現

- ❑ ひどい結婚と泥沼の離婚
  ◯ a terrible marriage and a messy divorce ☞ a messy situation「やっかいな事態」
- ❑ 離婚に終わったみじめな結婚
  ◯ a miserable marriage which ended in divorce
- ❑ 結婚トラブルの絶えない一生 ◯ a life full of marriage troubles
- ❑ 重婚 ◯ a bigamous [bígəməs] marriage
- ❑ できちゃった結婚[でき婚]
  ◯ a marriage that results from an unplanned pregnancy

▶ marriage から広がるボキャブラリー:動詞表現

- ❑ プロポーズする ◯ make a proposal of marriage
- ❑ できるだけ結婚を遅らせる
  ◯ delay marriage for as long as possible

- パパは結婚に反対だった。 ◎ Dad was opposed to my marriage.
- 娘の結婚に同意する ◎ agree to the marriage of my daughter
- アドバイスを求めて結婚カウンセラーのもとを訪れる
    ◎ visit a marriage counsellor for advice
- 結婚生活をやり直そうとする
    ◎ try to straighten out my marriage
- 10年の結婚生活の後、夫と別れる
    ◎ part from my husband after ten years of marriage
- 彼女の結婚生活は修復不可能だった。
    ◎ Her marriage was beyond saving.

▶「社会のしくみ」に関わる表現

- (社会的な傾向としての) 晩婚 ◎ the late age of marriage
- 平均結婚年齢の上昇 ◎ a rise in the average age of marriage [U]
- 結婚できる見通しが事実上ない若い男性
    ◎ a young man with no real marriage prospects ☞ a person of great prospects「将来大変有望な人」
- 王室間の縁組み ◎ a marriage alliance between royal families
- 入籍する ◎ register your marriage officially
- 地味婚 ◎ a plain subdued wedding ceremony

▶ ストーリー

John and Mary **got married to each other** more than thirty years ago and are in love as **the day they got married**. Their friends ask them what **the secret of a successful marriage** is. They answer that they have always **had a happy married life**, because **their marriage is based on understanding and tolerance**.

(ジョンとメアリーは30年以上前に結婚し、今も結婚当日のように愛し合っている。友人たちは結婚生活がそんなにうまくいっている秘訣は何かとたずねる。二人は、結婚生活が今までいつも幸せだったのは自分たちの結婚が理解と寛容に基づいているからだと答える。)

MARRIAGE

072　MEETING　C

> 会議は会社だけで行われるものでなく、生活空間において多種多様な話し合いが存在する。下記で紹介した表現、特に会議の運営に関わる表現はいろいろな話し合いの場に応用できるものである。
> ✲ 'meeting' は「集まり」を表す一般的な語であり、以下のようにさまざまな種類とそれらに相当する語がある。
> 例 a conference（会議）　a convention（代表者の大会）
> 　　a rally（大集会）　preliminary discussions（予備会議）
> 　　a social gathering（懇親会）　a class reunion（クラス会、同窓会）
> 　　a get-together of former classmates（以前の同級生たちの集まり）
>
> **>> BOSS; COMPANY; WORK**

▶ meeting から広がるボキャブラリー

- 抗議集会 ● a protest meeting
- 公開の集会 ● a public meeting
- 私的な会談 ● a private meeting
- 首脳会議［サミット］ ● a summit meeting
- 国連安全保障理事会の会議 ● a UN Security Council meeting
- ブリュッセルでのNATO国の会議
  ● a meeting of the NATO [néitou] nations in Brussels
- 内閣の緊急会議 ● an emergency meeting of the Cabinet
  ☞ an emergency exit「非常口」
- 株主総会 ● a shareholders' meeting ☞ a top shareholder「筆頭株主」
- 部門のミーティング；部局会議
  ● a departmental [di:pɑ:rtmént(ə)l] meeting
- 退屈な会議 ● a boring meeting

▶「会議の運営」に関わる表現

- 会議の議事（日程） ● the agenda of a meeting
- 議事録 ● the minutes [main(j)ú:ts] of a meeting
- 円滑に進められる会議 ● a well-run meeting
- 会議を召集する ● call a meeting ☞ close a meeting「閉会する」
- 会議の開会を宣言する ● <u>call a meeting to order</u>

出来事

- 会議の議長を務める ○ chair a meeting
- 会議に出席する ○ attend a meeting
- 会議で演説する ○ address a meeting ☞ address an audience「聴衆に演説する」
- 新しい会の最初の集まりを開く
  ○ hold the first meeting of a new society
- 会を一時中断 [休会] する ○ adjourn [ədʒə́ːrn] a meeting
- 会を延期する ○ postpone a meeting
- 会談を中止する ○ cancel a meeting
- 次の会の期日を確かめる ○ confirm the date of the next meeting
- 私は会議の時間ぴったりに着いた。○ I was on time for the meeting.
- ボブは我々の会議に遅れた。○ Bob was late for our meeting.
- 結局、会議は昨日 (予定していたのに) 行われなかった。
  ○ In the end, the meeting did not come off yesterday.
  ☞ このcome offは「予定していたことが行われる」の意味
- 会は定足数に足りなかった。
  ○ There was no quorum [kwɔ́ːrəm] at the meeting.
- その会議では各党の意見がかみ合わなかった。
  ○ There were differences of opinion among the parties at the meeting.

▶ ストーリー

I **hate meetings**, especially **those which seem to drag on for ever**. I have been to many **meetings in which no conclusion was reached**, and **time was wasted** by a small number of people **talking at length about nothing of importance**. In order to **keep meetings short and to the point**, they **should be held** in a sealed room, with a limited supply of oxygen.

(私は会議が嫌いだ。特にいつまでも長引きそうな会議が。私は今まで、何の結論にも達せず、くだらないことを長々と話す少数の人たちによって時間が浪費される会議に何度も出席してきた。会議を短く、要を得たものにするためには、封鎖した部屋で酸素の供給を制限して行うべきである。)

MEETING

073 MISTAKE · · · · · · · · · · · · · C

> 誤りは避けるべきものであると同時に避けられないものでもある。'mistake' に関わる表現を「許されない誤り」(重大なもの) と「許される誤り」(ささいなもの) という視点から整理して紹介した。どれも日常頻繁に使うものばかりである。
> ✲ 'a mistake' は「誤り、間違い」を表す一般的な語であり、類義語の 'an error' は正確さや客観的な基準から見た誤りを指す形式張った語である。例 a typographical error (= a typo) 印刷ミス
>
> **>> APOLOGY; DIFFICULTY; FAILURE**

▶「許されない(重大な)誤り」に関わる表現

- ❏ 不注意による誤り[ケアレスミス] ○ a careless mistake
- ❏ 大きな誤り ○ an enormous mistake
- ❏ 根本的な誤り ○ a fundamental mistake ☞ fundamental human rights「基本的人権」
- ❏ 明白な誤り ○ an obvious mistake
- ❏ 愚かな誤り ○ a foolish mistake
- ❏ 代償の大きな誤り ○ a costly mistake ☞ costly「高価な、犠牲の大きい」
- ❏ 高くつく誤り ○ an expensive mistake ☞ a costly mistake とほぼ同義
- ❏ 重大な誤りをおかす ○ make a serious mistake ☞ 上の「〜な誤り」はすべて make と共に用いることができる。
- ❏ 誤りを重ねる ○ make mistake after mistake ☞ time after time「何度も」
- ❏ 自分の誤りを包み隠す ○ cover up my mistakes ☞ cover up bribery「わいろをもみ消す」
- ❏ ボブの誤りを指摘する ○ point out Bob's mistake
- ❏ メグの誤りを根にもって彼女を怨む
  ○ hold Meg's mistake against her ☞ hold sth against sb「〈過去のよくない行いなど〉を持ち出して誰かを非難する」

▶「許される(ささいな)誤り」に関わる表現

- ❏ つづりの誤り ○ a spelling mistake
- ❏ よくある誤り ○ a common mistake
- ❏ 正真正銘の誤り ○ a genuine mistake

- おかしやすい誤り ◯ an easy mistake to make
- 誤って何かをする ◯ do something by mistake
- 自分の誤りに気づく ◯ realize my mistake
- 自分の誤りを認める ◯ acknowledge my mistake
- 自分の誤りを直す ◯ correct my mistake
- 今後誤りを避ける ◯ avoid a mistake in the future
- 誤りをおかす危険を減らす
  ◯ reduce the risk of a mistake being made
- 決して再び同じ誤りをおかさない
  never make the same mistake again
- 誤りをわびる ◯ apologize for a mistake
- 浅はかな誤りに対して償いをする
  ◯ make amends for a thoughtless mistake
  ☞ thoughtless behaviour「軽率なふるまい」
- 彼らの結婚は誤りであった。◯ Their marriage was a mistake.

▶決まり文句

- 誰でも誤りはある。◯ Anyone can make a mistake.
- 言っておくが、これが最後のチャンスだ。
  ◯ Make no mistake. This is your last chance.
  ☞ 自分の発言を強めて、相手に警告するような場合に用いる
- ボブとメグはつき合っている。マチガイナイ！
  ◯ Bob and Meg are seeing each other, and no mistake!

▶ストーリー

Some mistakes are so minor that **we can overlook them**. Other **mistakes are very easy to make**. Even if someone **makes a stupid mistake**, we should perhaps **forgive them for it**, especially if they **learn from it**.

(誤りの中には、見逃してもよいくらい非常にささいなものもある。また一方で非常におかしやすいものもある。誰かが愚かな誤りをおかしたとしても、特にその人がそこから学ぶのなら、私たちはそれを許すべきであろう。)

074 MONEY   U

> 金は出たり入ったりしながら生活空間を巡っていくものである。金に関わる表現も「入る」と「出る」という2つの視点から整理してみると非常に覚えやすくなる。生活空間において 'money' に関わる表現がどのように用いられるかよくわかるだろう。
>
> **>> ECONOMY; SHOPPING; WORK**

▶「入ってくる金」に関わる表現

- たくさん稼ぐ ◎ earn a lot of money
- 印税で大きく儲ける ◎ make a lot of money from book royalties
- 銀行に自分の金を預け入れる ◎ put your money into the bank
- 慈善のために金を集める ◎ raise money for charity ☞ raise funds「資金を調達する」
- 多くの金を産み出すプロジェクト
  ◎ a project which produces a lot of money
- 自分が投資した金で利子を得る
  ◎ earn interest on the money I have invested
- 手っ取り早く儲けようと株を買う
  ◎ buy some stocks in an attempt to make some quick money
  ☞ このquickは「すぐ現金になる」の意味。in an attempt to do「〜しようとして」
- できる限りたくさん貯金しようとする [節約しようとする]
  ◎ try to save as much money as possible

▶「出ていく金」に関わる表現

- 口座から金をおろす ◎ draw (out) money from an account
- 損 [損失] を出しているホテル ◎ a hotel that is losing money
- 新しい会社に多くの金を出資する
  ◎ invest a lot of money in a new company
- 自分が借りた金に対して利子を支払う
  ◎ pay interest on the money I have borrowed ☞ 前置詞onに注意
- 新しいプロジェクトのために金を出す
  ◎ put up money for a new project ☞ put /sth/ up「〈金〉を提供する」

- 驚くほど早く金を使い果たす
  - **go through** money **at an alarming rate** ☞ go through three jars of jam in a week「ジャム3瓶を一週間で使い果たす」
- 困っている友人に金を貸す **lend money to a friend in need**
  - ☞ A friend in need is a friend indeed.「まさかの時の友こそ真の友」《諺》
- 高くついた誤り **a mistake that cost a lot of money**
- 私は自分の金を手放したくない。
  - **I do not want to part with my money.** ☞ part with *sth*「やむなく〈物〉を手放したり、売り払う」
- 金で買える最高のワイン **the best wine money can buy**

▶決まり文句

- 支払った金に見合うものを買う **get value for money**
- 私は金のなる木じゃあるまいし。**I am not made of money.**
- 金のなる木はない。**Money does not grow on trees.**
  - ☞ *sth* does not grow on trees「〈物〉が簡単には手に入らない」
- 私はどんどん金を儲けている。**I am making money hand over fist.**
  - ☞ hand over fist「どしどし、どんどん」(金を手にしたり失ったりする様)
- 彼は有り余るほど金を持っている。**He has money to burn.**
- 知っての通り、金がものをいうんだよ。**Money talks, as you know.**

▶ストーリー

I asked my students if they said 'zeikin o harau' or 'zeikin o osameru'. Almost all of them said the former. The former suggests **paying taxes somewhat unwillingly**; the latter suggests **gladly paying taxes for the good of society**. When you consider **how much tax money is wasted or stolen**, 'harau' seems the better choice.

(自分の学生に「税金を払う」と言うのか「税金を納める」と言うのか聞いてみた。彼らのほぼ全員が前者だと言った。前者はしぶしぶ税金を支払うという感じがし、後者は社会の利益のために喜んで税金を支払うという感じがする。どれぐらいの税金が無駄に使われたり、盗まれているかを考えると、「払う」と言うほうがよいように思えるのだが。)

075 MOVIE　C

> 映画は生活空間における娯楽の中心の一つである。ここでは、新聞や雑誌などでよく用いられる 'movie' 関連の表現を紹介した。
> ✣ 'movie' は米語であり英国では 'film' を用いるが、今日では 'movie' が英語圏で映画を表す語として一般的に用いられている。しかし 'film' のほうが応用範囲が広く、例えば、「記録映画」は 'a documentary film' とは言えるが 'a documentary movie' とは言わない。
> ✣ 複数形で 'go to the movies' のように用いられた場合、「映画館に何か映画を見に行く」という意味になる（類例☞*）。
>
> **>> ENJOYMENT; HOBBY; MUSIC; TELEVISION**

▶ movie から広がるボキャブラリー：名詞表現

- 無声映画 ○ a silent movie
- ホラー映画 ○ a horror movie
- ヤクザ映画；任侠映画 ○ a gangster [yakuza] movie
- 探偵映画 ○ a detective movie
- スパイ映画 ○ a spy movie
- アクション冒険映画 ○ an action-adventure movie
- 警官をパロディにした映画 ○ a spoof cop movie ☞ spoof [spúːf]「もじり、パロディ」
- ポルノ映画 ○ a blue movie
- ソフトコアのポルノ映画 ○ a soft-core porn movie
- ハードコアのポルノ映画 ○ a hard-core porn movie
- 喜劇映画 ○ a comedy
- ミュージカル（の映画）○ a musical
- 映画の冒頭シーン ○ the opening scene of a movie
- ラストシーンがロマンチックな映画
  ○ a movie with a romantic closing scene

▶ movie から広がるボキャブラリー：動詞表現

- 映画の製作と監督をする ○ produce and direct a movie
- 映画をロケで撮影する ○ shoot a movie on location ☞ on location

in Japan「日本ロケで」
- ❏ 映画を編集する ◯ edit a movie
- ❏ 映画のオリジナル・サウンドトラックを吹き替える
  ◯ dub over the original soundtrack of a movie ☞ be dubbed into Japanese「日本語に吹き替えられる」
- ❏ 映画にモンゴル語の字幕を加える
  ◯ add Mongolian subtitles to a movie ☞ subtitles「説明字幕、スーパー」
- ❏ ホリデーシーズンに映画を封切る
  ◯ release a movie during the holiday season
- ❏ 超大作映画で主役を演じる ◯ star in a blockbuster movie
- ❏ 映画デビューをする ◯ make my movie debut
- ❏ 映画で悪党を演じる ◯ play the villain in a movie
- ❏ 芸術雑誌で映画の批評を書く ◯ review a movie in an art magazine
- ❏ 映画を検閲する ◯ censor a movie
- ❏ 映画からセックス・シーンをカットする
  ◯ cut the sex scenes out of a movie
- ❏ その映画は今どこでやっていますか。
  ◯ Where is the movie showing?
- ❏ その映画は3カ月以上にわたり上映されている。
  ◯ The movie has been on for over three months.
- ❏ 息子が小さいときはよく映画に連れて行ったものだ。
  ◯ I would often take my son to the movies when he was little.*

▶ ストーリー

Sometimes I want to **show a video to my students**. But it is almost impossible to find **a movie I can show**. This is because **the language of movies**, especially **Hollywood movies**, is so **crude** and **vulgar**.

(時々私は自分の学生にビデオを見せたくなる。しかし見せられる映画を見つけるのはほとんど不可能である。これは映画、特にハリウッド映画、の台詞が非常に粗野で卑猥だからである。)

076 MUSIC · U

音楽も現代の代表的な娯楽の一つであるが、前項の映画よりも身近な存在と言えるだろう。ここで紹介した表現もみなさんが自分で直接使えるものになっている。
✱ 曲としての音楽について述べる場合、ふつう 'the' を伴う (☞*)。数える場合は、'a piece of music' 'two pieces of music' と言う。

>> ENJOYMENT; HOBBY; MOVIE

▶ music から広がるボキャブラリー：名詞表現

- ダンス音楽 ○ dance music
- フラメンコ音楽 ○ flamenco music
- 軽古典音楽 light ○ classical music
- 感傷的な音楽 ○ sentimental music
- 即興で作った音楽 ○ extemporized music ☞ extemporize [ikstémpəràiz] *sth*「〈物事〉を即席でやる、作る」
- 明るい照明とうるさい音楽 ○ bright lights and loud music
- 宗教音楽の録音（テープ、CDなど）○ recordings of religious music
- リラックスさせてくれるBGM
  ○ background music that helps me to relax

▶ music から広がるボキャブラリー：動詞表現

- 音楽を聴く耳がある；音楽がわかる ○ have an ear for music
  ☞ have no ear for music「音楽がわからない」
- 作曲する ○ write music
- 楽譜を読む ○ read music ☞ この music は「楽譜」の意味
- オリジナル性の高い曲を作曲する ○ compose very original music
- ドラマ/詞に曲をつける ○ set a drama / a poem to music
- 大勢の聴衆に自分自身の曲を演奏する
  ○ play my own music to a large audience
- 自分なりにその曲を解釈する
  ○ interpret the music in an original way*
- 映画を音楽だけで楽しむ ○ appreciate a film for the music alone*

- メグと音楽の趣味が一致する ◯ share Meg's taste in music
- 音楽を聞いてとても癒される ◯ find music very soothing
  ☞ a soothing voice「なだめるような声」
- 音楽のリズムに合わせてゆっくりと動く
  ◯ move gently to the rhythm of the music*
- 口論している隣人の騒音をかき消すために音楽 (の音) を大きくする
  ◯ turn up the music to drown out the noise of the neighbours arguing* ☞ turn down the music「音楽 (の音) を小さくする、下げる」 drown my sorrows in drink「酒で寂しさを紛らす」
- その曲は大きさと強烈さが高まっていくように思われた。
  ◯ The music seemed to swell in size and intensity.*
- 音楽がうるさくて誰の声も聞こえなかった。
  ◯ No one could be heard above the music.*

▶決まり文句

- あなたの話を聞いていると、とてもうれしくなる。
  ◯ What you say is music to my ears.
  ☞ be music to my earsは「私の耳に心地よく響く」の意
- 遅かれ早かれ、あなたは自ら責任をとらなければならないだろう。
  ◯ Sooner or later, you will have to face the music.

▶ ストーリー

A lot of people say that they **are tone-deaf**, and they **cannot hum a tune**, or that they **cannot appreciate music**. In fact, people who **have normal hearing and speech** cannot **be tone-deaf**. It is possible that they **have had no musical training or education**. But this is not the same as **being tone-deaf**.
(多くの人が、自分は音痴で、曲をハミングして歌うことができないとか、あるいは音楽がわからないという。実際は、正常に聴き話すことができる人たちが音痴であるはずはない。そのような人たちは音楽の訓練や教育を受けてこなかった可能性がある。しかし、それは音痴であることとはまた別の話である)

MUSIC

077 NEWSPAPER [PAPER] ･･････ C

> メディアが多様化した現在でも、新聞はあらゆる情報の入手源、すなわち生活空間の核の一つである。ここではやや専門的なものもあるが、毎日目にする新聞に関わる表現を押さえておこう。'newspaper' は単に 'paper' とも言う。
>
> ✱ 'a story in the paper'（新聞の記事）と 'a story on page 19'（19面の記事）の違いに難しさを感じる人が多いが、前者は「入れ物（新聞）の中に記事が入っている」イメージであり、後者は「記事が表面（ページ）に乗って［載って］いる」イメージである。
>
> **>> BOOK; TELEVISION**

▶ newspaper [paper] から広がるボキャブラリー：名詞表現

- ❏ 地方紙 ○ a regional newspaper ☞ regional disparities「地域格差」
- ❏ 地元紙 ○ a local newspaper
- ❏ くだらない新聞 ○ a trashy newspaper ☞ a trashy novel「三文小説」
- ❏ 評価の高い新聞 ○ a well-respected newspaper
- ❏ 新聞と他のメディア ○ newspapers and the other media
- ❏ 雑誌、定期刊行物、新聞
    ○ magazines, periodicals, and newspapers
- ❏ 新聞と広告産業 ○ the newspaper and advertising industries
- ❏ 新聞記事の情報源 ○ the source of a newspaper story

▶ newspaper [paper] から広がるボキャブラリー：動詞表現

- ❏ 毎朝ネット新聞を読む ○ read an online newspaper every morning
- ❏ インターネットで新聞記事を検索する
    ○ search for a newspaper article online ☞ online は副詞
- ❏ 紙の新聞の衰退 ○ the decline of the dead tree press ☞ dead tree「（電子版に対して）印刷された」
- ❏ 新聞の発行部数が減った。
    ○ Newspaper circulation has decreased. ☞ a newspaper with a circulation of 1,000,000「発行部数100万部の新聞」
- ❏ 新聞に記事を掲載する ○ publish an article in a newspaper

- ❏ 新聞に全面広告を出す ○ take out a full-page ad in a paper
  ☞ take out an advertisement「広告を出す」
- ❏ 新聞広告を見て問い合わせる
  ○ respond to a newspaper advertisement
- ❏ 新聞(社)の謝罪広告 ○ an apology published by a newspaper
  ☞ an apology published in a newspaper「新聞に掲載された謝罪」
- ❏ 新聞を二つ折りにする ○ fold a newspaper in two
- ❏ 全紙がその記事を載せた。○ All the papers carried [covered] the story. ☞ carry the news「そのニュースを報じる」
- ❏ 新聞の配達が雪のため遅れた。
  ○ Newspaper deliveries were delayed by the snow.

▶ 新聞のパーツ

- ❏ 見出し ○ the headlines
- ❏ 四面の全国ニュース ○ national news on page 4
- ❏ 五面下の地方ニュース ○ regional news at the bottom of page 5
- ❏ 十四面隅の地元ニュース ○ local news in a corner of page 14
- ❏「編集長への手紙」面 ○ the letters-to-the-editor page
- ❏ 最終面のテレビ番組表 ○ the TV guide on the back page
- ❏ 物議をかもす話題についての論説
  ○ an editorial on a controversial topic
- ❏ 地元紙での「求人欄」 ○ 'situations vacant' in the local newspaper

▶ ストーリー

The mainstream Japanese press and TV vary **their reporting on people** according to race, nationality, age, sex, job title, position in society, and so on. **Such reporting is biased reporting**, and **is easy to notice** if you **read the newspapers and watch television carefully**.

(日本の主要な新聞やテレビ局は、人種、国籍、年齢、性別、会社の肩書き、社会における地位などによって人々に関する報道の仕方を変える。このような報道は偏った報道であり、気をつけて新聞を読んだりテレビを見たりすれば容易に気づくことである。)

078 PARCEL [PACKAGE] ･････････ C

> 現代人の生活空間において、品物を送ったり、受け取ったり、包んだり、さらにそれらのためにサインしたりする場面は意外に多い。さらに、コンビニエンス・ストアや宅配サービスの広がりと共に、もはや「郵便局 (Post Office)」は時代遅れになりつつあるようだ。
> ✽米国では 'parcel' の代わりに 'package' と言うのが普通だが、英国では 'parcel' と 'package' の両方が用いられる。
>
> **>> ROAD; TRAIN**

▶ parcel から広がるボキャブラリー：名詞表現

- 大きい正方形の小包 ● a large square parcel ☞ a T-shirt with square patterns「四角い模様のついたTシャツ」
- 茶色の紙にくるまれた小包 ● a parcel wrapped in brown paper
- 赤十字社からの小包で食いつないでいる難民
  ● refugees who are surviving on Red Cross parcels ☞ survive on charity「施しを受けてなんとか生活する」
- 宅配便で配送された小包
  ● a parcel that was delivered by courier
- 小包爆弾 ● a parcel bomb

▶ parcel から広がるボキャブラリー：動詞表現

- 代金引換 [代引き] で小包を受け取る
  ● receive a parcel by cash on delivery
- きれいなリボンで小包をしばる
  ● tie up a parcel with some pretty ribbon ☞ tie /sth/ up は「〈物〉をしっかりくくる」の意味
- 小包に名前と住所を書く ● write the name and address on a parcel
- 小包に切手を貼る ● put stamps on a parcel
- 小包を送るためにコンビニに行く
  ● go to the convenience store to send off a parcel
- 手紙を小包とは別に送る
  ● send a letter separately from the parcel ☞ send /sth/ off「〈物〉を

発送・郵送する」
- 小包が郵便で到着した。 ○ A parcel arrived through the post.
- 特使が持ってきた小包をサインして受け取る

   ○ sign for a parcel that has come by special messenger

   ☞ sign for sth は「〈手紙・小包など〉の受領証明として署名をする」こと
- 小包のひもを切る ○ cut the string on a parcel
- 小包をX線の機械に通す

   ○ put a parcel through an X-ray machine
- ドラッグの入った小包がぱっと開いた。

   ○ The parcel containing drugs burst open.

▶ 決まり文句

- 私は小さい一区画の土地を所有している。

   ○ I own a small parcel of land. ☞ このparcelは「土地の一区画」の意
- この政策が改革の肝[眼目]だ。

   ○ This policy is part and parcel of the reforms.

   ☞ part and parcel of sth で「〈物事〉の重要部分、眼目」

▶ 関連表現

- 不在連絡票を受け取った。

   ○ I received [got] a notice of nondelivery while I was away.

   ☞ 自分が直接受け取らなくてもこのように言える

▶ ストーリー

These days it is very easy to **send parcels**, or even **large items of luggage**. You only have to go to **your local convenience store** and **give them the parcel**. It will probably **be sent off the same day**, and **be delivered the next day**. This is **an unbelievably efficient service**.

(最近では、小包はもちろん大きな荷物でさえもとても簡単に送ることができる。地元のコンビニに行って小包を預けるだけである。それは恐らく即日発送され、次の日に配達されるであろう。これは信じられないほど効率的なサービスである。)

079　PET　　　　　　　　　　　　　　　C

ペットは疲れた現代人を癒してくれる貴重な存在の一つである。近年の「ペットブーム」がそれを物語っており、広告やCMにも犬やネコは頻繁に登場している。動物の好き嫌いに関わらず、ここに紹介した程度の表現はマスターし、ボキャブラリーの幅を広げておこう。
✱〈決まり文句〉であげた 'pet' の形容詞的用法に注意。

>> **FAMILY; HOME; LOVE**

▶ pet から広がるボキャブラリー：名詞表現

- ペットにえさをやる ○ feed my pet ☞ feed my baby「子供に食事を与える」
- ペットの世話をする ○ look after a pet
- リスをペットとして飼う ○ keep a squirrel as a pet
- ペットをかわいがる ○ pamper a pet ☞ pamper a child「子供を甘やかす」
- find a lost pet ○ いなくなったペットを見つける ☞ get lost「道に迷う」
- ペットのウサギと仲良くする
  ○ have a close relationship with my pet rabbit
- タマ を「ペット」としてよりも「仲間の動物」と見なす
  ○ regard Tama as an 'animal companion' rather than a 'pet'
- うちのペットを家族の一員であると考える
  ○ consider our pet to be one of the family
- ペットがいなくなって非常に悲しい
  ○ feel very sad at the loss of a pet ☞ feel sad about his death「彼の死を悲しむ」
- ペットのふんを拾う[片づける] ○ pick up my pet's droppings
- (毎年の) 予防接種を打つためペットを獣医のところに連れて行く
  ○ take my pet to the vet's to get his shots ☞ vet's「動物病院」
- 病気のペットを永眠させてくれるよう獣医に頼む
  ○ ask the vet to put my sick pet to sleep ☞ put *sb* to sleep「〈人〉を眠らせる」

▶ 関連表現

- 珍しい [外来の] ペット ○ an exotic pet ☞ exotic plants「外来植物」

- 家の中で飼うペット（家猫など） ◯ a household pet
- 捨てられたペット ◯ an abandoned pet ☞ an abandoned car「乗り捨てられた車」
- 家の中に舞い込んできたセキセイインコ
  ◯ a budgie which flew into our house
- ヘビをペットにする［かわいがる］ ◯ make a pet of a snake
- 犬を去勢する ◯ neuter my dog
- 猫の卵巣を除去する ◯ spay my cat
- ペットボトル ◯ a plastic bottle
  ☞ 日本語の「ペットボトル」の 'PET' は 'polyethylene terephthalete'（ポリエチレンテレフタレート）の略だが、英語では普通 a plastic bottle と言うので注意

▶決まり文句

- テレビのワイドショーは私の大嫌いなものの一つだ。
  ◯ TV gossip shows are one of my pet hates.
  ☞ a pet hate《英》[a pet peeve《米》] は「虫の好かないもの・人」の意味
- 私は持論を説明した。◯ I explained my pet theory. ☞ pet は「お気に入りの、得意の」の意味。
- ボブは自分の得意なお題目をしゃべりまくった。
  ◯ Bob went on about his pet subject.
  ☞ go on about sth「〈物〉についてとりとめなくしゃべる」。上3例の 'pet' は、聞いている方に「退屈さ」や「いらだち」を連想させる

▶ストーリー

I found our cat, Mr. Suzuki, after he **had been abandoned**. He **is very easy to look after**. In fact, he basically **takes care of himself**. There is an old English saying that **'a dog is a man's best friend'**. Although Mr. Suzuki is a cat, he is certainly **one of my best friends**.

（我が家の猫であるミスター鈴木を見つけるのは、彼が捨てられた後だった。彼はとても世話がしやすい。現に彼は基本的に自分で自分の面倒を見るのである。英語に「犬は人間の最良の友である」ということわざがある。ミスター鈴木は猫であるが、彼は間違いなく私の最良の友の一人である。）

080 POLITICS ⓤ

生活空間の中で頻出する 'politics' に関わる表現を集めてみると、好ましくない意味を表すものが多く驚かされる。これらは現代の世相を映し出しているとも言えるだろう。新聞・ニュースで毎日のように話題に上るものでもあり、しっかりマスターしておきたい。
✼基本的に 'politics' の形で ⓤ 扱いであるが、複数扱いされる場合もあり、用例で確認しておこう (☞*)。

>> ECONOMY; GOVERNMENT; COUNTRY / NATION

▶ politics から広がるボキャブラリー：名詞表現

- 政党政治；党派活動；政党の駆け引き ◯ party politics
- 地方政治 ◯ local politics
- 急進的な政治 ◯ radical politics ☞ a radical reform「抜本的改革」
- 環境保護主義政治；環境保護政策 ◯ green politics
- 国際政治；世界政治 ◯ global politics
- 国内政治 ◯ domestic politics
- 民主党の政策 ◯ the politics of the Democratic Party
- 議会政治 ◯ parliamentary politics
- 政治と行政 ◯ politics and administration
- 会社での処世術；対人工作 ◯ office politics
- あなたはどの政党を支持して [政治についてどう考えて] いますか。
  ◯ What are your politics?*

▶ politics から広がるボキャブラリー：動詞表現

- 政界に入る ◯ go into politics ☞ go into business「事業を始める」
- 政治に対して深い興味を持つ ◯ have a deep interest in politics
- 好んで政治を論じる ◯ like to talk politics ☞ talk business / sports「商売の話をする/スポーツを語る」
- 政治には興味がない。 ◯ Politics do [does] not interest me.*
- 地方政治の腐敗を一掃する ◯ clean up local politics
- 悪徳政治家を政界から引退させる
  ◯ force a crooked politician to retire from politics ☞ a crooked

cop「悪徳警官」
- ❏ 政治の話題を避ける ◎ steer the conversation away from politics
  - ☞ steer sb away from sth「〈人〉を〈物事〉から引き離す」の応用
- ❏ 選挙民の願いを無視する一方で策を弄して私利を図る2つの政党
  ◎ two parties playing politics while ignoring the wishes of the electorate ☞ play doctor「お医者さんごっこをする」
- ❏ 政治と宗教を一緒くたにする ◎ mix politics and religion

▶ 関連表現

- ❏ すべての政治家に疑いを抱く
  ◎ feel suspicious of all politicians ☞ be suspicious of sb/sth「〈人/事〉に疑念を抱く、不審に思う」
- ❏ 自分の支持する政治家に投票する
  ◎ vote for the politician I support
- ❏ 当選しなかった政治家 ◎ a politican who failed to get elected
- ❏ 自分の選挙区に頻繁に戻る政治家
  ◎ a politician who frequently returns to his constituency
- ❏ 政治家と大企業との癒着
  ◎ the connection between politicians and big business
- ❏ 政治家に裏切られた思いの有権者
  ◎ an electorate [iléktərət] which feel betrayed by their politicians

▶ ストーリー

Many people **are not very interested in politics. Politics can certainly be boring**, and all too often we find that '**politics' means politicians playing politics for their own interests**. But nevertheless, **it is perhaps our duty to understand and follow politics**.

(多くの人が政治にあまり興味を持っていない。政治は確かに退屈な場合があるし、「政治」といえば政治家が私利私欲のために策を弄することを意味する場合があまりにも多い。しかしそれにもかかわらず、政治を理解し、それに注目していくことは、ひょっとしたら我々の義務かもしれない。)

081 QUALITY / QUANTITY ····· CU

質が求められるのは食べ物だけではない。'quality of life'（生活の充実度）という表現に代表されるように、サービスや制度など生活空間の中であらゆるものが対象になる。

対立概念である「量」(quantity) と合わせて論じられる場合も多く、この2語に関わる代表的な表現を合わせてマスターしておきたい。

- quality: 品質を指す場合☞ U、特定の特徴や特性を指す場合 ☞ C
- quantity: 基本的に☞ U、「部分」や「分け前」に近い意味のとき ☞ C
  （頻出する 'a ～ quantity of' の形にも注意☞*）

>> **DRINK**(酒類); **DRINK**(清涼飲料); **FOOD**

▶ 「質」(quality) に関わる表現

- ❏ 質の悪い服 ○ clothes of poor quality U
- ❏ 優れた品質の商品 ○ goods of excellent quality
- ❏ その品は質が悪い。○ The goods are of inferior quality.
- ❏ どこかエロチックなところがある絵
  ○ a painting with a certain erotic quality
- ❏ 最高級の食べ物とサービス ○ top quality food and service ☞ この
  qualityは「高品質の」の意味の形容詞。a quality newspaper「高級紙」
- ❏ 品質管理のシステム ○ a system of quality control
- ❏ 患者の（質的な）生活水準 ○ a patient's quality of life
- ❏ 価格を安く抑え品質を高く保つ
  ○ keep the price low and the quality high
- ❏ 可能な限り質の高い野菜を手に入れようとする
  ○ try to obtain the best possible quality of vegetables
  ☞ the best -est「考えうる最高の」（いろいろな形容詞の最上級がくる）
- ❏ 教育の質を改善する ○ improve the quality of education
- ❏ ダイアモンドの特性 ○ the special qualities of a diamond C
  ☞ personal qualities「個性」

▶ 「量」(quantity) に関わる表現

- ❏ 情報の量 ○ the quantity of information U

- ごく小量の毒 ◎ a tiny quantity of poison*
- かなりの量の食べ物 ◎ a considerable quantity of food*
- 膨大な量の仕事をこなす ◎ do a vast quantity of work*
- ある薬の量を測る ◎ measure the quantity of a certain medicine
- 食糧を大量に買う ◎ buy food in large quantites ⓒ
  - ☞ ×'in *big* quantities' とは言わないことに注意
- 金鉱石の鉱床を大量に見つける
  - ◎ find deposits of gold ore in quantity ☞ このdepositは「(金・鉱物などの) 鉱床、埋蔵物 堆積物」の意味。glacial deposits「氷河堆積物」
- 食物の輸入量が半分になった。
  - ◎ Imports of food halved in quantity. ☞ halveは「半減する」という動詞

▶ quality を用いた対句

- 質と量の改善 ◎ an improvement in quality and quantity
- 製品の品質とコスト ◎ the quality and cost of the product
- 製品の信頼性と品質を保証する
  - ◎ guarantee the reliability and quality of a product
- コストは大きさ、量、そして品質次第である。
  - ◎ Cost depends on size, quantity, and quality.
- 高品質で効率的そして役に立つサービスを提供する
  - ◎ provide a high quality, efficient and helpful service

▶ ストーリー

Whether to **concentrate on quality or quantity**? Should I buy **one top-quality shirt**, or **three shirts of lower quality**? I myself tend to **go for quantity rather than quality**, as long as **the quality is not too low**. Of course, the ideal is to **find top quality at a low price**.

(質と量どちらを重視すべきか。最高級のシャツを一枚買ったほうがよいのか、あるいは低品質のシャツを三枚買ったほうがよいのか? 私自身、その質があまりにも低くなければ、どちらかというと質より量を求める傾向がある。もちろん、理想は低価格で最高級のものを見つけることだが。)

082　RELIGION　　　　　　　　　　C U

> 日本では宗教についての意識が希薄な面もあるが、英語圏では'religion'は間違いなく生活空間の核の一つである。なじみのないものもあるかと思われるが、以下の表現は確実に押さえておきたい。
> C　特定の宗派やいろいろな宗教について述べる場合 ☞ C
> U　宗教一般や信仰・信仰心について述べる場合 ☞ U
>
> **>> DEATH; LIFE**

▶ religion から広がるボキャブラリー：名詞表現

- 国家宗教；公式の宗教 ○ a state religion ☞ state ceremonies「公式行事」
- 個人的な宗教 [信条] ○ a personal religion
- 宗教への没頭 ○ a preoccupation with religion ☞ their main preoccupation「彼らの主な仕事」
- 信教の自由 ○ freedom of religion Ⓤ
- 国家による宗教への干渉 ○ interference by the state in religion
  ☞ interfere in *sth*「〈事〉に干渉する」の名詞表現
- 宗教により分裂させられた国 ○ a country divided by religion
- 一神教 ○ a monotheistic religion
- 多神教 ○ a polytheistic religion
- 宗教とカルトの違い
  ○ the difference between a religion and a cult
- 比較宗教学 ○ the comparative study of religion ☞ with comparative comfort「比較的快適に」
- 道徳 [人の道] を教える宗教 ○ a religion which teaches morality
- 世界の偉大な宗教の一つ ○ one of the great religions of the world

▶ religion から広がるボキャブラリー：動詞表現

- 宗教を信じる ○ believe in religion
- 信仰を実践する ○ practise a religion
- 厳格に信仰に従う ○ strictly observe a religion
- 宗教と政治をめぐって争う ○ fight over religion and politics
- 私たちはすべての宗教に対して寛大であるべきだ。

- ○ We should <u>be tolerant towards</u> all religions. [C] ☞ be tolerant of sb's mistakes「〈人〉の失敗に対して寛大である」
- ❏ 信仰の自由を享受する ○ enjoy freedom of religion
- ❏ 国家と宗教を分離する ○ separate the state and religion
- ❏ 私は宗教に関心がない [無頓着だ]。○ I <u>am indifferent to</u> religion.

▶ 関連表現

- ❏ 信仰の厚い人 ○ a religious person
- ❏ 宗教的な生活 [信仰生活] を送る ○ lead a <u>religious life</u>
- ❏ 宗教的思想の歴史 ○ the history of religious thought
- ❏ 宗教の原理主義者 ○ a religious fundamentalist

▶ 決まり文句

- ❏ ボブは運動を生きがいにしている。
  ○ Bob <u>makes a religion of</u> exercise.
  ☞ make a religion of sth「〈事〉を後生大事にする」
- ❏ 私は細心の注意を払ってその仕事を行った。
  ○ I did the job <u>with religious care</u>.
- ❏ 宗教はアヘンである。
  ○ Religion is the opium of the masses. [U] ☞ Karl Marxの言葉

▶ ストーリー

If we **'pray' for something** for purely selfish reasons, this is not **an example of praying**, but **of making a wish**. Such an action is **not connected to religion, but to superstition**. If we **pray for help in time of difficulty**, or **pray for others to be helped**, this is **an example of prayer**.

(もし私たちがただ利己的な理由のために何かを求めて「祈る」なら、これは祈りではなく願いをかけている例なのである。このような行動は宗教ではなく迷信に結びついたものである。もし私たちが困っているときに助けを求めて祈るか、あるいは他の人たちが助けの手をさしのべられることを祈るなら、これが祈るということの例なのである。)

083 ROAD 〔C〕

> 道は生活空間の基盤となるインフラであり、以下のような位置や案内や行動に関わる表現を構成する要素としても重要である。
> ✻ここには含めなかったが、'road'には「(成功への)道、手段」という比喩的な意味もある。
> 例 the road to success 成功への道　the road to ruin 荒廃への道
> The road to hell is paved with good intentions.
> 地獄に続く道は善意で舗装されている。(諺)
>
> **>> ACCIDENT; AMBULANCE / FIRE BRIGADE / POLICE; CAR; TRAVEL**

▶ road から広がるボキャブラリー

- 狭く曲がりくねった道路 ◯ a narrow, winding road
- でこぼこの未舗装道路 ◯ a rough unpaved road ☞ paved「舗装された」
- 何とか通行可能な道路 ◯ a road that is scarcely passable ☞ Her French is passable. 「彼女のフランス語はなんとか通じる」
- 穴ぼこだらけの道 ◯ a road which is full of potholes
- 道幅を広げる ◯ widen a road
- 新しい道路の建設 ◯ the construction of a new road
- 道路のインフラに投資する ◯ invest in road infrastructure [ínfrəstrÀktʃər] ☞ infrastructureとは経済活動や社会生活の基盤を形成する構造物(水道・電気・公共交通機関など)を指す

▶「位置」に関わる表現

- さらに道を進んで[進んだところに] ◯ further up the road
- 道の真ん中を歩く ◯ walk in the middle of the road
- 道端に何かが見える ◯ see something on the side of the road
- 道の両側に植樹する ◯ plant trees on both sides of a road
- 道路の反対車線を走る ◯ drive on the wrong side of the road
  ☞ the wrong side of a sheet of carbon paper「紙の裏側」

▶「ナビ(案内)」に関わる表現

- 詳細な道路地図 ◯ a detailed road map

- その区域の道に精通している ◯ know the roads of the area
- 北へ向かう道を走る ◯ drive on the road going north
- 本道へとつながる道をたどる
  ◯ follow a road which <u>leads to</u> the main road
- この道からそれて脇道に入る ◯ <u>turn off</u> this road into a sideroad
- 裏道を走り続けて本道を避ける
  ◯ <u>keep to</u> the back roads and avoid the main roads
- 大通りの混雑と交通渋滞を避ける
  ◯ avoid the congestion and traffic jams on the main roads
- どの道を行ったらよいのかわからない
  ◯ do not know which road to choose
- 間違った道を選ぶ ◯ take the wrong road
- 間違った角を曲がった後、ランプ（高速出入り口）をバックする
  ◯ <u>reverse up</u> a slip road after taking a wrong turning ☞ reverse /sth/ up「〈道〉を逆に進む」

▶「行動」に関わる表現

- 運転中他の車にかっとなりやすい ◯ <u>have a tendency to</u> road rage
- メグはひどく無謀[乱暴]な運転手だ。
  ◯ Meg is a terrible road hog. ☞ 道路の真ん中を運転するなど
- 交通安全に注意を払う ◯ <u>pay attention to</u> road safety
- 警察の道路封鎖に車を止める ◯ <u>stop at</u> a police road block

▶ ストーリー

The road was a very demanding one. It was narrow and winding, and also **very bumpy. When we reached the mountains, the hairpin bends were really sharp**. But **Meg handled the car with skill**, as **we ate up the miles**.

（その道路はすごく運転技術を要するものだった。狭くて、曲がりくねっていて、さらにすごくでこぼこしていた。山に着くと、数あるヘアピンカーブは本当に急だった。しかし、目的地までの距離をぐんぐん縮めながら、メグはうまく車を操縦していった。）

084　SEASON　　Ⓒ

> 日本だけでなく、英語圏にも四季の移り変わりがはっきりしている地域は多い。気候の面だけでなく精神面にも大きな影響を与える 'season' は生活空間の Core Nouns の一つと言えるだろう。
>
> 　日本語で「〜シーズン」と言うように、'season' は「季節」だけでなく「(〜の)時季」の文脈でも用いられる。四季全体だけでなく、各季節(春夏秋冬)に関わる頻出表現も紹介した。
>
> ✱ 春夏秋冬は以下のような ⒸⓊ の区別がある。
>
> Ⓒ/Ⓤ ｛ 個別に扱ったり、「〜の春」などと特定の呼び方をする場合 ☞ Ⓒ
> 　　　 季節を自然現象として述べる場合 ☞ Ⓤ
>
> **>> HOLIDAY; WEATHER**

▶「季節」に関わる表現

- 一年の四季 ◯ the four seasons of the year
- 雨季；梅雨 ◯ the rainy season ☞ The rainy season has set in.「梅雨入りした」 for a rainy day「まさかの時のため」
- ホリデーシーズン ◯ the holiday season
- 海水浴場の閑散期 ◯ the off-season at a seaside resort
- 観光(客)シーズン真っ只中に ◯ at the height of the tourist season
  ☞ be at the height of one's popularity「人気絶頂にある」
- 牡蠣(かき)が旬の季節 ◯ the oyster season
- 季節外れの果物を買う ◯ buy fruit that is out of season
- イチゴが旬になった。◯ Strawberries have come into season.

▶「春」に関わる表現

- 雨がちの春 ◯ a wet spring Ⓒ
- よく晴れた春の日 ◯ a beautiful spring day
- 春に咲く花 ◯ the flowers that come out in spring Ⓤ
- 遅く来る春 ◯ a spring that is late in coming

▶「夏」に関わる表現

- 真夏に；夏の真っ盛りに ◯ at the height of summer
- 1999年の春と夏に ◯ in the spring and summer of 1999

- ❏ 夏の10週間に ◯ for ten weeks in the summer
- ❏ 夏に海辺での長い休暇をとる
  ◯ have a long seaside holiday in the summer
- ❏ 夏の夕方の突然の雷雨
  ◯ a sudden thunderstorm on a summer evening

▶ 「秋」に関わる表現

- ❏ 初秋に ◯ early in the autumn [fall《米》]
- ❏ 秋の新しい装い ◯ the new autumn fashions
- ❏ 秋の作物を採り入れる ◯ <u>bring in</u> the autumn harvest ☞ bring in a new tax law「新税法を導入する」
- ❏ 秋の色彩を楽しむ ◯ enjoy the autumn colours

▶ 「冬」に関わる表現

- ❏ 真冬に ◯ <u>in the depths of</u> winter ☞ in the depths of the recession「不況の真っ只中に」
- ❏ 穏やかな冬 ◯ a mild winter
- ❏ 厳しい冬 ◯ a harsh winter
- ❏ 雪のまったくない冬 ◯ a winter without any snow
- ❏ 吹雪の到来 ◯ the coming of the winter storms
- ❏ 冬の衣類を買う ◯ buy winter clothing

▶ ストーリー

People often **ask what one's favourite season is**. I myself **like spring and autumn best**. I like **watching out for the first signs of spring**, and **the days that become longer and warmer**. **I like autumn** because I **like to look at the leaves turning yellow and red**.

(人はしばしば一番好きな季節は何かとたずねる。私自身は春と秋が一番好きである。私は春の訪れの気配に注意を払い、日がだんだん長く暖かくなっていくのを見るのが好きである。秋が好きなのは、木の葉が紅葉するのを見るのが好きだからである。)

085 SEA ··· [C][U] / SEASIDE ··· [U]

> 海は「娯楽」の対象・場所としてのイメージが強いが、一方では守るべき「環境」として話題に上ることが非常に多くなっている。ここでも、この2つの視点から 'sea' と 'seaside' に関わる表現を時事性の高いものも含めて紹介した。
>
> ✻ 'sea' については以下の[C][U]の区別に注意。
>
> [U]
> ┌ 波の状態について述べる場合 ☞ [C]
> │ （通常 'a ～ sea' の形で用いられる。〈ストーリー〉を参照）
> └ 水の広がりあるいは自然現象としてとらえた場合 ☞ [U]
> 　（通常 'the sea' の形で用いられる）
>
> ✻ 'sea' と 'seaside'
> 'sea' にも「海辺」の意味があるが、'seaside' は「陸が海と出会うところ」というイメージが強くなる。ふつう 'the' をつけて用いられる。
>
> **>> COUNTRY / COUNTRYSIDE; ENVIRONMENT; HOLIDAY; TRAVEL; WEEKEND**

▶「娯楽」に関わる表現

❏ 休日の行楽客でいっぱいの海水浴場 [シーサイドリゾート]
　◯ a seaside resort full of holidaymakers

❏ 我が家の毎年恒例の海辺で過ごす休暇
　◯ our family's annual seaside holiday

❏ かつて流行っていた海辺のホテル
　◯ a once-fashionable seaside hotel ☞ once-famous「昔有名だった」

❏ 休暇に（保養や海水浴などで）海辺に行く
　◯ go to the seaside for my holidays ☞ 前置詞に注意

❏ 海辺で数日を楽しむ ◯ enjoy a few days at the seaside

❏ 海が見えるホテルの部屋 ◯ a hotel room with a sea view

❏ 海を見晴らす別荘 ◯ a holiday house overlooking the sea [U]

❏ 海をこよなく愛する ◯ have a great love of the sea

❏ 海辺へ日帰り旅行をする ◯ take a one-day trip to the seaside
　☞ a two-day trip「一泊二日の旅」

❏ 海に近いホテルに滞在する ◯ stay in a hotel close to the sea

❏ 毎年多くの遊泳者が海で行方不明になっている。
　◯ A large number of swimmers are lost at sea every year.

▶「環境」に関わる表現

- 海水の侵入を防ぐための堤防を作る
  - ◯ build seawalls to keep out the sea ☞ keep /sth/ out「〈物〉が入り込まないようにする」
- 海を埋め立てて陸にする [干拓する] ◯ reclaim land from the sea
  ☞ reclaim iron from scrap「鉄くずから鉄を再生利用する」
- 海上のタンカーから漏れ出た油 ◯ an oil spill from a tanker at sea
- 瀬戸内海の赤潮 ◯ a red tide on the Inland Sea
- 海を汚染する ◯ pollute the sea
- 海をゴミ箱のように考える
  - ◯ consider the sea as a kind of garbage can
- 未処理の下水を海に流し込む
  - ◯ pump untreated sewage into the sea ☞ untreated「(廃液・有毒物などが) 未処理の」
- 多くの種類の海鳥のすみかを破壊する
  - ◯ destroy the habitat of many kinds of sea birds
- 乱獲により海の生態系のバランスを乱す
  - ◯ disturb the ecological balance of the sea by overfishing
- 海洋資源の有効活用を図る
  - ◯ try to use the resources of the seas efficiently

▶ ストーリー

When I was a young boy, we **used to live at the seaside**. In fact, **our house was almost on the beach**. When **the sea was very rough, it used to come right up the beach and into our house**. Still today, more than any other sound, I **love the sound of the waves** — **the waves of a calm sea**, or **the waves of a rough sea**.

(私が少年だったとき、私たちは海辺に住んでいた。というよりも家はほとんど砂浜の上にあった。海がすごく荒れると、浜を昇ってよく我が家に浸水してきた。今日でも私は他のどんな音よりも波の音が好きである。それが穏やかな海の波であっても荒れた海の波であっても。)

086 SHOPPING　　　　　　　　　　　U

> ひと口に買い物と言っても、現代ではその対象や買い物をする場所により千差万別の感がある（場合によっては、同じ行為にもかかわらず「買い物」と「ショッピング」のように区別される）。ここでは、日常生活の空間で「買う」行為一般に関してよく用いられる表現を紹介した。
> 〈関連表現〉で取り上げたクレームに関する表現も要注意。
> **>> DEPARTMENT STORE / SUPERMARKET; HOUSEWORK; MONEY**

▶ shopping から広がるボキャブラリー：名詞表現

- ❏ ショッピングモール ◯ a shopping mall
- ❏ 複合型ショッピングセンター ◯ a shopping complex ☞ a cinema complex「シネコン」complexは「複数の施設が入った複合ビル」を言う
- ❏ 地域の大手ショッピングセンター
  ◯ a major regional shopping centre
- ❏ ウィンドーショッピングをしに行く ◯ go window shopping
- ❏ 商品を比べながら買物をする ◯ do comparison shopping
- ❏ クリスマスの買い物をすべて終える
  ◯ finish all the Christmas shopping
- ❏ 空港で免税の買い物をする
  ◯ do my duty-free shopping at the airport
- ❏ いらない服を衝動買いする
  ◯ buy unnecessary clothes on impulse ☞ an impulse buyer「衝動買いをする人」

▶ shopping から広がるボキャブラリー：動詞表現

- ❏ 買い物リストを作る ◯ make a shopping list
- ❏ 少し買い物をする ◯ do a bit of shopping
- ❏ 買い物を手伝う ◯ help out with the shopping
- ❏ 買い物に繰り出す ◯ set out on a shopping expedition
- ❏ 派手に買い物をしに出かける ◯ go on a shopping spree ☞ a spree「ばか騒ぎ」have a spree「浮かれ騒ぐ、痛飲する」

- 買い物に繰り出した後へとへとに疲れる
  - feel exhausted after a shopping expedition
- その老婦人は買い物袋をいくつも持ってすごく重そうにしている。
  - The old lady is weighed down with shopping bags.
  - ☞ be weighed down with sth「〈物〉で押しつぶされそうになる」

▶ 関連表現

- 服を選ぶのに一緒に三越に買い物に行く
  - go shopping together at Mitsukoshi to choose some clothes
  - ☞ go skiing / swimming などと同じ用法。「〜に」はto〜でないことに注意
- 私は万引きの容疑で逮捕された。 ○ I was arrested for shoplifting.
- ほしい物が満足できる価格で見つかるまでは店を見て回る価値がある。
  - It's worth shopping around until you find what you want at the right price.
- 腐った卵を買う ○ buy eggs that are off
- すっぱいミルクに文句を言う ○ complain about milk that is sour
- 賞味期限を過ぎたベーコンを返品する
  - return bacon that is past its 'best-by' date
- 腐ったトマトのお金を返してもらう
  - get a refund for some rotten tomatoes
- 安物買いの銭失い。 ○ Buy cheap and waste your money.
  - ☞ buy cheapは「安く買う」の意味

▶ ストーリー

I often **go shopping for food at the local supermarket**. I **do not really like shopping**, so I try to finish as quickly as possible. I find that **making a shopping list beforehand makes shopping easier**. It also **cuts out impulse buying**, so it **saves me money**.

(私は地元のスーパーマーケットによく食べ物を買いに行く。私は本当は買い物が好きではないので、できるだけ早く終わろうとする。あらかじめ買い物リストを作ると買い物がもっと簡単になる。そうすることにより衝動買いもしなくなるので、お金の節約になる。)

087 SLEEP ... C U

眠りは時間的に我々の生活の三分の一をしめる大変重要なものであり、「夢」と同じように、いずれの言語でも「眠り」に関することわざやイディオムは多いようである。ここでは 'sleep' を用いた日常的な表現を中心に紹介した。'sleep' とコロケーションを作る語句とその用法まであわせて押さえておきたい。

- ひと眠り（の時間）を意識して述べる場合 ☞ C
- 眠りについて一般的に述べる場合 ☞ U

>> DAY / NIGHT; DREAM

▶「安眠」に関わる表現

- すぐうとうとしてしまう ◯ easily drop off to sleep
- 深い眠りに落ちる ◯ fall into a deep sleep ☞ fall into a doze「うとうとする」
- 夜ぐっすり眠る ◯ have a good night's sleep
- 毎晩8時間眠る ◯ get eight hours' sleep every night
- 日中に睡眠時間を見つける
  ◯ find time for a sleep in the middle of the day C
- 私は寝つきがよい。◯ Sleep comes easily for me. U
- 音楽のおかげで眠れた。◯ The music sent me to sleep. ☞ send Bob to his death「ボブを死に追いやる」

▶「睡眠不足・寝つきの悪さ」に関わる表現

- 私は睡眠不足で悩んでいる。◯ I am suffering from a lack of sleep.
- 寝不足で目がかすんでいる。◯ I am short of sleep, and bleary-eyed.
  ☞ be short of money「お金が足りない」
- ほんの少ししか寝ていない ◯ get only a short period of sleep
- 寝つけない ◯ cannot get to sleep
- いびきをかく ◯ snore in my sleep
- 寝言を言う ◯ talk in my sleep
- 睡眠障害がある ◯ have a sleep disorder
- 寝ぼけて歩く ◯ walk in my sleep
- 私はぐっすり眠ることが必要だ。◯ I am in need of a good sleep.

☞ be in great need「大変お金に困っている」
- ボブを眠りから目覚めさせる ○ rouse Bob from his sleep
- 起こされた後、もう一度眠ることができなかった。
    ○ I could not get back to sleep after I was woken up.
- ボブは睡眠中に突然亡くなった。 ○ Bob died suddenly in his sleep.

▶ 関連表現

- 昼までゆっくり寝ている ○ sleep in until midday
- ぐっすり眠る ○ sleep soundly
- 眠りが浅い ○ sleep lightly
    ☞ 上の3例のsleepは動詞
- 毎晩同じ夢を見る ○ have the same dream every night
- 夜遅くまでぱっちり目が覚めている ○ be wide awake late at night
- ちょっとうたた寝をする ○ grab a quick nap ☞ このgrabは「飲食物・睡眠などをすばやく取る」という意味。 cf. grab a lunch (No.027)
- かなり眠気を催す ○ feel rather drowsy
- 右腕がしびれた。 ○ My right arm went to sleep. ☞ 比喩的な表現

▶ 決まり文句

- そのことでくよくよしてはいけない。 ○ Don't lose any sleep over it.
- 昨夜は熟睡した。 ○ Last night I slept like a log. (動詞)

▶ ストーリー

Some people seem to **need very little sleep**, and **sleep just a few hours a night**. In most such cases, we find that such people have the ability to **take very short naps during the day**, and in this way **catch up on the sleep** that they do not get at night.

(ほとんど睡眠を必要としなくて、毎晩2、3時間しか眠っていないように思われる人がいる。そのような人たちはたいていの場合、日中にこまぎれの睡眠をとる能力があり、そうすることにより夜の睡眠不足を取り戻しているのである。)

088 SOCIETY ... C U

社会は形として意識されることはないが、漠然と我々の生活空間を指す場合、あるいは「〜社会」のように、時代や文化の特徴を一括りにして呼ぶ場合にしばしば用いられる。ここでもこの2つの視点から 'society' に関わる表現を紹介する。

- 社会のタイプや特定の会、協会、組合などを指す場合 ☞ C
- 社会の構造について述べる場合や、「社交界」などのように共通の信念としきたりで成り立っている集まりや交際を指す場合 ☞ U

>> COUNTRY / NATION; ECONOMY; GOVERNMENT; POLITICS

▶ society から広がるボキャブラリー

- 文明社会 ◯ a civilized society C ☞ a civilized nation「文明国」
- 豊かな社会 ◯ an affluent society ☞ an affluent family「裕福な家族」
- 公正な社会 ◯ a just society ☞ a just war「正しい戦争」
- 閉鎖社会 ◯ a closed society ☞ behind closed doors「密かに、非公開で」
- 伝統的な社会 ◯ a traditional society
- 封建制社会 ◯ a feudal society ☞ the feudal system「封建制度」
- 識字率の高い社会 ◯ a highly literate society
- 識字率の低い社会 ◯ a society with a low level of literacy
- 近代的な産業社会 ◯ a modern industrial society
- 戦後の日本社会 ◯ postwar Japanese society
- 友達とのつき合いを楽しむ ◯ enjoy the society of my friends U
  ☞ seek the society of sb「〈人〉との交際を求める」

▶「社会のしくみ」に関わる表現

- （階層間の）流動性のある社会
  ◯ a society with social mobility
- 皆が平等の権利を持っている社会
  ◯ a society in which everyone has equal rights
- 多くの不平等がある社会 ◯ a society with many inequalities
- ある社会の中で一般的な考え方
  ◯ a way of thinking that is common within a society

- ❏ 社会に対する移民の影響
  - ⬥ **the impact of immigrants on a society** ☞ an impact on *sth*「〈物事〉の影響、効果」
- ❏ 社会における若者の役割 ⬥ **the role of young people in society**
- ❏ 社会の構造的な変化を起こしうる要因
  - ⬥ **factors which can cause structural changes in society**
  - ☞ structural defects「構造上の欠陥」
- ❏ 社会全体に影響を与える政治的な決定
  - ⬥ **political decisions which affect the society as a whole**
- ❏ 社会に対して危険を及ぼす病気
  - ⬥ **a disease which poses a danger to society** ☞ pose a threat to *sth*「〈物事〉に脅威をもたらす」
- ❏ 社会における宗教の役割についてさまざまな意見を持っている
  - ⬥ **have differing views about the role of religion in society**
- ❏ 性犯罪者の社会復帰に反対する市民運動
  - ⬥ **a citizens movement against the return of sex offenders to society**
- ❏ 社会全体が大気汚染、騒音、交通事故の代償を払う。
  - ⬥ **Society at large pays for air pollution, noise, and road accidents.** ☞ at large は as a whole とほぼ同義
- ❏ 日本は今や多民族の社会だ。 ⬥ **Japan is now a multiracial society**
  - ☞ a homogeneous society「単一民族の社会」

▶ ストーリー

Gulliver's Travels, by Johnathan Swift, is **a social satire** which seeks to **examine and question the values of the society of Swift's time**. Much that people **accept as natural in their society**, when examined closely, often seems ridiculous.

(ジョナサン・スイフト作『ガリバー旅行記』は、スイフトの時代の社会の価値観を検討し異議を唱えようとした社会風刺文学である。人々が自分の社会で当然と受け入れていることの多くが、よく調べると、ばかばかしく思われることがしばしばある。)

089 SPORT　　　　　　　　　　　　　　　　　C

スポーツは、するだけでなく観る娯楽として生活空間に欠かせないものである。ここでは実用面から、'sport' と共に用いる動詞に注目したい。特に〈使い分けのポイント〉と〈ストーリー〉では、各種競技と動詞の使い分けを解説してある。

✽ 基本的に C だが、単複で次のような大まかな使い分けがある。
- 特定の競技やスポーツの種類を指す場合 ☞ 単数形
- スポーツについて一般的に述べる場合 ☞ 複数形

>> ENJOYMENT; FITNESS; HOBBY

▶ sport から広がるボキャブラリー：名詞表現

- 観て楽しむスポーツ [観戦スポーツ] ◯ a spectator sport ☞ a mere spectator「単なる傍観者」
- 体がぶつかりあうスポーツ ◯ a contact sport ☞ ラグビー、柔道など。close contact「濃厚接触」
- 屋外スポーツ [アウトドア・スポーツ] ◯ outdoor sports
- アマチュアのスポーツ ◯ amateur sports
- プロのスポーツ ◯ professional sports
- 競技 ◯ a competitive sport ☞ competitive prices「競争力のある価格」
- 冬季スポーツ ◯ winter sports
- 水上スポーツ ◯ water sports
- オリンピック競技 ◯ an Olympic sport

▶ sport から広がるボキャブラリー：動詞表現

- スポーツを始める ◯ <u>take up</u> a sport ☞ 趣味として始めること
- 多くのスポーツをする ◯ play a lot of sports
- スポーツ観戦を楽しむ ◯ enjoy watching sports
- スポーツに熱中する ◯ <u>go in for</u> sports ☞ go in for sth「〈事〉に(趣味・習慣として)こっている」
- スポーツが好きである ◯ be fond of sports
- 何か (習慣的に) 運動をやっていますか。◯ Do you do any sports?

▶「社会のしくみ」に関わる表現

- スポーツ界 ◎ the world of sports [the sporting world]
- 新聞のスポーツ面 ◎ the sports page of a newspaper
- テレビのスポーツ番組 ◎ sports programmes on TV
- テレビによるスポーツ報道 ◎ sports coverage by television
- スポーツ雑誌 ◎ a sports magazine
- スポーツ解説者 ◎ a sports commentator ☞ a political commentator「政治解説者」
- スポーツのプロモーター ◎ a sports promoter

▶「〜をする」動詞の使い分けのポイント

- テニス / 野球 / フットボール / ラグビー / ゴルフをする
  ◎ play tennis / baseball / football / rugby / golf
- スキー / スケート / ハイキング / ロック・クライミングに行く
  ◎ go skiing / skating / hiking / rock climbing
- 柔道 / アーチェリー / バレエをする
  ◎ practise judo / archery / ballet
- 競技 / オリンピックの試合 / 100メートル走のトレーニングをする
  ◎ train for a competition / the Olympic Games / the 100 metres

▶ ストーリー

In this Unit I have made a major exception to my rule of 'minimum slash marks'. Notice that we '**play sports**' that have a field or a playing area. We '**go -ing**' in the case of **outdoor sports** that have no specific areas. We '**practise archery**' because it is not **a game**. It is **a skill** which we **improve by repeated practice**.

(この項では「できるだけスラッシュマークを使わない」という原則に大きな例外を設けた。競技場や運動する場所のあるスポーツをする場合は 'play sports' ということに注意すること。特定の場所を持たない屋外スポーツの場合は、'go ing' という。'practise archery'というのは、アーチェリーが試合ではないからである。アーチェリーは練習を繰り返すことにより向上する技術である。)

SPORT

090 STRESS U

> 現代人の生活はストレスに満ちており、その回避と解消が大きな課題となっていると言えるだろう。ここではストレス「を受ける」「に対処する」という視点から、'stress' に関わる表現を整理した。中でもストレスに対処する動詞表現は重要である。
>
> ✴ 'stress' には、心理的重圧の「ストレス、精神的な緊張」の他、頻度は低いが、「物理的重圧」から比喩的に派生した「強調」の意味もある。
>
> 例 put [lay] stress on something あることを強調する
>
> **>> DIFFICULTY; FAILURE; WORK**

▶「ストレスを受けること」に関わる表現

- 重度のストレス ○ a high level of stress
- ストレスの身体的症状 ○ the physical symptoms of stress ☞ cold symptoms「風邪の諸症状」
- (何かの問題で) ストレスを受けている期間 ○ a period of stress
- ストレスだらけの仕事 ○ a job that is full of stress
- 私は大きな感情的かつ精神的ストレスを受けている。
    ○ I am undergoing great emotional and mental stress.
    ☞ undergo an operation「手術を受ける」
- ストレスのため胃潰瘍になる
    ○ develop an ulcer because of stress ☞ develop cancer「ガンになる」
- ボブは重圧にあえいでいる。○ Bob is under stress. ☞ be under pressure「重圧を受けている」

▶「ストレスに対処すること」に関わる表現

- ストレスの警告となる予兆がわかる
    ○ recognize the warning signs of stress ☞ a sign of life「人の気配」
- 自分のストレスの原因がわかる
    ○ understand the causes of my stress
- メグがストレスに対処するのを手伝う ○ help Meg cope with stress
- ストレス軽減のために運動する ○ exercise in order to relieve stress
- ストレス処理法を教えてくれる特別講習会に通う

○ go to special stress management classes
❏ 深呼吸の訓練をすることによりストレスをコントロールする
○ control my stress by doing deep breathing exercises
❏ ストレス解消法として買い物を選ぶ
○ favour shopping as a means of <u>getting rid of</u> stress ☞ get rid of sb/sth「(好ましくない)〈人/物〉を取り除く、追い払う」

▶ 対句表現

❏ 緊張と重圧 ○ tension and stress
❏ 不安とストレス ○ anxiety and stress
❏ 神経質とストレス ○ nervousness and stress
❏ 精神的プレッシャーとストレス ○ psychological pressure and stress
❏ 私は落ち着かなくて[不安で]かなりストレスを感じている。
○ I am restless and feel a lot of stress. ☞ spend a restless night「眠れぬ夜を過ごす」
❏ ストレスと恐怖の徴候を示す ○ <u>display signs of</u> stress and alarm
❏ 私は現代生活のもたらす緊張に耐えられない。
○ I <u>cannot stand the stresses and strains</u> of modern life.
☞ 例外的にstressが複数形で用いられる決まり文句

▶ ストーリー

People say that **stress is a part of modern life**. But human beings, as a whole, have in all periods of history **experienced about equal levels of stress**. Five hundred or a thousand years ago people **worried about whether** their city would be destroyed and they would be sold into slavery. Today, we **feel anxiety and stress** because we are late for a meeting.

(ストレスは現代生活の一部であると人は言う。しかし人類すべてが、今までの歴史の中でどの時代もほぼ同じレベルのストレスを経験してきた。500年あるいは1000年前には、人々は自分の都市が破壊されるのではないか、自分たちが奴隷として売られてしまうのではないかと心配した。今日、私たちは会議に遅刻するという理由で不安とストレスを感じるのである。)

091 SUCCESS　　　　　　　　　　　 C U

成功の影には失敗があり、逆もまた然りである。この2つに関わる表現を総合的にマスターすることにより、自分の野心や人生計画、あるいは失望などについて英語で自由に話せるようになるであろう。ここでは、'success'を用いた「うまくいく/いかない」場合に関わる表現を整理した。

- 特定の成功事例などについて述べる場合 ☞ C
- 何かをうまくやり遂げることや、人生においてうまくいった経験について一般的に述べる場合 ☞ U

>> AIM; DIFFICULTY; FAILURE; LIFE; LUCK; WORK

▶「うまくいくこと」に関わる表現

- ❏ 計画の完全な成功 ◯ the total success of a plan
- ❏ 成功/自由の味をしめる ◯ get a taste of success / freedom ☞ この taste は「経験」の意味
- ❏ 大きな成功を達成する ◯ achieve great success ᵁ
- ❏ やることなすことすべて大当たりする
  ◯ make a huge success of whatever I do
- ❏ 成功へのカギを見つける ◯ find the key to success
- ❏ 辛抱強さが成功に不可欠の要素であることを知る
  ◯ know that patience is a vital element of success
- ❏ メグが私の計画に同意するよう説得することに成功する
  ◯ have success in persuading Meg to agree to my plan
- ❏ 生徒が大学入試に合格すること
  ◯ the success of students trying to get into university
- ❏ 女優として出世街道を突き進む
  ◯ have a series of successes as an actress ᶜ
- ❏ 私の人生は比類なき出世物語[サクセス・ストーリー]である。
  ◯ My life is one big success story.
- ❏ 私のプランは成功を収めた。◯ My plan met with success.
  ☞ meet with failure「失敗に終わる」。meet with *sth* は「〈事〉を経験する、〈事〉に遭遇する」の意味

▶「うまくいかないこと」に関わる表現

- うまくいく見込みがほどんどない ○ have little chance of success
- うまくいく望みがまあまあある
  ○ have a moderate hope of success ☞ a moderate success「まあまあの成功」
- 成功は期待できない ○ cannot expect success
- ボブの成功をねたむ ○ begrudge [bigrʌ́dʒ] Bob his success
  ☞ begrudge him this success「彼の今度の成功をねたむ」
- 彼は常に成功に見放されてきた。
  ○ Success has always eluded him. ☞ elude sb「〈人〉をうまくかわす」
- 資金難のため我々のプロジェクトの成功が危うくなった。
  ○ The shortage of funds imperilled the success of our project.
  ☞ imperil sb/sth「〈人/事〉を危うくする」

▶決まり文句

- あなたの成功の秘訣を教えてください。
  ○ Tell me the secret of your success.
- 一事成れば万事成る。○ Nothing succeeds like success.《諺》
  ☞ このsucceedは「成功する」ではなく、「続く、連続する」の意

▶ ストーリー

The saying, '**Nothing succeeds like success**' means that if we **achieve success in something, other successes are likely to follow**. If an actor makes a film that **is successful**, he is likely to get a chance to make another film that, hopefully, **will also be successful**. In this way, he **becomes successful** through **having achieved a series of successes**.

(「一事成れば万事成る」ということわざは、私たちが何かで成功すれば、次々と続いて成功する可能性が高いという意味である。もし俳優がある映画で主演して大当たりすれば、続けて映画で主演する可能性が高く、うまくいけばその映画も同じように当たるであろう。このように、彼は次々と成功することによって成功するのである。)

SUCCESS

092 TECHNOLOGY ･･･････ C U

科学技術は我々の生活空間の隅々にまで入り込んでいる。最近では一般向けのメディアでも科学技術の専門用語が当たり前のように用いられていることが多い。ここに紹介したさまざまな'technology'やそれに関わる表現をぜひマスターしておきたい。

- 何かを行うさいの個々の技術や方法について述べる場合 ☞ C
- 「応用化学」「先端技術」「工学」など科学技術の分野について述べる場合 ☞ U (複合語において 'tech' と略される場合が多い)

>> CELLPHONE; COMPUTER; E-MAIL / INTERNET; INDUSTRY / AGRICULTURE

▶ technology から広がるボキャブラリー：名詞表現

- ❏ 新しい技術 ◯ a new technology C
- ❏ 未来の [これからの] 技術 ◯ a future technology
- ❏ 有望な技術 ◯ a promising technology
- ❏ 高度な技術 ◯ an advanced technology
- ❏ 最新の技術 ◯ an up-to-date technology
- ❏ 時代遅れの技術 ◯ an out-of-date technology ☞ 特定の技術を言う
- ❏ 時代遅れの技術 ◯ outdated technology ☞ その分野
- ❏ 最先端の技術 ◯ leading-edge technology
- ❏ 真新しいだけの技術 ◯ new-fangled technology ☞ new-fangled ideas「奇をてらったアイディア」
- ❏ いわゆる「フェールセーフ・テクノロジー」
  ◯ a so-called 'fail-safe technology' ☞ fail-safe「誤作動や誤操作に対する自動安全制御」
- ❏ 核 (科学) 技術 ◯ nuclear technology
- ❏ 最近新しい技術により取って代わられた製造行程
  ◯ a manufacturing process recently overtaken by new technology
- ❏ 技術への科学の適用 [技術に科学を用いること]
  ◯ the application of science to technology U
- ❏ 社会に対する新興技術の影響
  ◯ the impact of emerging technologies on society

❏ 地デジの技術にはいくつかの規格がある。

◎ There are several variants of digital terrestrial television technology [DDTV]. ☞ a variant [vé(ə)riənt]「異形、変形、別形」

▶ technology から広がるボキャブラリー：動詞表現

❏ 新しい技術を採り入れる ◎ adopt new technology
❏ 最新の技術をその産業に応用する

◎ apply the latest technology to the industry

❏ 実証されていない技術の利点を誇張する

◎ make exaggerated claims for an untried technology

❏ 上司は未検証の技術に理解がある [よく受け入れる]。

◎ The boss is receptive to untested technologies.

❏ うちの会社は革新的な技術を受け入れたがらない。

◎ Our company is resistant to innovative technologies.

❏ encourage innovation in technology ◎ 技術革新を奨励する
❏ 新しい技術は私たちにさまざまな恩恵をもたらしてきた。

◎ New technology has brought us a variety of benefits.

❏ 新しい技術が作り出す機会から恩恵を得る

◎ benefit from the opportunities which new technologies create

❏ 現代科学技術に投資する ◎ invest in modern technology
❏ ある新しい技術を軍事目的に利用する

◎ exploit a new technology for military purposes ☞ exploit children「子供を食い物にする」

▶ ストーリー

The pace of technological advance is unbelievably fast. No sooner have we **mastered a new technology** than we find **it is out of date**. Trying to **keep up with new technological developments** is almost impossible.

(科学技術の進歩するペースは信じられないほど速い。我々が新しい技術を習得したかと思うと、それは時代遅れになっている。新しい技術の進展についていこうとしてもほとんど不可能である。)

093 TELEVISION · · · · · · · · · · · · Ⓒ Ⓤ

> メディアが多様化した現在でもテレビは物理的(受像器)にも娯楽(番組)としてもお茶の間の中心的存在である。ここでは後者に関わる実用的な表現と最新技術に関わる話題を中心に紹介する。
> - テレビを電化製品 (a television set) として考える場合 ☞ Ⓒ
> - テレビ放送のシステムや組織や技術について述べる場合 ☞ Ⓤ
>
> ✱番組などがテレビに映っている場合は 'on' を用いることに注意。
>
> **>> NEWSPAPER; MOVIE**

▶「視聴者」に関わる表現

- テレビ番組の視聴率 ◯ the audience ratings for a TV programme
- テレビをつける ◯ turn on the TV Ⓒ
- テレビを消す ◯ turn off a TV set
- テレビでドラマを見る ◯ see a drama on television
- テレビの画面がほこりをたくさん集めるようだ。
  ◯ The screen of the TV set seems to collect a lot of dust.
- テレビで9時のニュースを見る ◯ watch the 9 o'clock news on TV
- テレビの全国放送に出る ◯ appear on national television Ⓤ
- リモコンを手にテレビの前に座る
  ◯ sit in front of the TV set with the remote control in my hand
- そんな近くでテレビを見ると目が悪くなるよ。
  ◯ If you sit so close to the television, you will damage your eyesight.

▶「最新技術の話題」に関わる表現

- 液晶テレビ ◯ a liquid crystal television
- アナログ放送から地デジテレビへの変更
  ◯ the change from analogue broadcasting to digital terrestrial television [DDTV]
- ハイビジョンテレビはそれほど高くない
  ◯ HDTVs [high definition televisions] are not so expensive.
- 衛星チャンネルでニュースを見る

- ○ watch the TV news on a satellite channel
- ❏ パソコンでテレビ番組を録画する
  - ○ record a TV programme on my computer
- ❏ テレビの映り［受信状態］がどこかおかしい。
  - ○ There is something wrong with the TV picture.
- ❏ このあたりはテレビの映り［受信状態］がよくない。
  - ○ We do not get good TV reception in this area.
- ❏ デジタル・テレビ放送とは何なのかわからない。
  - ○ I do not understand what digital television broadcasting is.
- ❏ 我が家はケーブルテレビに加入している。○ We have cable (TV).

▶「テレビを観ての反応」に関わる表現

- ❏ 毎週放映されるテレビ番組を興味深く追っていく
  - ○ follow a weekly TV programme with interest
- ❏ テレビで見聞きすることを何でも信じる［テレビの見すぎである］
  - ○ believe everything one sees and hears on TV
- ❏ 私はテレビのニュースを疑ってかかる。
  - ○ I am sceptical about the TV news.
- ❏ 私はテレビのクイズ番組に死ぬほど退屈している。
  - ○ I am bored to death with the quiz shows on TV.

▶ ストーリー

When I get home, I **turn on the TV**, and **watch anything that is on**. I **don't usually bother with the TV guide**. But there are some so-called '**television personalities**' who **appear on TV** so often that I **have got fed up with seeing their faces**. When they **come on**, I immediately **change channels**.

(私は帰宅するとテレビをつけて、映っているものを何でも観る。たいていは番組表のやっかいにはならない。しかし、顔を見るのもうんざりするほどテレビによく出る、いわゆる「テレビ・タレント」がいる。彼らが出てくると、すぐにチャンネルを変えてしまう。)

094 THANKS (複数形)

> **感**謝は謝罪と共に対人関係においてきわめて重要であり、その表現の仕方は英語においても実に多彩である。'thanks'を用いた直接的な表現に加え、それ以外の関連表現を多数紹介した。
>
> また、ここでは用例に含まれた「話す行為を表す動詞」に注意しよう（☞*）。sayやtell以外の動詞には特に注意すること。'smile my thanks'（微笑みで感謝を表す）のような表現も話す行為の一部（'nonverbal communication'として）と考えよう。
>
> **>> APOLOGY; BEHAVIOUR; LANGUAGE**

▶ thanks から広がるボキャブラリー：動詞表現

- 感謝を表す［述べる］ ◯ express my thanks* ☞ express my anger「怒りの気持ちを表す」
- 微笑みで感謝を表す ◯ smile my thanks* ☞ 'Thank you,' Meg smiled.「『ありがとう』と言ってメグは微笑んだ」
- 感謝の言葉をつぶやく ◯ mumble my thanks* ☞ mumbleは口の中でもごもご言うこと
- 全員に心からの感謝の意を表する
   ◯ extend sincere thanks to everyone* C ☞ extend condolences「お悔みを述べる」
- ボブに特別な感謝の言葉を述べる
   ◯ have a special word of thanks for Bob*
- （私たちは）メグに感謝します。 ◯ Our thanks go to Meg.
- 私はありがとうと言って彼に本を返した。
   ◯ I returned the book to him with thanks.
- 心からの感謝と拍手喝采を受ける
   ◯ receive grateful thanks and applause
- みんなから本当に感謝される ◯ truly earn everyone's thanks
- みんなの感謝に礼を言う ◯ acknowledge everyone's thanks*
- 感謝を期待せずに仕事をする ◯ do a job without expecting thanks
- メグの感謝を軽くあしらう ◯ brush aside Meg's thanks*
- お礼を言うのを忘れる ◯ forget to say thanks*

- ❏ 一言もお礼を言わずパーティを去る
  - ◯ leave a party without a word of thanks

▶ 関連表現

- ❏ 感謝祭を祝う ◯ celebrate Thanksgiving Day
- ❏ メグに礼状[お礼の手紙]を送る ◯ send Meg a thank-you note
- ❏ 報いられない仕事を引き受ける ◯ take on a thankless task
- ❏ あなたのおかげで私たちはうまくいった。
  - ◯ Thanks to you, we succeeded.
- ❏ 私たちはうまくいった。あなたのおかげではないけどね。
  - ◯ We succeeded. No thanks to you.
  - ☞「別に誰か・何かのおかげでなく[いなくても・なくても]」の意味
- ❏ 感謝の意を表する
  - ◯ express my gratitude*; show my appreciation*
- ❏ 自分がどれだけありがたく思っているかボブに伝える
  - ◯ tell Bob how grateful I feel*
- ❏ ボブのこれまでの親切に非常に恩義を感じる
  - ◯ feel very indebted to Bob for the kindness he has shown me
  - ☞ feel indebted to *sb* for *sth*「〈事〉に関して〈人〉に恩義を感じている」
- ❏ 自分を援助してくれたこと対して他の人たちにありがたく思う
  - ◯ feel thankful to others for the help given me
  - ☞ 上の2つが同じ構文であることに注意

▶ ストーリー

Today, Bob Smith is retiring from our company. He has been working for us for thirty years. I know **you all join me in expressing our thanks to him for his many years of hard work. As a token of appreciation I wish to present him with this small gift.**

(今日、ボブ・スミス氏が我が社を去ります。彼は30年間我が社に勤めてきました。皆さんも私と共に彼の長年の激務に感謝の意を表してくれるものと思います。感謝のしるしに、私は彼にこのささやかな贈り物をしたいと思います。)

THANKS

095 TIME · C U

> 時はつかみどころのない概念である。英語でも 'time' に関わる表現は無数に存在するが、生活空間においては以下のように「機会」「時期・期間」に分けて整理しておくと、自分の計画や行動に関して話すさい大いに役立つだろう。
>
> C ┌ 特定の時間・期間・機会を指す場合 ☞ C
> U └ 何かのために利用可能な、または必要な時間の量を指す場合 ☞ U
> （ただし C と U の区別が曖昧なこともある。下の用例を参照のこと）
>
> **>> DAY / NIGHT; EVENING / MORNING; HOBBY**

▶「機会」に関わる表現

❏ 有名な場所を初めて訪問するとき
　◯ the first time to visit a famous place
❏ 泣く時間と笑う時間 ◯ a time for tears and a time for laughter ©
❏ 時折メグをひょっこり訪ねる
　◯ drop in on Meg from time to time ☞ drop in on *sb* / at *spl*「(予告もなしに)〈人/場所〉を訪ねる、立ち寄る」
❏ ボブに最後に会ったときのことを覚えている
　◯ remember the last time I met Bob
❏ 本を読む暇 [時間] がまったくない
　◯ never find the time to read books
❏ あなたは自分の言葉を後悔するときが来るであろう。
　◯ The time will come when you will regret your words.

▶「時期・期間」に関わる表現

❏ 時間不足；時間の欠如 ◯ a lack of time
❏ ヘンリー国王の時代に ◯ in the time of King Henry
❏ 十分な時間 ◯ a reasonable amount of time ⓤ
❏ ちょうど列車の出発に間に合う ◯ be just in time to catch the train
❏ メグと楽しく過ごす ◯ have a good time with Meg
❏ 仕事をするとき時間を節約する方法を見つける
　◯ find a way to save time when doing a job ☞ save (you) 500 yen

214

「500円の節約になる」
- 十分な時間の余裕を残して仕事を終える
  - ◯ finish my work in good time ☞ このgoodは「十分な、かなりの」の意味。have a good night's sleep「ひと晩ゆっくり寝る」
- 趣味に多くの時間を費やす ◯ spend a lot of time on my hobby
- 交渉に十分な時間を割り当てる[時間の余裕を見ておく]
  - ◯ allow adequate time for negotiations ☞ allow two hours for transfer「乗り換えに2時間みておく」
- ボブのために時間を割く ◯ make time for Bob
- 無用な仕事をして時間を無駄にする
  - ◯ waste time doing useless tasks
- 多くの時間とエネルギーを食われてしまう
  - ◯ take up a lot of time and energy
- (ふいに仕事の) 休暇を取る ◯ take time off work
  - ☞ take a few days off work「(あらかじめ予定して2、3の日休暇を取る」
- マイペースで物事を行う ◯ do things in my own time

▶決まり文句

- 一歩ずつ順を踏んで着実に行う ◯ take things one step at a time
- 一度に一つずつ物事を行う ◯ do things one at a time
- 機は熟した。◯ The time is ripe.
- ボブはとっくに来ていてもよい頃である。
  - ◯ It's high time Bob was here.

▶ストーリー

We **are all ruled by time**. We never seem to **have enough time to do the things we want to do**. We should relax more, and **spend less time worrying about how to make time for all the things we cannot find time to do**.

(私たちは皆時間に支配されている。私たちはしたいことをする時間が十分あるとは決して思えない。私たちはもっと気を楽にして、やる暇がないことにどう時間を割こうかと心配する時間を減らすべきだ。)

096 TRAIN ・・・・・・・・・・・・ C

> 公共の移動手段は本項の 'train' と共に 'plane' が代表的なものである。しかも英語表現でも、ここで紹介した用例の多くで 'train' と 'plane' を入れ替えて用いることができる。
>
> 例 the next plane for ...、miss the plane など
>
> しかし、'train' のほうがより我々の生活空間の核に近い乗り物と言え、本書ではこちらを取り上げた。一部「地下鉄」の用例も加えてある。
>
> ✳ 次のような英米の差異に注意。
>
> 地下鉄:《英》the Underground, the Tube (俗称) —《米》the subway
> (横断用の) 地下道:《英》subway —《米》an underpass
>
> **>> ACCIDENT; CAR; HOLIDAY; TRAVEL**

▶ train から広がるボキャブラリー:名詞表現

- 蒸気機関車 ◯ a steam train
- 電車 ◯ an electric train ☞ 一般的には単に a train でよい
- ディーゼル機関車 ◯ a diesel train
- 急行列車 ◯ an express train
- 各駅停車 (の列車) ◯ a local train
- 通勤電車 ◯ a commuter train
- 大阪行きの列車 ◯ the Osaka train ; the train for Osaka
- 青森行きの列車 ◯ a train bound for Aomori ☞ eastbound「東行きの」
- 5番ホームからの次の列車 ◯ the next train from platform 5
- 京都への最終列車 ◯ the last train to Kyoto
- 函館への夜行列車 ◯ the night train to Hakodate
- 長い列車の旅 ◯ a long train journey
- 落書きだらけの地下鉄車両
    ◯ a subway train covered in graffiti ☞ ニューヨークの地下鉄など

▶ train から広がるボキャブラリー:動詞表現

- 列車に乗る ◯ catch a train; take a train ☞「乗ってどこかに行く」の意味
- 列車に乗り込む ◯ get on [in] a train
- 列車に乗り遅れる ◯ miss the train
- 列車に間に合うように急いで行く ◯ rush off to catch a train

モノ

- モスクワからパリまで列車に乗って行く
  - take the train from Moscow to Paris
- 飛行機の代わりに高速列車で行く
  - travel by high-speed train <u>instead of</u> plane
- あなたは違う列車に乗っています。 ○ You are on the wrong train.
- 列車に群がって乗る ○ <u>crowd on to</u> a train ☞ crowd in to a shop「店になだれ込む」
- 次の駅で列車を乗り換える ○ <u>change trains</u> at the next station
  ☞ trainsと複数形であることに注意
- 列車の窓から外を見る ○ <u>look out of</u> the train window
- 行楽シーズンの期間、列車を増発する
  - <u>run more trains</u> during the holiday season
- 非常（停止用）ボタンを押して列車を止める
  - stop a train by pressing the emergency button
- 列車は駅を出発した。 ○ The train <u>pulled out of</u> the station.
- プラットホームに立って列車が入ってくるのを見る
  - stand on the platform watching a train <u>pull in</u>
- 列車は今到着予定である。 ○ The train <u>is due now.</u> ☞ My baby is due in June.「私の子供は7月に生まれる予定だ」
- 列車は脱線した。 ○ The train was derailed.
- 電車で行くより地下鉄に乗ったほうが速い。
  - It's quicker by Tube [subway] than by ordinary train.

▶ ストーリー

If I have a choice, I **prefer travelling by train, rather than by plane**. I really **enjoy looking out of the window of a train** and **seeing the scenery go past**. Also, **in a train**, you can **get up** and **stretch your legs**. In a plane, you cannot really do this.
(もし選べるなら、私は飛行機より電車で旅行するほうが好きである。私は列車の窓から外を見て、風景が過ぎていくのを眺めるのが実に楽しい。また、列車では立ち上がって足を伸ばすことができる。飛行機ではこれは事実上できない。)

TRAIN

097 TRAVEL ... U

距離の長短、娯楽かビジネスかなど、目的・形態により旅行はさまざまな過程をへて行われる。ここで紹介した「計画・手配」関連の用例は、旅行だけでなく日常のあらゆる場面に応用できるだろう。

また、'travel' は本書で最も相互参照項目が多い語である。それらをすべてマスターすれば、生活空間の核となる英語が大きく向上していることになる。

✱〈関連表現〉であげた旅行を表す類義語と前置詞 'on' に注意。
  a trip   ☞ 比較的短い旅行で、行き先と目的に重点
  a journey   ☞ 長距離の旅行で、目的地に行くことに重点
  an excursion ☞ 短期間の、団体での観光旅行
  an outing   ☞ ちょっとした遠出やピクニック

>> CAR; COUNTRY/COUNTRYSIDE; SEA/SEASIDE; HOLIDAY; HOTEL; TRAIN; WEEKEND

▶「計画・手配」に関わる表現

- 旅行代理店に行く ◯ go to a travel agent's
- 旅行保険に入る ◯ take out travel insurance ☞ take out a loan「ローンを組む」
- 旅行パンフレットをいくつか見る [見て検討する]
  ◯ look at some travel brochures
- すべての旅行本と旅行ガイドをていねいに調べる
  ◯ carefully study all the travel books and travel guides
- インドへの旅行はビザが必要だ。◯ Travel to India requires a visa.
- 旅行 [移動] の手段を選ぶことができる
  ◯ have a choice of method of travel
- 団体旅行が最も安いと結論を出す
  ◯ decide that group travel is the cheapest
- 平日旅行の特別運賃を調べる
  ◯ look at special fares for midweek travel
- 国内旅行より海外旅行に興味がある
  ◯ be more interested in overseas travel than in domestic travel
- エコノミークラスの旅行は拷問のようなものだと考える
  ◯ regard economy class travel as a kind of torture

- 秘書に自分の旅行と宿泊の手配をすべてさせる
  - ○ get my secretary to arrange all my travel and accommodation
- 旅行の手配をするのが嫌いだ ○ hate making travel arrangements
- 旅行のチケットをすべてクレジットカードで支払う
  - ○ charge all my travel tickets to my credit card ☞ charge it to me [my account]「自分の勘定に付ける」

▶ 関連表現

- 旅行のための旅行がしたい ○ want to travel for travel's sake
  - ☞ 旅行に行くこと自体が目的だということ。最初のtravelは動詞（次の例も）
- 無性に旅行がしたくなる ○ have a compulsion to travel ☞ under compulsion「強制されて」
- 出張に出かけている ○ be away on a business trip
- 発見の旅に出かける ○ set out on a journey of discovery
- 奈良に修学旅行に行く ○ go on a school excursion to Nara
- 子供たちを動物園への遠出に連れて行く
  - ○ take the kids on an outing to the zoo ☞ take them on a picnic「彼らをピクニックに連れて行く」

▶ ストーリー

Basho called **the compulsion to travel** 'the cloud-moving wind'. Many people certainly **have an urge to travel**. They **are not happy staying at home**, but **are always away on some journey**, or **planning their next trip**. They often **spend hours looking at travel brochures** with a dreamy expression on their faces.

(芭蕉は無性に旅をしたくなる気持ちを「片雲の風」（雲を動かす風）と呼んだ。多くの人々が確かに旅をしたい衝動を持っている。彼らはじっと家にいるのに満足せず、つねに家を留守にして何らかの旅に出ているか、あるいは次の旅を計画しているのである。彼らはしばしばうっとりとした表情を顔に浮かべながら何時間も旅行パンフレットを見て時間を過ごす。)

098 WEATHER ... U

天候とその変化は、現代の科学技術をもってしても我々の自由にはならない。ここでも、各種天候状態の表現をもとに、'weather' が我々の生活に及ぼす影響に関わる表現を紹介した。

✴ 「天候一般」を表す場合、しばしば 'the' を伴う。

✴ 'in all weathers [weather《米》]' という表現がよく用いられるが、これは「どんな天候でも」という意味である。

✴ 英語全体に関わる注意事項として、Uの名詞でも、「いろいろな種類 (kinds of ～)」を表すときは複数形になる場合がある。

　例 the wines of France (フランスのいろいろなワイン)
　　 = the different wines of France

>> HOLIDAY; SEA / SEASIDE; SEASON

▶ weather から広がるボキャブラリー：名詞表現

- 不安定な [不順な；変わりやすい] 天候 ◯ unsettled weather
  ☞ The problem is still unsettled. 「その問題はまだ未解決だ」
- 素晴らしい [とても良い] 天気 ◯ lovely weather
- 好天続き ◯ a spell of fine weather ☞ a dry spell「日照り続き」
- 乾燥して、安定した天候状態 ◯ dry, settled weather conditions
- どんよりした天候状態 ◯ overcast weather conditions ☞ an overcast sky「曇った空」
- (何かをするのに) 都合の悪い天候 ◯ adverse weather conditions
  ☞ an adverse wind「逆風」
- 荒れ模様の [陰険を極めた] 天候 ◯ inclement [inklémənt] weather
- いやな天気 ◯ vile weather
- (雨風で) ひどい天気 ◯ terrible weather
- 悪天候；荒天 ◯ foul weather ☞ foulは主に「汚い、不正な」の意味
- 熱帯低気圧がもたらした雨 [雨天]
  ◯ rainy weather caused by a tropical depression ☞ an anticyclone「熱帯性高気圧」

▶ 「生活への影響」に関わる表現

- 天気を予報する ◯ predict the weather

- 天気が許せばピクニックに行く
  - go on a picnic, weather permitting
- 気まぐれな天気のためピクニックを中止する
  - cancel the picnic because of the vagaries of the weather
  - ☞ vagaries「とっぴな考え・行い」
- 天候のため困難な状況にある
  - be in difficulties due to the weather
- 悪天候によるすべての便の欠航
  - cancellation of all flights because of bad weather
- ひどい咳をもたらす天候 ○ weather that brings on bad coughing
- 天気予報を決してあてにしない
  - never rely on the weather forecast
- いつも天気の話ばかりしている
  - be always going on about the weather
- 天気が悪いと文句を言う ○ complain about the weather
- 冷たい、雨降りの天気は本当に私を憂うつにする。
  - The cold, wet weather really gets me down. ☞ get /sb/ down「〈人〉を落ち込ませる」

▶ ストーリー

We can both see **it is raining hard**, so why do you say to me, **'It's really terrible weather today'**? Perhaps **this custom of commenting on the weather** dates back to societies in which **the weather was important**, but **very changeable**. **A long spell of cold weather** could mean starvation. I wonder if people who live in the Sahara greet each other with, **'It's really hot and sunny today'**.

(二人とも激しく雨が降っているのがわかるのに、どうして一人が必ず「今日は本当にひどい天気ですね」と言うのか。 天候についてひとこと言うこの習慣は、天気が重要でありつつも非常に変わりやすかった社会にまでさかのぼる。長期にわたる寒い天候は飢餓を意味しかねなかった。サハラ砂漠に住んでいる人たちは、「今日は本当に暑くて日がよく照りますね」などと言って挨拶をかわすのだろうか。)

099　WEEKEND　C

> 週が日曜から始まるという考え方はほぼ米国と日本だけのものであり、英語圏では日曜から始まるのが一般的である。'this week' や 'next week' 'next Sunday' などと言う場合はこのことを念頭においていただきたい。したがって、日曜日に 'I will see you next week.' と言った場合、これは2通りに解釈できることになるので要注意！
> ここでは週末の計画や過ごし方に関わる表現を中心に紹介する。
>
> **>> ENJOYMENT; HOBBY; HOLIDAY; WORK**

▶ weekend から広がるボキャブラリー：名詞表現

- 忙しい週末 ○ a busy weekend
- 落ち着ける週末 ○ a relaxing weekend
- 祭日の重なる週末 ○ a holiday weekend
- 三連休の週末 ○ a long weekend ☞ 金曜か月曜を休んで取る、あるいは祝日による三連休を指す
- 夏期休暇中盤の三連休の週末 (金曜か月曜が休み)
  ○ a three-day weekend in the middle of the summer holidays
- 情事の週末 ○ a dirty weekend 《英》
- 週末旅行 ○ a weekend trip
- 週末のゴルフ ○ a weekend game of golf
- 販売テクニックについての週末セミナー
  ○ a weekend seminar on sales techniques
- 週末の買い物客でいっぱいのショッピングモール
  ○ a shopping mall full of weekend shoppers
- トップ経営者向けの週末セミナー
  ○ a weekend retreat for top executives ☞ 別荘やホテル等で催されるもの。retreatは「避難場所、保養所」の意味

▶ weekend から広がるボキャブラリー：動詞表現

- 週末はあけておくのが好きだ。○ I like to keep my weekends free.
- (週末前に) よい週末を！; また来週！ ○ Have a nice weekend!
- 週末の間［週末旅行に］出かける ○ go away for the weekend

出来事

- 週末が（悪）天候にたたられて台無しになる
  - ○ have my weekend ruined by the weather ☞ have *sth* done (by *sb*/*sth*)「〈〈人／物〉に〉〈物事〉を…される、…してもらう」
- 海辺で週末に一休みする ○ take a weekend break at the seaside
- 週末の特別行事を催す ○ hold a special weekend event
- 週末にメグに会う ○ see Meg at the weekend
- 今度の週末は計画がない ○ have no plans this coming weekend
- 週末の間することがない
  - ○ have nothing to do during the weekend
- 友人たちと週末を過ごす ○ spend the weekend with my friends
- 私は週末（を通して）勤務する。○ I am on duty over the weekend.
- 週末に仕事をする ○ work on weekends
- 平日は開いているが、週末は閉まっている店
  - ○ a shop which is open on weekdays but closed at the weekend
- 週末の渋滞を避けるため金曜の夜に出発する
  - ○ leave on Friday night to avoid the weekend traffic
- 先週末は家にいた。○ I stayed at home last weekend.
- 週末の邪魔をしてすいません。○ Sorry I disturbed your weekend.
  - ☞ Do not disturb!「起こさないでください」(ホテルの客室のドアにかける掲示)

▶ ストーリー

I **stayed at home all last weekend**. I **like relaxing weekends**, so always **try to keep my weekends free**. But usually I have to **play weekend golf with business associates**, or **go to some kind of weekend seminar organized by the company**. When things are busy at work, I **have to work at the weekend**.

(私は先週末ずっと家にいた。私は落ち着ける週末が好きなので、常に週末はあけておくようにしている。しかしたいていは、ビジネスパートナーと週末のゴルフをするか、会社が催す何らかの週末セミナーに出なければならない。仕事が立て込んでいるときは週末に働かなければならない。)

100　WORK　Ⓤ

> 仕事といえば、「こなすべき課題」と「会社の業務」という2つの面がある。ここでも、作業としての仕事の種類と会社でのスケジュールを中心に'work'をもとにした表現を紹介した。
>
> ✻ 類義語に'job'があるが、これは「収入を伴う特定の具体的な仕事」を意味し、Ⓒ扱いとなることに注意。'work'には「具体的な仕事」の他「精神的な仕事、労力」も含まれⓊ扱いとなる。したがって、英語で「仕事をする」と言う場合、状況によって次のように使い分けることになる：
>
> 　　do a job（ある特定の仕事をする）— do some work（何か仕事をする）
>
> **>> BOSS; COMPANY; HOLIDAY; WEEKEND**

▶ work から広がるボキャブラリー：名詞表現

- ❏ 激務；重労働 ◯ heavy work
- ❏ 軽度の仕事；楽な仕事 ◯ light work
- ❏ その日その日の仕事 ◯ day-to-day work ☞ on a day-to-day basis「1日単位で」
- ❏ 臨時の仕事 ◯ extra work
- ❏ 時間外労働；残業 ◯ overtime work ☞ work overtime「残業する」
- ❏ 大変な[労力を要する]仕事 ◯ demanding work ☞ Meg is always very demanding.「メグはいつもすごく注文が多い」
- ❏ 危険な仕事 ◯ dangerous work
- ❏ 肉体労働 ◯ physical work
- ❏ 骨の折れる仕事 ◯ backbreaking work
- ❏ 汚れ仕事；人のいやがる仕事 ◯ dirty work
- ❏ いい加減な仕事 ◯ sloppy work ☞ sloppy clothes「だらしない服装」
- ❏ 几帳面な仕事 ◯ meticulous work ☞ a meticulous account「詳細な説明」
- ❏ 細心の注意を要する仕事 ◯ delicate work ☞ a delicate matter「デリケートな事柄」

▶ work から広がるボキャブラリー：動詞表現

- ❏ 8時に仕事を始める ◯ begin work at eight o'clock

組織

- ボブは今仕事中［勤務中］である。◯ Bob is now at work.
- 昼食休みの間仕事を止める ◯ stop work for a lunch break
- 緊急の仕事を処理する ◯ deal with some urgent work
- その日一日の仕事を終える ◯ finish the day's work
- 仕事を自宅に持ち帰る ◯ take some work home
- 長時間の労力をプロジェクトにつぎ込む
  ◯ put many hours of work into a project
- 多くの労働経験［職歴］を持つ ◯ have a lot of work experience
- よく働いたとボブを誉める ◯ praise Bob for his hard work
- その芸術家の一年間の努力の成果をよく表す展示会
  ◯ an exhibition which represents a year's work of the artist

▶決まり文句

- これを手っ取り早く片づけなさい。
  ◯ You will make short work of this. ☞ 実質的な命令文
- 彼は生まれてこの方一度も仕事をしたことがない。
  ◯ He has never done a stroke of work in his life.
- あなたは、①手一杯の仕事がある。②難題を抱えている。
  ◯ You have your work cut out for you.

▶ストーリー

I leave home at seven and **get to work** just before nine. We **start work** at nine sharp. First I **check to see if** there is **any urgent work I have to deal with**. Then I **get down to the more routine tasks**. The job I do is just **rather simple and boring office work**. However, **the pay is good**, and we **never have to do overtime**.

(私は7時に家を出て、9時ちょうど前に職場に着く。我が社では9時きっかりに始業だ。最初に、処理すべき緊急の仕事があるかどうか確かめる。それから私はより日常的な業務にとりかかる。私がする仕事はどちらかというと単純で退屈な事務仕事である。しかしながら、給料は良く、我が社では決して残業をしなくてもよい。)

索 引

A

abandoned 183
Abraham Lincoln 123
abrupt 52
absorbing 132
abstract 34
absurd 147
abusive 154
accelerator 45
accidental 70
accommodation 219
accuse ～ of 42
achievable 28
achieve 29, 83, 206, 207
acid rain 101
acknowledge 171, 212
acne 149
action-adventure 174
activate 49
address 169
add ～ to 121, 175
add to 98
adjourn 169
adjust 127
adjust to 77
administration 184
admirable 28
adolescent 57
adopt 56, 57, 75, 209
adopt ～ to 26
advance 209
advanced 208
advantage 90, 91, 96
adverse 220
advertisement 179
advertising 178
aerobic 115
affect 99, 201
affection 95
affluent 200
after-dinner walk 79
agenda 168
agent 218
aggressive 39
agree to 167, 206
agree with 117
air-conditioned 136, 140
airy 137
aisle 73
alert 115
alliance 167
allied 66
allow ～ for 215
all the rage 111
all the vogue 111
amateur 202
amidst 64
amuse 29
amusing 151
analyze 82
and no mistake 171
a never-ending series of 80
animation freak 133
anniversary 70, 145
annoy 42
annual 61, 79, 194
anxiety 205
anything to do with 133
apologies for 32
apologize for 171
apologize to ～ for 25
appear 210, 211
appetizing 116
applause 212
application 208
apply ～ to 209
appreciate 35, 96, 119, 152, 176, 177
appreciation 213
appropriate 161
archery 203
arise 76, 77
arose 76
arouse 94
arrange 219
arrangements 219
arrested ～ for 31
arthritis 149
artificial 154
artist 225
as a last resort 30
assess 43
assign ～ to 42
asthma 149
as ～ as possible 65, 85, 166, 172
as a token of 213
as a whole 66, 201, 205
as fit as a fiddle 115
as luck would have it 163
as much money as possible 172
athlete 114
athlete's foot 149
atmosphere 140
at an alarming rate 173

at first sight 161
at large 201
at length 169
at present 31
at the bottom of 179
at the height of 192
at the mains 92
at the risk of -ing 101
at the weekend 223
at weekends 137
at work 24, 223, 225
aubergine 121
audience ratings 210
aurora 158
autocratic 42
available 120
averaging 125
avian influenza 113
avoid 24, 77, 113, 171, 191, 223
a bit of 81, 162, 196
a carton of 74
a catalogue of 81
a change for the better 52
a change of clothes 58
a circle of 119
a considerable quantity of 187
a couple of 85, 86
a drink or two 84
a friend in need 173
a hint of 32
a kind of 132, 195, 218
a large catch of 112
A large number of 194

a life-and-death struggle 159
a matter of life or death 71
a never-ending series of 80
a pair of 59
a piece of 34, 35, 112, 176
a run of bad luck 163
a second helping of 117
a series of 206, 207
a small parcel of 181
a spell of 220, 221
a tiny quantity of 187
a tissue of lies 156
a variety of 209
a vast quantity of 187
a work of 34

B

baby 57
backbreaking 224
background 108, 176
back ～ into 44
badly cooked 78
balance 131, 195
balanced 74, 131
balance of power 53
baldness 109
bald patch 127
ballet 203
ban 41
bankrupt 60
bank robbery 31
bar 141
barbeque 79, 113, 117
based on 94, 166

base fee 47
bathtowel 37
beach 195
beard 105, 124
because of 26, 49, 51, 130, 148, 204, 221
befall 81
beforehand 197
begrudge 207
behave badly 39
believe in 90, 162, 188
beneficial 53
benefit 66, 90, 115, 209
benefit from 152, 209
betray 160, 161
Better luck next time! 163
beyond my wildest dreams 83
beyond saving 167
be 'in' 111
be admitted to 138, 139
be afraid of 105, 106
be allowed home 139
be all messed up 127
be amused by 151
be an enthusiastic collector of 133
be arrested for 197
be at death's door 71
be away from 137
be a collector of 133
be a slave to 111
be a slave to fashion 111
be based on 48, 167
be befuddled with 84

be blessed with 162, 163
be bored by 151
be bored to death with 211
be captivated by 151
be caught out in 156
be comfortable in 155
be connected to 49, 97, 189
be crazy about 133
be discharged from 139
be doomed to 107
be down on my luck. 163
be dressed in 58
be due 33, 217
be dying 71
be dying for 85
be dying of 87
be economical with 157
be embarrassed by 151
be excited by 151
be expecting 56, 145
be faced with 77
be fascinated in 133
be filled with 95
be fond of 202
be fortunate enough to 91
be frightened by 151
be full of 50, 63, 95, 159, 190, 204
be full of character 55
be glowing with 130
be going out 161
be held in police custody 31

be incapable of 156
be indifferent to 189
be interested by 150
be interested in 218
be involved in 95
be in ~ condition 138
be in difficulties 89, 221
be in difficulty 77
be in good condition 115
be in good physical and mental health 130
be in hospital 139, 149
be in love 145, 160, 167
be in luck 162
be in need of 198
be in shape 115
be in time to 214
be just in time to 214
be keen on 133
be late for 169
be late in coming 192
be likely to 207
be lost at sea 194
be loyal to 67
be lucky enough to 130
be music to my ears 177
be not made of money 173
be off 197
be on 175, 211
be on duty 103, 223
be on his deathbed 71
Be on one's behaviour 39
be on their way 31
be on the verge of 71

be on time. 32
be on time for 169
be opposed to 167
be out of fashion 111
be out of luck 162
be out of season 192
be out of shape 115
be overflowing with 96
be past its 'best-by' date 197
be posted to 136
be proud of 159
be puzzled by 151
be receptive to 209
be resistant to 209
be responsible for 70
be ruled by 95
be rushed to 30, 138
be satisfied by 151
be sceptical about 211
be seeing each other 161, 171
be short of 198
be stunted by 124
be surprised by 151
be taken to 138
be thrilled by 151
be tolerant towards 189
be under stress 204
be unfit fo 113
be unsuitable for 26
be weighed down with 197
be well known 105
be wide awake 199
be withdrawn from sale

73
biassed 179
bigamous 166
birdwatching 133
bird flu 113
blackout 92
blame ~ for 123
bland 116
blatant 156
bleached 126
bleary-eyed 198
blend 121
blocking feature 49
blow-dry 126
blue 174
blush 156
body moisturizer 37
boil 149
book [reserve] a room 140
boost 89
boring 151, 158, 168, 185, 225
bossy 43
boss around 43
bound for 216
brainstorming 146
brake 45
break the bad news 152
brief 32
brilliant 146
bring about 53
bring home to 137
bring in 193
bring on 221
bring up 145, 155

brochures 218, 219
bronchitis 149
brotherly 160
browse 97
brunch 79
brush aside 212
Brussels sprouts 121
BSE 113
budgie 183
bugs 63
built-in camera 46
bullying 42
bumpy 191
bureaucratic 154
burst open 181
buy a round of drinks for 85
buy cheap 197
by accident 24, 25
by cash on delivery 180
by cellphone 47
by computer 63
by mistake 171
by plane 217
by pure chance 51
by the sea 135

C

cabinet 168
cable 211
call back 49
call charges 48
call it an evening 103
cancel 135, 169, 221
cancellation 221
cannot afford 135
cannot be accounted for 30
cannot stand 143, 205
cannot thank you enough 153
cannot understand the first thing about 62
can get by 155
can hold his drink 84
captivating 151
careless 170
carelessly 93, 96
carelessness 24
care for 56
carpentry 133
carry out 39
carry the story 179
caused by carelessness 24
cause of 25, 70, 107, 129, 148
celebrate 145, 213
censor 41, 175
chair 169
changeable 221
change for the better 53
change trains 217
charge 47
charity 153, 172
chat into 47
cheat 71
check 114, 125, 131
checked pattern 59
check ~ out of 41
check in to 141
check out of 141
check to see if 226

cheeks 105
chemical 27, 100
chemical fertilizers 120
cherish 160
chew 117
chicken pox 149
child's play. 57
children's bathtime 37
chilly 102
chopped 121
chores 142
circulation 178
civilized 200
clean-shaven 164
clean up 184
clear away 79
closed 200
close in on 68
close to 194, 210
closing scene 174
cloud 129, 219
clutch 45
coffee break 103
cold 149
collapse 61
collapsing 88
collide 45
comedy 174
come down with 148
come into fashion 110, 111
come into season 192
come near to 82
come of 108
come off 75, 169
come on 211

come out 157, 192
come over 99
come true 82
come up 146
come up to my expectations 39
come with 62
comfortable 29, 129, 137, 140, 155
command of the language 155
commentator 203
comment on 221
committee 123
common 170, 200
common-law 144
commonsense 75
community 66, 131
commute 65
commuter 216
comparative 188
compassion 153
compatible 63
competition 72, 203
competitive 101, 202
complain about 197, 221
complex 196
complexion 126
compose 176
compulsion 219
compulsory 90, 91
computer nerd 133
conceive 56, 77
concentrate on 132, 187
concept 125
concern 150

conclusion 169
conference 168
configure 96
confirm 169
confirm button 47
connections 108
connect to 47, 96
connoisseur 35
conservation 100
considerable 187
consider 〜 as 195
consider 〜 to be 182
consist of 75
constipation 117
constituency 185
construction 190
consult 40, 75
consume 89, 92, 125
consumption 92, 112, 113
contact 202
contain 40, 147, 181
contaminate 93, 100
contamination 113
contemporary 34
continue to 89, 125
continue with 146
control my anger at 95
controversial 179
convalescence 130
convenience store 72, 180, 181
convention 168
convert 〜 into 141
convince 〜 of 157
convincing 157

cope with 53, 148, 204
corporate 101
correct 171
corrupt 31
costly 170
coughing 221
courgette 121
courier 180
courtesy 153
cover 41, 179, 216
coverage 48, 203
cover up 170
craggy 104
crash 62, 74
create 76, 77, 154, 156, 209
creatures 100
creep into 32
critical 30, 138
criticize 91, 147, 155
crooked 184
crops 107
cross 105
crowd on to 217
crude 175
cube 86
cubist 34
cucumber 121
curative 131
cure 28, 106, 149
cure for cancer 28
custom 221
cut ～ into 113, 121
cut ～ out of 175
cut off 93
cut out 197

D

damage 100, 210
dance 176
dangerous 93, 224
dare to 105
dating site 49
day-to-day 224
deal with 225
dear 119
debate 131
debut 175
decide 57, 218
decide on 29
decipher 154
decisions 201
declare 80, 160
decline 27
decline of 72
decorated 137
deep breathing 205
defeat 67, 162
defend ～ against 67
deforestation 100
delay 166, 179
delicate 126, 130, 224
deliver 180
delivery 179
demand 32, 33
demanding 191, 224
demand to 141
democratic 123
denounce 39
deodorant stick 37
departmental 168
Department of Cardiology 139

Department of Gastro-Enterology 139
Department of Obstetrics and Gynecology 139
Department of Ophthalmology 139
Department of Orthopedic 139
Department of Otolaryngology 139
Department of Pediatrics 139
Department of Urology 139
depend on 107, 187
deposits of gold ore 187
derailed 217
describe 148
desert 129, 144
desertification 100
deserve 152
designated numbers 48
destroy 64, 65, 67, 88, 92, 119, 129, 195, 205
detailed 190
detect 156
detective 174
deteriorate 48, 89, 101
deterioration 130
develop 54, 100, 125, 146, 150, 151, 204, 209
developed 66
development 100, 125, 151, 209
devices 142, 143

diabetes 149
diagnose 148, 149
dial 48, 49
dice 121
did me the kindness to 153
diesel 216
dietary 75
dietician 75
differences of opinion 169
difference between 157, 188
differing 201
digest 117
digestion 117
digital television broadcasting 211
dilute ～ with 86
direct 174
dirty 222, 224
dirty old 164
discover 25, 28, 156
discovery 219
discriminate against 165
disease 106, 113, 148, 201
disheartened 107
dismiss 33, 162
disorder 198
display 46, 49, 150
display signs of 205
disregard 152
disruptive 38
distinguished 108
distinguish between 161
disturb 195, 223

divide 188
divorce 159, 164, 166
dizzy 84
documentation 62
domestic 184, 218
Don't judge a book by its cover. 41
Don't lose any sleep over 199
donate my collection to 35
double click 62
download 47, 49, 63
downmarket 72
downright 81
doze off 147
do a one-hour workout 115
do my daily shopping 73
do my weight training 115
do not bother with 211
do not have the faintest idea 147
do not turn a hair 127
do the -ing 143
drag ～ into 63
drag on 169
dramatic 52
drank himself to death 71
draw (out) ～ from 172
drill for 93
drink like a fish 113
drink myself to sleep 71

drink oneself to 71
drink to 128
drop in on 214
drop off to sleep 198
drowning 159
drown out 177
drowsy 199
dub over 175
due to 221
dull 158
during the weekend 223
dust 143
(dust) jacket of a book 41
duty-free 196
dye 127

E

earn 172
earnest 104
ease 158, 159
eat out 141
eat up 191
eccentric 54
ecological 195
economy class 218
edit 175
editorial 179
efficient 187
eggplant 121
elaborate 78
elections 150
electorate 123, 185
elegant 154
element 90, 147, 206
elementary 90
elude 207

embargo 88
embarrassing 151
embroider 156
emergency 138, 139, 168
emergency button 217
emphasis 52
emphasize 91
empty 36, 136
encounter 51, 76, 77
encourage 124, 209
endow ～ wit 35
enduring 118
end in 106, 166
enemy 66, 67, 119
enjoy ourselves 99
enlightened 100
enmity 118
enormous 170
entitled 40
environmental 52, 75
equipment 143
equipped with 46
error 170
Esperanto 154
establish 61
estranged 144
evident 98
exaggerated 209
examine 201
excellent 111, 140, 155, 186
exchange 47
exchange ～ with 147
exchange names and addresses 25
excitement 159

exciting 151
exclusive 135
excursion 218, 219
executives 222
exercise 75, 115, 131, 148, 189, 204, 205
exhausted 197
exhibition 225
exotic 120, 182
expand 61, 88, 89
expedition 196
experience 61, 70, 107, 128, 153, 158, 160, 205, 225
experience great grief at 95
experience which formed 54
expert 89
exploit 209
express 55, 70, 94, 160, 212, 213, 216
expression 83, 104, 127, 219
express condolences on 70
extemporized 176
extend 212
extended 109
extra 224
extract 96
eyebrows 105
eyelashes 105
eyesight 210

F

face upwards 104

facilities 115, 140
factors 75, 201
faculty 90
fad 74
fail-safe 208
fail to 25, 185
faithful 119
fall into a sleep 198
fall in love 161
fall in with 147
familiar 147
family-run 140
fanatic 115
fares 218
farfetched 147
fascinating 132
fashionable 111
fatal 24, 69
fateful 69
fatty 112, 113
favour 165, 205
favourite 102, 117, 127, 193
feed 182
feel ～ loyalty to 67
feel at ease 77
feel a warm glow of 128
feel ill at ease 77
feel indebted to ～ for 213
feel loyalty to 67
feel loyalty towards 67
feel run down 149
feel sad at 182
feel satisfaction at 95, 99

feel suspicious of 185
feel thankful to ～ for 213
feign 71, 148
fell head-over-heels in love 161
fertile soils 26
feudal 200
fight over 188
figure 165
filter ～ from 97
filter out 81
finance 60, 123
financial 76, 80
find out 83, 148, 156
find the source of 76
fire 42
fizzy 86
flamenco 176
flee 159
flick through 40
flirt with 164
flourished 26
flowery pattern 59
fluently 155
fly into 183
fold ～ in two 179
follow 75, 110, 114, 185, 191, 207, 211
fondly 161
food poisoning 112
foolish 170
forceful 55
force quit 62
forecast 125, 221
forehead 105

forestry 26
forget to 93, 212
forgive 171
former 42, 43, 136, 168, 173
forthcoming 33
for ～1's sake 219
for ～ purposes 209
for my life 159
for their own interests 185
for the sake of 53, 85, 129
for the weekend 222
foster 124, 136
foul 220
four-star 140
foyer 141
fragile 129
free-market 88
freedom 188, 189
freeze 62
friendly 66, 119, 140
frightening 151
frighten ～ to death 71
from cover to cover 40
from morning to [till] night 103
from the word go 81
from time to time 214
frozen 62, 112, 117, 120
frustration 143
fulfil 29
full of 65, 130, 166, 194, 222
fundamental 170

fundamentalist 189
funds 207
furniture 143
further up 190

G

gain pleasure from 98
gangster 174
garbage can 195
garbled 96
gathering 109, 168
geek 133
gender-free 164
generally 48
generate 92, 146
generosity 153
genuine 34, 170
get-together 168
get～ clear 146
gets ～ down 221
get ～ done 142
get ～ to 219
get a discount of 48
get a job 108
get a refund 135, 197
get a taste of 206
get back to sleep 199
get confused 83
get down to 225
get elected 185
get fed up with 211
get good TV reception 211
get his shots 182
get into 36, 206
get married 109, 145, 167

get one's own way 39
get out of 37
get over 148
get rid of 149, 205
get tired 149
get to 225
get to sleep 198
get up 102, 217
get value for money 173
gifted 56
give up 107
gladly 173
glance through 40
global 184
global standard 46
global warming 100
glossy 127
glued to 47
GNP 89
goods 97, 186
go off 25
government of the people, by the people, for the people 123
go away 222
go a long way 155
go by the book 41
go flat 86
go for 131, 187
go for a walk 79, 115
go from bad to worse 145
go in for 132, 202
go in to 184
go north 191
go on 53, 196, 221

go on about 183, 221
go on a diet 75
go on a shopping trip to 73
go on holiday 135
go on vacation 135
go out of fashion 110
go out on shopping expeditions 73
go past 217
go skiing 197
go some way 155
go through 173
go up 93
go without 87
grab a quick lunch 79
grab a quick nap 199
gradual 107
graffiti 216
grateful 212, 213
gratitude 152, 213
grave 76
green 184
gregarious 54
gross national product 89
growth industry 125
growth of 72
grow up 57, 108
grudging 33
guarantee 187
guest 141
gulp down 87, 117

H

habitat 195
hairdresser's 127

hairpin bends 191
haltingly 155
halve 187
handheld 46
handle 45, 191
handset 46
handsome 164
hand over fist 173
hang ～ out 143
hang up 48, 49, 58
hard-core 174
Hard luck! 163
haricot beans 121
harm 55, 100
harsh 193
haute cuisine 74
have ～ forwarded to 47
have ～ serviced 45
have access to 97
have an affair 161
have an appointment 102
have an ear for 176
have an interest in 133, 184
have an obsession about 133
have a clear idea of 146
have a close relationship with 182
have a crush on 161
have a good time with 214
have a great time 99
have a love for 160
have a love of 160, 194

have a relationship with 161
have a sale 72
have a skeleton in the closet [cupboard] 109
have a taste for 58
have a tendency to 191
have difficulty (in) 77
have difficulty in 77
have difficulty with 77
have enough time to 215
have fun 99
have good taste 58
have my hair permed 127
have no choice but to 61
have no idea 147
have no idea how to 96
have on 59
have success in 206
have to face the music 177
have your work cut out for you 225
hay fever 149
head 122
headlights 45
headlines 179
healthful 131
healthy 75, 131
hearing 177
heartfelt 33
heart transplant 139
heat up 36, 117

heavy 27, 224
helpful 187
help out with 142, 196
hepatitis 149
high 158
high-calorie 74
high-protein 74
high-speed 217
high blood pressure 149
high in fibre 74
hilly 64, 65
hit-and-run 24
holding 60
hold ~ against 170
hold an auction 35
holidaymakers 194
Hollywood 175
Home, Sweet Home. 137
hopeless 106
hopelessly 160
hope to 83
horizontal stripes 59
horror 174
horticulture 26
host 79
hotel with 115
household 183
huge 206
humble 32
hum a tune 177
hurt 101
hybrid car 44

I

I'll show them who's boss. 43

ice-cold 86
idealistic 28
identify 107
idle away 102
ignition 45
immediate 28, 108
immense 98
immoral 157
impact 201, 208
imperil 207
impressionist 34
improvement 27, 52, 187
impulse buying 197
indecisive 42
infatuation 161
in-law 145
incentives 89
inclement 220
incorrect 155
incorrectly 155
increase in 76, 92, 122
indecisive 43
index 41
indoor 115
inefficient 31
inequalities 200
infant 57
infatuation 161
infected with 113
inflation 89
informal 154
information superhighway 97
infrastructure 190
ingenious 146
ingredients 121

initial 28
injustice 95
Inland Sea 195
innovation 209
innovative 60, 209
input 48
input 〜 into 63
insincere 33
instead of 217
insurance 25, 60, 131, 218
interesting 150
interference 188
interpret 82, 176
intimate 118
introduce 89, 93
introduction 41
investigate 25, 70
investment 89, 91
invest 〜 in 172
invest in 61, 190, 209
invite 〜 for 79
invite 〜 out for 85
in an attempt to 172
in an original way 176
in a computer 63
in a corner of 179
in a tall glass 86
in a terrible mess 137
in charge of 145
in deep recession 88
in delight 104
in exasperation 127
in front of 210
in good time 215
in moderation 85

In my day 68
in my own time 215
in one's face 105
in strange taste 137
in sufficient time 106
in the case of 81
in the depths of 193
in the end 107, 163, 169
in the face 105
in the middle of 65, 68, 82, 140, 190, 198, 222
in the mountains 135, 140
in the time of 214
in the west of 66
in tiles 37
in times of 76
in time of 189
iron 143
iron and steel industry 27
irrational 38
irrigation 26
isolation 138
issue 95
is in shape 115
is often full of 63
is out of shape 115
It's high time 〜 215
I need a bath! 37

J
join 213
join 〜 for 79
journey 218, 219
jump at 50
junk 117

just 200

K
keep 〜 free 222, 223
keep 〜 on 59
keep in good health 131
keep in shape 115
keep in touch with 136
keep my number 48
keep on 63, 96
keep out 195
keep the wheels of 〜 turning 27
keep to 75, 191
keep up with 110, 111, 209
Keep your hair on! 127
key to success 206
kumquat 121

L
labour-saving 142, 143
lack 95
lack of 91, 114, 148, 198, 214
lakeside 140
launch a new product 73
lay down 〜 for 67
lay on 93
leading 66, 73
leading-edge 208
lead a 29, 158, 159, 189
lead the life of Reilly 159
lead to 31, 38, 51, 191
lean 112
leave 〜 on 93

leftover 79, 117
lend out 41
lethal injection 70
letters-to-the-editor page 179
let ～ be your guide 95
liberalization 89
lie on my face 104
life-threatening 148
light 224
light-headed 84
lightly 199
light textile 27
light up 104
like a dream come true 83
like a log 199
lingering 70
liquid crystal 210
literacy 200
literate 200
liver 107
lives in a dream 83
live apart from 144
live a full life 99
live under one roof 109
live with 164
local 30, 89, 138, 178, 179, 181, 184, 197, 216
locate 97
log in [on] to 63
log off [out of] 63
long-lasting 118, 129
long established 72
long for 136
long phone call 48

look after 182, 183
look at 105, 193, 218, 219
look back on 158
look for 39, 75, 87
look forward to 57, 87, 134
look of 105, 129
look out of 217
loquat 121
lose ～ to 144
lose control of 45
lose face 105
lose my feeling of 95
lose my husband to 144
lottery 51, 83
lovable 54
lovely 57, 65, 220
love ～ with all my heart 57
Love is blind. 161
low-carbohydrate 74
lucked out 163
luck out in the end 163
lunch break 225
luxurious 37, 140
luxury 158, 159

M

made in heaven 166
made possible by 26
mad cow disease 113
mainstream 179
maintain 114, 115, 130, 150
maintenance 114
main entrance 141

majority 99
makes my hair stand on end 127
make ～ clear 29
make amends for 171
make a contribution to 89
make a pet of 183
make a proposal 166
make a religion of 189
make claims for 209
make do with 79
make friends 46, 119
make love 160
make me feel at home 137
Make no mistake. 171
make short work of 225
make time for 215
make yourself at home 137
mall 196
man-made 80
manage 60, 61
manageable 126
management structure 60
manager 141
manage to 105
manpower 27
manual labour 165
manufacturing 27, 89, 208
marine 100, 101
marketplace 53
Mars 158

marshy 64
mash 121
master 155, 209
maternity 138
measles 149
measure 80, 187
media 178
medical 149
medicine 187
meet with 206
mend 143
menswear department 72
messy 166
meticulous 224
microeconomics 89
middle-aged 164
migraine 149
mild 193
military 27, 80, 106, 209
minced 113
Minister of Agriculture 123
Minister of Defence 123
Minister of Education 123
Minister of Finance 123
Minister of Foreign Affairs 123
Minister of Health 123
Minister of Health, Labor and Welfare 123
Ministry of Health, Labour and Welfare 131
Ministry of the Environment 101
minor 171
minority 99
minutes 168
miserable 106, 129, 166
mixture 121, 128, 161
mobile home 136
model planes 133
moderate 207
modern art 34
money talks 173
money to burn 173
Mongolian 175
monotheistic 188
mop 143
moral 157
morality 188
more by luck than by ability 163
morning, noon, and night 103
morning person 103
motivation 150
mountainous 64
movement 201
multi-racial 201
mumble 212
mumps 149
musical 174

N

national 89, 154, 179, 210
nationalized 27
nationwide 48
nationwide chain 72
NATO 168
navy beans 121
necessary for 124
negative 125
neglect 145
neglect to 131
negotiations 107, 215
nervousness 205
network 48, 62, 63, 66
neuter 183
never done a stroke of work 225
never dream of 83
new-fangled 208
newborn 57
newly married 145
new edition 40
nibble at 116
nightmares 82
night person 103
no-confidence motion 122
nondelivery 181
nonverbal communication 212
nothing but 33, 117
nothing like 37
nothing more than 51, 83, 123
Nothing succeeds like success. 207
notice 179, 181
not ... one ounce of 157
not a flicker of 95
not grow on trees 173
nourishing 117

nowhere near 157
no one could be heard above 177
No such luck! 163
nuclear 109, 208
nurse 85, 148
nursing 136
nutritional 86

O

obnoxious 54
observe 38, 188
obsession 133
obtain 186
obvious 123, 170
occur to 147
off-season 192
off-the-top-of-the-head 147
office procedures 53
office work 225
of importance 169
of my lifetime 134
oil spill 195
old-fashioned 65
Olympic 202
once-fashionable 194
once in my life 158
one-day trip 194
one-touch dialling 49
one and only 51
one at a time 215
one in a million 51
One man's meat is another man's poison. 113
one step at a time 215

on ～ night 223
on a business trip 219
on a network 63
on holiday 134, 135
on impulse 196
on location 174
on my cell 47
on my computer 63
on television 210
on the back page 179
on the brink of 61
on the Internet 97
on the spur of the moment 73
on weekdays 223
on weekends 223
open ～ to 89
operation 139
opium of the masses 189
opposition party 123
ordinary 111, 159, 217
organize 79, 223
original 53, 175, 176
origins 154
outlet 73
out-of-date 208
outbreak 30
outburst 94, 95
outdated 208
outdoor 202
outing 218, 219
outlet 48
outright 106
outstrip 125
outwardly 94

out of character 55
out of date 209
out of friendship 119
out of kindness 152
overall 28, 114, 125
overcast 220
overcome 76, 77, 95
overcooked 116
overdue wor 50
overfishing 100, 195
overindulge in 117
overlook 140, 171, 194
overseas 47, 61, 218
overtake 208
overthrow 122
overtime 224, 225
over ～ holidays 134
over our cellphones 47
over the weekend 223
oyster 192
ozone layer 100

P

pacemaker 47
pack 58
pack of lies 156
painless 75
pamper 182
panic 62
paramedics 30
parliamentary 131, 184
part and parcel of 181
part from 167
part with 173
passable 190
passion 161
passionate 160

passion fruit 121
password 62
patch 63
patience 206
patient 186
pay 225
paying 132
pay ∼ for 131
pay attention 106
pay attention to 101
pay fo 201
pay for 90, 165
peel 121
pent-up 94
performance 89
permanent 118
persimmon 121
persist with 156
personality 55
persuade ∼ to 127, 206
pest-resistant 120
pet hates 183
pet subject 183
pet theory 183
pharmaceutical 27
philosophical 162
phone for 30
physical 90, 96, 114, 130, 204, 224
physical geography 67
pick up 47, 182
pimples 104
pinkish 59
plant 190
plan ∼ strategy 60
plan for 80, 81

plastic bottle 183
platonic 160
play around with 144
play down 80
play on 94
pleased 104
plenty of 53, 113
policy 28, 122, 123, 131, 181
policy on 100
polish 143
polite 154
political 34, 53, 60, 80, 107, 201
polka dots 59
pollute 101, 195
pollute with 101
pollution 201
polytheistic 188
pomegranate 121
population 124, 125
porn 174
poses ∼ to 201
possess 157
postpone 169
poultry 112
pour ∼ for 85
powerless 101
practise 188, 203
praise ∼ for 39, 225
pray 189
pre-prepared 143
precocious 56
predict 220
preface 41
prefer 217

pregnant 57
preliminary discussions 168
prepare for 69, 81
preschooler 57
present 155
present ∼ with 213
preserve 65, 100, 120
press 179
pressure 149, 205
presume on 153
preteen 57
preventive 131
price 186
primary 90
Prime Minister 123
professional 202
profuse 32, 33
prolong 159
promise 122, 161
promising 208
promote 124, 203
promotion 50
properly cooked 116
prospective 144
prospects 167
protest 168
provider 48
provincial chain 72
psychological 205
publish 40, 178
pull in 217
pull out of 217
pump ∼ into 195
puppet 122
purchase 35, 97

pursue 132
put ［lay］ stress on 204
put ～ into 172, 225
put ～ out to air 143
put ～ through 181
put ～ together 159
put ～ to sleep 182
put down 40
put on 40, 58, 103
put on sale 40
put on weight 75
put up ～ for 172
put your mind at ease. 77
puzzling 151

Q
qualified 30
Queen Mary 159
quench 87
question 31, 201
quorum 169

R
radical 52, 184
rainy 192, 220
raise 108, 122, 172
rally 168
ran out 162
rapid 49, 53
rather than 65, 95, 131, 156, 182, 187, 217
rationing 93
raw 112
realize 43, 82, 171
real character 55
reasonable 115, 131, 214
reboot 62

reception 48, 211
recipe 129
reclaim ～ from 195
recognize 105, 204
recommendation 122
reconsider 91
recover 45, 69, 88, 138
recovery 89
recover control of 45
recover from 148
recurring 82
reduce 24, 171
reduction 124
red tide 195
refined sugar 116
reflect 55
reflects 55
refresh 87
refugees 180
refuse to 33
regain 94, 130, 150
regain control over 94
regard ～ as 81, 142, 182, 218
regime 114
regional 178, 179, 196
register 167
regular 52, 126, 131
regulations 131
rejoice in 162
relatives 119
relaxed education 91
relaxing 222, 223
release 94, 175
reliability 187
relieve 204

religious 90, 176, 189
rely on 26, 221
remember 67, 70, 151, 161, 214
remote control 210
renew 119
repair 44, 132
repay 152, 153
reporting 179
report ～ to 24, 30
represent 225
representative 123
require 55, 218
require ～ for 27
rescue 61, 81
reservoirs 93
resign 42
resign from 122
resort 30, 135, 192, 194
resources 195
respond to 80, 179
restless 205
result from 166
retard 124
retire 130
retirement 132, 136
retire from 184
retreat 222
retrieve 63
return 102, 197, 201
return ～ to 212
return from 134
return to 185
reunion 79, 168
reveal 156
reverse discrimination

165
reverse up 191
review 175
revive 86
rheumatism 149
rich in 116
right-hand 164
right click 62
rise in 92, 167
roast 113
rock climbing 203
role 91, 201
romantic 174
rough 64, 154, 190, 195
rouse 199
routine 225
royalties 172
rubber duck 37
rugged 64
ruin 79, 99, 130
ruined by the weather 134
ruin ～ by -ing 50
rule over 67
rumour 157
run ～ efficiently 60, 61
run in 109
run into 76
run more trains 217
run out 162
rural 158
rush ～ to 81
rush off 216

S

sacrifice 129
Safari 97
sales techniques 222
salty 116
satellite channel 211
satisfying 151
saturated fat 74
save face 105
save money 172, 197
save time 214
savour 85
scenery 217
scientific approach 26
scope for change 53
seafood 112
search ～ for 105
search for 31, 97
secondhand 44
see little of 127
see through 156
self-made 164
selfish 38
send off 180
sensible 52, 111
sensitive 56
sentimental 84, 176
sent ～ to sleep 198
separate 180, 189
separately 180
serious injury 24
serve 112
serve ～ to 85
service area 48
settled 220
settle down 108, 109
set ～ to 176
set a target for 125
set my cell to silent mode 47
set off on 65
set out on 196, 219
set up 29, 61, 122, 123
sew 143
sewage 195
sexually transmitted disease 149
sexual prejudice 165
sex offenders 201
shaky 88
shampoo 126
shared files 63
shareholder 168
share one's taste in 177
sharp 191, 225
sheer 51, 128
shoot 174
shoplift 73
shoplifting 197
shop around 197
shop at 110
shop for 58
shop in 73
shortage 207
shoulder-length 126
show a video 175
show in her face 55
shrink 89
sign for 181
silent 174
sincerity 55, 153
single-parent 108
single bed 141
sip 87
site 49

situated 64, 140
situations vacant 179
sit down to 103
sit face-to-face with 105
skilfully 157
skill 191
skim through 40
skip 79
slam ～ loudly 45
slanting 103
slim 51
slip 191
slip by 50, 51
sloppy 224
slow down 124
sluggish 88
smuggle ～ into 67
snatch 128
snore 198
snowy 64
so-called 208
social mobility 200
social satire 201
soft-core 174
soils 26
solution 25, 106, 147
somewhere between 157
some bath and shower gel 37
some bath soap 37
sooner or later 177
soothing 177
sore throat 149
sound 88, 104, 125, 175, 195
soundly 199

sour 197
south-facing 137
so to speak 41
spay 183
speak the same language 155
special needs 56
spectacular 80
spectator 202
speech 177
speedometer 45
spelling 170
spending 122, 125
spend ～ -ing 69, 73, 103, 143, 215, 219
spend ～ on 91, 132, 133, 215
spicy 116
spoil 57, 99
spoilt 39
spoof 174
spouse 145
spread 27
spread in to 65
spree 196
spy 174
square 180
squeeze 121
stable 88, 138
stained 58
stake 61
standardize 154
standard of living 89
stand a chance of 51
stare ～ in the face 71
stare death 105

stare into 105
starving 117
star in 175
state 28, 44, 188, 189
statement 157
stay away from 113
stay up 41, 69
steam 216
steer ～ away from 185
stick my head out of the window 104
stick to 75
stiff 84, 115
stiff neck 149
stimulate 98, 150
stimulus 151
stir 86
stomach ulcer 149
stop at 191
storms 193
straighten out 167
streaming 97
stresses and strains 205
stretch 217
stretcher 30
strictly 188
strike up 118, 119
striped pattern 59
stripes 59
stroke 139
structural 201
struggle with 154
stunning 110
stupid 171
substantial 79
subtitles 175

suburbs 65
succeed 107, 162, 207, 213
succeed through 152
successful 146, 166, 167, 207
such-and-such 35
suffer 107, 139
suffer from 117, 148, 149, 198
suggest 41, 65, 146, 173
suitable for 116, 132
suite 141
summit 168
sunny 221
superstition 189
supply ～ to 92
supply electricity to 92
supportive 144
suppress 94
suppression 157
supreme 128
surprising 151
surrealistic 34
surrounding 64
survive on 180
suspects 31
swallow 116, 117
swell in size and intensity. 177
swerve 45
sympathy 152
symptoms 148, 204
syndrome 149

T

take ～'s chances 50
take ～ in (my) stride 77
take ～ off 69
take ～ on 219
take ～ out to 79
take ～ to 175, 182
take action 106
take an interest in 150
take a one-day trip 194
take a swig of 87
take care of 183
take delight in 99
take down 41
take no chances 106
take off 58
take on 213
take out 45, 179, 218
take over 61
take place 52
take pleasure in 99
take responsibility 43
take up 132, 133, 202, 215
talk to 47
tap out 49
tasks 215, 225
tasteless 116
tax 122, 123, 173
tear ～ out 127
teenager 57
Tell me the secret of your success. 207
temporary 136
tempting 116
tender 113
tend to 105, 187
tension 205

tepid water 36
terminal 139
terrorism 106
That's just my luck! 163
That's life! 159
the ～ establishment 34
There is no place like home. 137
There is something wrong with 211
the amount of 48
the best of friends 119
The day will come when 68
the eldest 109
the greatest happiness of the greatest number 128
the joy of -ing 57
the lates 110, 111, 209
the latest thing 111
the love of my life 161
the luck of the draw 163
the main breadwinner 109, 144
the military-industrial complex 27
The more things change, the more they remain the same. 53
the second printing 40
the three R's 91
The time is ripe. 215
The time will come when 214

索 引 245

the vagaries of the weather 221
thirst-quenching 86
thorough 98
thrilling 151
through the post 181
throw away 97
throw the baby out with the bath water 37
throw the book at 41
thunderstorm 193
tie up 180
toddler 57
toilet-train 57
tolerance 153, 167
tone-deaf 177
torture 218
toss back 85
total 80, 81, 106, 112, 206
touch 153
Tough luck! 163
tourism 125
tourist 192
toy department 72
to the point 169
to the rhythm of 177
to the west of 66
traditional 27, 74, 109, 165, 200
train for 203
train spotter 133
transfer ～ to 42
trashy 178
treatment 149
trends in 110

trendy 111
trip 218
tropical depression 220
truly 212
trusted 119
try to 61, 65, 94, 96, 115, 127, 131, 142, 167, 172, 186, 195, 197, 223
turned off 47
turning 191
turnip 121
turn ～ into 133
turn ～ off 92, 93
turn ～ on 92
turn off 93, 191, 210
turn on 210, 211
turn out to be 81, 83
turn up 177
TV gossip shows 183
two slices of 112
typo 170

U

ulcer 204
ultimate 28
unattached 164
unbelievably 209
uncontrollable 94
uncooperative 38
under-representation 165
undercooked 116
undergo 139, 204
underlying 28
under police escort 31
undesirable 38
undying 160

unemployment 89
unexpected 52
unfaithful 144
unforeseen 76
unhappiness 129
unnecessary 196
unpaid leave 42
unpaved 190
unplanned pregnancy 166
unpredictable 38
unsettled 220
untested 209
untimely 70, 71
untreated sewage 101, 195
unusual 132
unwillingly 173
UN Security Council 168
up-to-date 208
upgrade 63
upmarket 72
upright 54
up to 141
urban 48, 101, 158
urbanization 27
urge 219
urgent 225
urge ～ on 165
used to 195
useless 215
utter 156

V

vacation 135
vacuum cleaner 143

values 201
value 〜 at 35
vanity mirror 127
varied 74
vegetarian 74, 116
vertical stripes 59
via a compute 63
vigorous 124
vile 220
villain 175
vital 206
vote 〜 in 123
vote 〜 out 123
vote for 185
vote it out 123
vow 160
vulgar 154, 175

W
wait for 30, 103
wake up 82, 199
wake up to find 138
walk down 73
walk round 47
war-torn 66
warm 〜 up 84
warning signs 204
war aims 29
wash down 117
waste 169, 173, 197
waste time -ing 215
watch out for 193
Watch your language! 155

waves 195
wavy 126
weather permitting 221
weenie 133
welfare 66, 131
well-being 114
well-cooked 78
well-marbled 112
well-off 108
well-respected 178
well-run 168
wet 192
What have you done to 〜!? 127
Where is the movie showing? 175
whirlpool 36
WHO 131
wholesome 117
who the boss is 43
widen 190
widespread 52
winding 190, 191
window shopping 73
wind up 61
win more by luck than by ability 163
wipers 45
wipe 〜 clean 97
with-it 110
within easy walking distance of 73
without hesitation 85

with any [a bit of] luck 162
with a 〜 personality 55
with a very wide range of 72
with care 99
with gratitude 152
with great difficulty 77
with interest 211
with low mileage 44
with one's my heart 161
with religious care 189
wooded 64, 65
work for 43
working-class 108
work for 43, 69, 102, 108
work through 79
World Health Organization 131
wrapped in 180
wreck 50
wrinkled 104
write a 〜 constitution for 67
written 33, 154

X
X-ray machine 181

Y
year-round 114
You are the boss. 43

Z
zoo 219
zucchini 121

索 引 247

著者紹介

クリストファ・バーナード（Christopher Barnard）
元帝京大学教授

カリブ海のセント・ルシアに生まれる。イギリスで学び、ケンブリッジ大学を卒業。その後、アメリカのコーネル大学で言語学の修士号を取得したほか、テンプル大学でも教育博士号を取得する。日本では言語教育や辞書学の分野で幅広い著作活動を行っている。

著書に、『英語句動詞文例辞典』『ルミナス英和辞典』（執筆）『ライトハウス英和辞典』（執筆）（以上、研究社）、『続・句動詞の底力』『句動詞の底力』『日本人が知らない英文法』『英文法の意外な穴』『単語力がなくても英文を読みこなす法』（共著）（以上、プレイス）、*Language, Ideology, and Japanese History Textbooks* (RoutledgeCurzon) などがある。

100の超基本名詞で広がる
英語コロケーション2500

2010年5月31日　初版発行	2024年5月8日　五刷発行

著　者	クリストファ・バーナード
発行者	山　内　昭　夫
発　行	有限会社 プレイス
	〒112-0006 東京都文京区小日向 4-6-3-603
	電話　03 (6912) 1600
	URL　http://www.place-inc.net/
印刷・製本	シナノ印刷株式会社

カバーデザイン／吉本拓也（吉本意匠）　　本文DTP／Studio G
©Christopher Barnard / 2010　Printed in Japan
ISBN 978-4-903738-22-2
定価はカバーに表示してあります。乱丁本・落丁本はお取替いたします。